THE PRIZE

THE PRIZE

Who's in Charge
of America's Schools?

Dale Russakoff

Houghton Mifflin Harcourt

BOSTON   NEW YORK

2015

Copyright © 2015 by Dale Russakoff

All rights reserved

For information about permission to reproduce selections from this
book, write to Permissions, Houghton Mifflin Harcourt Publishing
Company, 215 Park Avenue South, New York, New York 10003.

www.hmhco.com

Library of Congress Cataloging-in-Publication Data is available.
ISBN 978-0-547-84005-5

Book design by Brian Moore

Printed in the United States of America
DOC 10 9 8 7 6 5 4 3 2 1

To Matt, Sam, and Adam, and in memory of my parents

Contents

THE PRIZE

I

The Pact

December 2009–July 2010

L ATE ONE NIGHT in December 2009, a large black Chevy
Tahoe moved slowly through some of the most violent neighborhoods of Newark, New Jersey. In the back sat two of the
nation's rising political stars — the Republican governor-elect, Chris
Christie, and the Democratic mayor of Newark, Cory Booker. The
pair had grown friendly during Christie's years as United States attorney in Newark in the early 2000s and remained so, even as their national parties had become polarized to the point of gridlock in Washington. Booker had invited Christie to ride with him on this night in
a caravan of off-duty cops and residents who periodically patrolled the
city's busiest drug corridors.

The caravan started out on once-vibrant Orange Street in the Central Ward, across from a boarded-up housing project so still and silent
it appeared dead. Baxter Terrace was home to both white and black
industrial workers in the 1940s, when factories in Newark made seemingly everything — leather, plastics, cigars, textiles, dyes, hats, gloves,
beer, electrical instruments, jewelry, chemicals, military clothing. As
Newark's manufacturing collapsed, and as whites fled to the suburbs,

Baxter became all black and poor, overtaken in subsequent years by violent gangs and drug dealers.

The volunteer patrolmen turned left on Bergen Street, which led to the South Ward, Newark's poorest and most violent. The street was punctuated with small tire and auto-body shops variously bearing Italian, Brazilian, and Spanish family names, with one gleaming exception — a small commercial development anchored by an Applebee's and a Home Depot, Newark's lone big box store. At almost every intersection, telephone poles bristled with signs offering cash for junk cars or for houses — "no equity, no problem." One stretch of Bergen, a middle-class shopping district in the 1960s, was now home to Tina's African Hair Braiding, Becky's Beauty Salon, a preowned-furniture store, Family Dollar, Power Ministry Assembly of God, Aisha's New Rainbow Chinese Halal Food, and a Head Start center. By far the biggest and most prosperous-looking establishment was Cotton's Funeral Service and the adjacent Scentiment Florist.

Driving through Newark was like touring archaeological layers of despair and hope. Downtown still had artifacts of the glory days before World War II, when Newark was among the nation's largest cities, with one of the highest-grossing department stores in the country. The majestic, limestone Newark Museum, endowed by the store's founder, Louis Bamberger, still presided over downtown, as did the Italian Renaissance–style Newark Public Library, built at the turn of the twentieth century. Run-down and vacant buildings now dominated the streetscapes, but five colleges and universities, including Rutgers–Newark and New Jersey Institute of Technology, held out potential for a better future. And Mayor Booker was aggressively recruiting development — the first new hotels in forty years, the first supermarkets in twenty. Soon Panasonic and Prudential Insurance would be building new office towers. A Whole Foods would come later. The momentum stopped far short of Newark's neighborhoods, however.

The ostensible purpose of the ride-along was for Booker to show the governor-in-waiting one of his crime-fighting techniques. But

Booker had another agenda. His own rise in politics had coincided with, and been fueled by, a national movement seeking radical change in urban education, leading Booker to envision an audacious agenda for Newark and for himself. He would need Christie's help.

The state had seized control of the city's schools in 1995, after investigators documented pervasive corruption and patronage at the top, along with appalling neglect of students. Their conclusion was encapsulated in one stunning sentence: "Evidence shows that the longer children remain in the Newark public schools, the less likely they are to succeed academically." Fifteen years later, after the state had compiled its own record of mismanagement, fewer than forty percent of third through eighth graders were reading or doing math at grade level. Yet in all those years, no governor had returned the reins. That meant that within weeks, Christie, upon his inauguration, would become the overlord of the Newark Public Schools and its $1 billion annual budget.

Booker had listened carefully as Christie spoke in his campaign of his commitment to struggling cities, frequently reminding voters that he was born in Newark. The Christies had moved to the suburbs in 1967, when he was four, weeks before the eruption of cataclysmic riots that still scarred the city emotionally and physically. Booker asked his driver to detour from the caravan's route to Christie's childhood neighborhood, where the governor-elect said he had happy memories of taking walks with his mother, his baby brother in a stroller. The Tahoe pulled to a stop along a desolate stretch of South Orange Avenue. Its headlights illuminated a three-story brick building with gang graffiti sprayed across boarded-up windows, rising from a weedy, garbage-strewn lot. Across the street loomed dilapidated West Side High School. Almost ninety percent of its students lived in poverty, and barely half of the freshmen made it to graduation. Violence permeated children's lives. In separate incidents the previous year, three West Side students had been shot and killed by gangs. One year before that, on a warm summer night, local members of a Central American gang known as MS-13, wielding guns, machetes, and a steak knife, had murdered three college-bound Newark youths execution-style and badly maimed a fourth. Two of the victims and the survivor were West Side graduates.

Christie had made urban schools a prominent issue in his campaign. "We're paying caviar prices for failure," he'd said, referring to Newark's schools budget, of which three-quarters came from the state. "We have to grab this system by the roots and yank it out and start over. It's outrageous."

There was little debate that the district desperately needed reform. The ratio of administrators to students was almost twice the state average. Clerks made up thirty percent of the central bureaucracy, about four times the ratio in comparable cities. Even some clerks had clerks, yet payroll checks and student data were habitually late and inaccurate. Test and attendance data had not been entered for months, and computers routinely spat out report cards bearing one child's name and another child's grades, meaning the wrong students got grounded or rewarded.

Most school buildings were more than eighty years old, and some were falling to pieces—literally. Two nights before first lady Michelle Obama came to Maple Avenue School, in November 2010, to publicize her Let's Move! campaign against obesity—appearing alongside Booker, a national cochair—a massive brick lintel fell onto the front walkway.

What happened inside many buildings was even worse. The district had four magnet schools, two of which produced debating champions and a handful of elite college prospects. But in twenty-three of its seventy-five schools, fewer than thirty percent of children from the third through the eighth grade were reading at grade level. The high school graduation rate was fifty-four percent, and more than ninety percent of graduates who attended the local community college required remedial classes. Only 12.5 percent of Newark adults were college graduates, just over a third of the statewide rate.

Newark was an extreme example of the country's increasing economic and racial segregation. In a predominantly white state, and one of the nation's wealthiest, ninety-five percent of Newark students were black or Latino and eighty-eight percent qualified for free or reduced-price lunches. Forty-four percent of city children lived below the poverty line—twice the national average—and seventy percent were born to single mothers. An astonishing forty percent of newborns received inadequate prenatal care or none at all, disadvantaged before drawing their first breaths.

In the back seat of the Tahoe, Booker turned to Christie and proposed that they work together to transform education in Newark. With Christie's absolute legal authority and Booker's mayoral bully pulpit, they could close failing district schools, greatly expand charter schools, weaken tenure protections, reward and punish teachers based on their students' test scores. It was an agenda the incumbent Democratic governor, Jon Corzine, likely never would have embraced, out of loyalty to teachers' unions. Christie's upset victory over Corzine, in Booker's view, represented "a once in a lifetime chance to get the system on the right track."

They shared a belly laugh at the prospect of confounding the political establishment with an alliance between a white, suburban Republican and a black, urban Democrat. Booker warned that they would face a brutal fight with unions and machine politicians invested in the status quo. With 7,000 people on its payroll, the school district was the biggest public employer in a city of roughly 270,000. Shaking it up, Booker said, was sure to activate the same coalition that had foiled his first mayoral bid, spreading rumors that he was gay, Jewish, a closet Republican, and a Trojan horse for white, monied outsiders. Booker could barely see in the pitch dark, but as he described all that ugliness, he got the distinct impression that Christie was salivating.

"Heck, I got maybe six votes in Newark," the governor-to-be responded. "Why not do the right thing?"

Whatever their political differences, Booker and Christie agreed completely on public education. Both viewed urban school districts as beholden to public workers' unions and political patronage machines rather than children, and both were part of the growing national movement seeking to reinvent education. With backing from the nation's richest philanthropists and prominent politicians in both parties—including President Barack Obama—the self-dubbed education reform movement aimed to break up the old system with entrepreneurial approaches: charter schools, business-style accountability for principals and teachers based on students' test scores, and bonuses for top performers. There was significant public debate over the merit of these strategies. Research scientists questioned the validity of using test score data to measure teacher effectiveness. Moreover, decades of research had shown that experiences at home and in neighborhoods had far more influence on children's academic achievement than classroom instruction. But reformers argued that well-run schools with the flexibility to recruit the best teachers could overcome many of the effects of poverty, broken homes, and exposure to violence. They pointed to high-performing urban charter schools—including some in Newark—that were publicly funded but privately run, operating free of the district schools' large bureaucracies and, in most cases, also free of unions. Although a national study at the time found that only one in five charters in the country outperformed their district counterparts on standardized tests, Booker and other reformers said emphatically, "We know what works." They blamed vested interests for using poverty as an excuse for failure, and dismissed competing approaches as "incrementalism." Education needed "transformational change," they said.

Christie's response to Booker—"Why not do the right thing?"—reflected the righteous tone of the movement. Reformers likened their cause to the civil rights movement, well aware that many of their opponents were descendants of the old civil rights establishment: urban politicians determined to protect public jobs in cities where secure employment was rare.

It seemed that every side in the education debate had its eyes on a different prize. In impoverished cities, the school district with its bloated payroll was often the employer of first and last resort. Over the years in Newark, numerous politicians had actually taken to calling the district budget "the prize." Reformers saw in districts like Newark an opportunity to prove that systems built around unions and large public bureaucracies were themselves an obstacle to learning. At the heart of it all were the children and a question continually posed by their parents and teachers: Were the battles waged in their name really improving young lives?

The education of the poorest Americans has been a cause of the wealthiest since Reconstruction, when Northern industrialists built schools of varying caliber across the South for former slaves. Henry Ford created the Ford English School in 1913 to teach "basic reading and speaking comprehension skills" to mostly foreign-born factory workers. Early in the twentieth century, Andrew Carnegie's foundation developed the "Carnegie unit," or the credit hour, which became the currency of learning: to graduate from high school, students still must earn a certain number of credits, based not on what they have learned, but on time spent in classes.

In the most spectacular example of education philanthropy in the twentieth century, Walter Annenberg stood with President Clinton in the White House Rose Garden in late 1993 and committed $500 million to "guarantee our nation's future" by financing reforms in thousands of urban and rural schools. The Annenberg Challenge, as it was known, drew $600 million in matching contributions and reached more than 1.5 million children in thirty-five states. But the overwhelming verdict was that while the effort benefited many individual schools and children, it didn't dent the problems in the larger system.

Discontent over public education had been galvanized in 1983 by a five-alarm federal report, *A Nation at Risk,* announcing that American students had fallen significantly behind those in other industrialized countries, jeopardizing the nation's economic competitiveness. "If an unfriendly foreign power had attempted to impose on America the mediocre educational performance that exists today, we might well have viewed it as an act of war," the report said.

Top corporate leaders worked alongside governors to raise state academic standards and institute standardized testing to monitor student progress. Their efforts ultimately led to the No Child Left Behind law, signed by President George W. Bush in 2002, which dramatically expanded testing and required reporting of student scores by race and income level. That data documented a yawning gap between the academic achievement of poor and minority children and all others. In the late 1980s, a movement championed mainly by conservative Republicans sought to give parents in inner-city districts publicly subsidized vouchers to enroll children in religious or private schools.

In 1990, Teach for America began recruiting elite college graduates to teach for two years in the lowest-income communities. The goal was to develop a generation of future leaders dedicated to battling inequity in the education system, whether from inside or out. They were deemed "education entrepreneurs"—an oxymoron only a few years earlier—and many went on to found charter schools, new teacher and principal training programs, consulting practices, and other ventures intended to upend the existing system. By the end of the decade, they had some of the nation's largest fortunes behind them.

For generations, the foundations of deceased early-twentieth-century industrialists had dominated education philanthropy. Beginning in 2000, there was a rapid changing of the guard as living billionaires—Bill Gates of Microsoft, the Walton family of the Walmart fortune, Michael Dell of Dell computers, and Eli Broad, the California insurance and real estate magnate—became the nation's top donors to K–12 education. These spectacularly successful entrepreneurs, who mostly made their fortunes disrupting established industries with technology and new business models, were drawn to young reformers trying to do the same in public education. They defined the system itself as the problem.

"It was a change in the meaning of philanthropy," said Kim Smith, a cofounder of the NewSchools Venture Fund, a philanthropy financed by Silicon Valley venture capitalists. "In the past, if you gave money to, say, housing or the arts, the need would be perpetual. You didn't believe it would one day sustain itself. But this group of people understands leverage. If you get education right, you're going to get people jobs, reduce incarceration, et cetera. So the idea was to help people analyze what's not working and inspire entrepreneurs to solve problems."

They became known as "venture philanthropists" and called themselves investors rather than donors, seeking returns in the form of sweeping changes to public schooling. Employing management consultants and the kinds of analytic tools that fueled the rise of their companies, they pressed for data-driven accountability systems to measure the effectiveness of teachers and schools. President Obama and Secretary of Education Arne Duncan incorporated many of those goals into Race to the Top, a $4.3 billion initiative that induced states to expand charter schools and to tie teachers' evaluations, pay, and job security to growth in their students' standardized test scores. The stated goal was to put single-minded focus on what was best for children, even if at the expense of upending adult lives and livelihoods.

In the beginning, Democratic politicians almost universally spurned the cause, as did many African American leaders, perceiving these efforts as threats to the Democratic base in cities — unions, public sector jobs, and politicians who doled them out. They questioned the credibility of a movement to reform education for America's lowest-income black and brown schoolchildren that was led by white elites and financed by some of the richest men on the planet — labeled the "billionaire boys' club" by education historian Diane Ravitch, a onetime reformer who emerged as a prominent opponent of the movement she had once embraced. An early exception within the ranks of the voucher movement was Howard Fuller, whose long journey through civil rights activism, Black Power advocacy, the African liberation movement, and community organizing had led him to the cause of education in his native Milwaukee, where low-income and minority children were dropping out of district schools in droves. After doing battle as an activist and later as superintendent of schools, he resigned in 1995, declaring the district "hopelessly mired in the status quo."

But Fuller was an outlier, and reformers recognized they had a problem. Cory Booker couldn't have arrived at a more opportune time.

Booker had emerged from the first generation of black leaders born after the civil rights movement. His parents, who grew up in the segregated South and participated in sit-ins in the 1960s, were among the first African Americans to rise into management at IBM. They raised him and his brother in the almost all-white suburb of Harrington Park, about twenty miles from Newark. "We wanted our sons to learn to navigate in the larger world," recalled his mother, Carolyn Booker. "This, too, was part of the struggle."

Cory Booker made it look easy. Six foot three, gregarious and charismatic, he was an honors student, a football star in high school, and president of his senior class. One success followed another. He graduated from Stanford University, went on to Oxford as a Rhodes Scholar, and then to Yale Law School. Ed Nicoll, a forty-year-old self-made millionaire who was studying law at Yale, became one of his close friends. In class, where most students showcased abstract-thinking skills, Nicoll said, Booker spun folksy stories about his family, often ending with a point about social justice. "He got away with it and he enchanted everyone from left to right," Nicoll said. "In a class where everybody secretly believed they'd be the next senator or the next president of the United States, it was absolutely clear that Cory had leadership written all over him . . . Even back then, people said he'd be the first black president."

Instead of pursuing lucrative job prospects after law school, Booker went to Newark in 1997 to represent poor tenants, paid by a Skadden Foundation fellowship. He moved into low-income housing in an area of the Central Ward that was riddled with drugs and crime, organizing tenants to take on slumlords and growing close to a number of community activists. With their support, he ran for city council the next year, arguing that government was part of the problem —city hall looked the other way when slumlords gave money to the right politicians. Ed Nicoll took time off from his work in finance to help Booker raise money for his campaign. His advice was simple. Tell wealthy donors your own story: a privileged young African American moves to one of the nation's poorest cities to tackle the unfinished business of the civil rights movement. Booker found Nicoll's lesson invaluable.

"He was the first person who told me—and many people have said it since—that investors bet on people, not on business models, because they know successful people find a way to be successful," Booker said.

Booker raised more than $140,000, an unheard-of sum at the time for a Newark council race. In the spring of 1998, after a grassroots campaign that included knocking on every door in his ward, Booker, who had just turned twenty-nine, edged out four-term councilman George Branch in a runoff.

With his golden résumé and gritty surroundings, Booker quickly displayed a gift for attracting media attention. He was featured on *60 Minutes*, on the *CBS Evening News*, and in *Time* magazine for staging hunger strikes and camping out for weeks at a time in drug corridors to demand better security for law-abiding residents. "I moved onto the front lines, the last frontier for really, truly making justice happen, and that's in our inner cities," Booker said in an interview with Dan Rather.

He called his political philosophy "pragmatic Democratic," looking to government but also private and faith-based initiatives to address poverty. Departing further from the standard playbook for urban Democrats, Booker became an early champion of charter schools, arguing that the poorest children—like the richest—should be able to opt out of bad schools. He later took the even more unconventional step of embracing vouchers for private schools for the same reason.

Booker was a valuable asset for the almost universally white, rich, Republican voucher movement, which along with the charter movement introduced him to some of his major political donors. He began shuttling between two worlds: the troubled streets of Newark and the rarefied redoubts of wealthy donors, where he became a potent fundraiser and mesmerizing orator.

His education views won him an invitation in September 2000 to deliver a speech at the conservative Manhattan Institute for Policy Research. In an impassioned address, still featured on the institute's website more than a decade later, Booker depicted Newark residents as captives of self-dealing, nepotistic, patronage-dispensing politicians who ignored their needs. He said this was particularly true in the "repugnant" school system. "I define public education not as a publicly guaranteed space and a publicly run, publicly funded building where our children are sent based on their ZIP code. Public education is the use of public dollars to educate our children at the schools that are best equipped to do so—public schools, magnet schools, charter schools, Baptist schools, Jewish schools."

In Booker's view, that speech launched his national reputation. "I became a pariah in Democratic circles for taking on the party orthodoxy on education, but I found a national community of people who were feeling the same way, on the left and the right," he said. "In 2002, when I first ran for mayor, I had all these Republican donors and donors from outside Newark, many of them motivated because we have an African American urban Democrat telling the truth about education."

One of them was Ravenel Boykin Curry IV, then a thirty-six-year-old principal in a family-owned hedge fund in Manhattan. Curry, a Democratic supporter of charter schools who became one of Booker's most generous backers, confessed that he hadn't given a thought to Newark at the time. "It seemed hopeless," he said. "Everyone just looks out and sighs and thinks, 'There's nothing I can do.' Then this guy with great political skills who's willing to make the sacrifices we weren't willing to make comes along, and it reignites the old flame: 'Oh, yeah, we can still change the world.'"

Curry wrote Booker a check and introduced him to some of his Harvard Business School classmates. "They let Cory into their boardrooms and offices, introduced him to people they worked with in hedge funds," said a Democratic operative who worked with them. "As young finance people, they looked at a guy like Cory at this stage as if they were buying Google at seventy-five dollars a share. They were talking about him being the first black president before he even got elected to the city council, and they all wanted to be a part of that ride. If it was twenty-five years, that was fine. They were in."

In his 2002 campaign against four-term mayor Sharpe James—who embodied the urban machine politics Booker decried to the Manhattan Institute—Booker drew more than $3 million in contributions, from Republicans as well as Democrats. James turned the newcomer's fundraising against him, branding him an agent of rich, white outsiders, a time-honored way to inflame Newark voters' passions. According to an analysis by Think Progress, more than $565,000, in fact, came from Wall Street financiers and investors. James won the race, but by the smallest margin in his then thirty-two-year political career. A documentary about the hard-fought campaign, *Street Fight*—financed by Curry and made by his younger brother, Marshall—was nominated for an Oscar in 2005 and became a staple of Booker's political narrative. The campaign inspired Curry, Whitney Tilson, Charles Ledley, and John Petry, all hedge fund managers enriched by the late-1990s boom on Wall Street, to seek out and support more Democrats who embraced charter schools and opposed the influence of teachers' unions on the party. They ultimately formed a political action committee, Democrats for Education Reform, with Booker as one of their star fundraisers. The group's beneficiaries would come to include the 2004 U.S. Senate candidate from Illinois, Barack Obama.

When Booker ran for mayor again in 2006 with even more outside backing, Sharpe James dropped out rather than face likely defeat, and Booker beat his stand-in, state senator Ronald Rice Sr., in a landslide.

Once in office, Booker surprised reformers by paying little attention to the school district, telling them his hands were tied because of Governor Corzine's union allegiances. Instead, he set out to recruit charter schools, using his magic with donors to raise $20 million in 2008 for a Newark Charter School Fund to support the sector's growth. Money came from the Bill and Melinda Gates Foundation, the Walton Family Foundation, the Doris and Donald Fisher Fund of the Gap clothing store fortune, hedge fund titan Julian Robertson's foundation, and Laurene Powell Jobs, the wife of Apple founder Steve Jobs, as well as from four local foundations. With Booker's encouragement, Newark spawned some of the top charter schools in the country, including fifteen run by the nationally respected networks Uncommon Schools and KIPP.

New Jersey's troubled urban schools provided rich source material for Christie's run for governor in 2009. The issue of education reform had strong crossover appeal for a Republican candidate in a heavily Democratic state. Christie used it to aggressively reach out to black and Hispanic parents concerned about schools in inner cities where Republicans rarely campaigned. He also fired up his Republican base by lambasting the state teachers' union, the New Jersey Education Association, by far the biggest political donor in the state, boasting that he refused even to interview for its endorsement. "To get your endorsement I'd have to sell out the children of New Jersey," he recalled saying.

He explained his passion for the issue in terms of his life experience. His ancestors had come from Italy and Ireland, finding opportunity in Newark. But as he was about to start kindergarten, the city was in rapid decline, and the family moved to suburban Livingston, New Jersey. He has often said that he believed he owed his success in life to his escape from the Newark schools—adding that it happened only because his parents were able to borrow $1,000 from each of his grandmothers for a down payment on a $22,000 home. "I remember being told by my parents that we were moving so that I could go to a good school," Christie said.

The Newark public schools had a reputation for excellence well into the 1950s, when Philip Roth graduated from the predominantly Jewish Weequahic High School and Amiri Baraka (then LeRoi Jones), the late African American poet, playwright, and revolutionary, graduated from the predominantly Italian American Barringer High. But the schools declined in tandem with the city amid a convergence of forces that, viewed from the present, resemble a series of plagues.

In the bullish aftermath of World War II, the federal government aggressively promoted the growth of suburbs, with home mortgage subsidies and construction of new interstate highways to whisk middle-class breadwinners to and from jobs in urban centers. It helped families like the Christies achieve the American dream — a better life for their children.

But the dream had an underside. The policies fostered an epochal exodus of more than 100,000 white Newark residents in the 1960s that flipped the city's racial makeup in one decade from two-thirds white to two-thirds black. It was the fastest and most tumultuous turnover of any American city except Detroit or Gary, Indiana. Once a thriving industrial hub where successive waves of immigrants found work and rose into the middle class, Newark lost factories to the suburbs, the South, and beyond.

The economic base collapsed near the peak of the Great Migration of black families from the Deep South, removing a ladder of opportunity climbed by earlier-arriving ethnic groups. In all, 160,000 men, women, and children came north to Newark, most from rural areas and with limited educations. A pattern of well-documented racial discrimination barred the new arrivals from the dwindling supply of good jobs.

Black families increasingly crowded into slums, where the federal and city governments were carrying out a strategy intended to revive cities: urban renewal. As in many distressed communities, Newark leaders used federal funds to bulldoze dilapidated buildings to make way for high-rise office towers, spacious civic plazas, public housing for the displaced poor, and commuter highways for an increasingly suburban workforce. Louis Danzig, Newark's urban renewal director, was a national leader of the movement and proved so masterful at securing aid from Washington that Newark cleared more slums and displaced a higher percentage of residents than any other city. The theory was that slums bred crime, disease, and sloth, and that new housing would help eradicate all that—and poverty, too. "Good houses make good citizens," Danzig said.

Not surprisingly, it wasn't that simple. In Newark and elsewhere, urban renewal became known as "Negro removal." A state investigation later found that despite the massive dislocation, the great majority of federal money benefited moderate and middle-income residents, businesses, and downtown colleges and institutions. The planners and developers destroyed long-standing neighborhoods and relegated residents to five large housing projects in Newark's Central Ward, including three high-rise silos with no ground-floor restrooms and minimal grass or open space, making it almost impossible for parents to supervise children. By the late 1960s, more than eighteen thousand residents were jammed into a one-and-a-half-mile radius, virtually all of them low-income African Americans or Hispanics—"one of the most volatile [ghettoes] anywhere on the eastern seaboard," according to testimony before the U.S. Commission on Civil Rights.

"Our city was set up to fail," said Clement Price, a professor of African American and Newark history at Rutgers and a respected civic leader. "It was planned failure—in public education, in housing, and in job opportunity."

It certainly began to look that way to Louis and Ella Mae Sherrer, who came north during the Great Migration and settled in Newark in the 1950s. Louis became a union plumber and started a home improvement business, and Ella worked in a hospital cafeteria. They bought a house two blocks from Orange Street, a vibrant thoroughfare with plentiful shopping and movie theaters. "You never needed to go downtown," said Ella. On walks there, she and her three children passed home after home of families she knew well—"houses all the way from here to there," she said.

Then, in the late 1950s, the state unveiled plans for Interstate 280, one of two federal highways linking downtown to the western suburbs. It would slice Orange Street and surrounding neighborhoods to pieces; seven miles west, there would be an exit for Livingston, the Christies' future home. Barbershops, theaters, and stores began closing even before the route opened. Families who could afford to move did so—the federal home loan program had redlined almost all of Newark, deeming it too risky for mortgages or lending, making renovations unaffordable—and in time the Sherrers' neighborhood was pocked with abandoned houses, many occupied by squatters and drug dealers.

Turmoil engulfed the public schools as white children left en masse, black children arrived from the South, and widespread redevelopment displaced many families. African American students comprised ten percent of the district in 1940, fifty-five percent in 1961, and seventy-one percent in 1967.

"I remember how differently they started treating us," said Antoinette Baskerville-Richardson, a Weequahic High School student in the late 1960s, who later became a teacher and, after retiring, president of the school board. Weequahic's racial composition reversed in the 1960s, from eighty-one percent white at the beginning of the decade to eighty-two percent black by the end. Baskerville-Richardson recalled the district building a fence around the school, with the result that students couldn't congregate after dismissal. "It was as if we were animals," she said.

The school district allowed the remaining white students to transfer out of predominantly African American schools, where substitutes taught up to a quarter of the classes. "In schools with high Negro enrollments," the NAACP reported in 1961, "textbooks were either not available or so outmoded and in such poor condition as to be of no value as a text . . . We found that some class libraries consist of nothing but comic books."

Although black residents were approaching a majority in the city, they were politically powerless to force local officials to address evidence of police brutality, substandard housing, or collapsing public education. An Italian American political machine, which became dominant in the early 1960s, displacing Irish bosses, tightly controlled city hall and the schools, along with patronage jobs, contracts, and—it was well known—lucrative kickbacks from organized crime. Former U.S. representative Hugh Addonizio, the mayor at the time, famously explained his motivation for leaving the prestige of Congress to run such an impoverished city: "There's no money in Washington, but you can make a million bucks as mayor of Newark."

On the night of July 12, 1967, Newark exploded in six days of riots that many longtime residents still call "the rebellion," an uprising against racial oppression. The immediate spark was a brutal police beating of a black taxi driver who was rumored—falsely—to have died. A crowd of more than three hundred hurled rocks and Molotov cocktails at the police station where the driver was being held, and officers attacked with nightsticks and shields. Rioters smashed windows, burned buildings, and looted stores, laying waste to large swaths of the Central Ward. The state and local police and National Guard responded with indiscriminate gunfire that, according to multiple investigations, killed men, women, and children who were on stoops and sidewalks and inside apartments and cars. Eyewitnesses reported that the National Guard ransacked and shot up stores with signs posted to indicate they were black-owned; looters had spared many of them. Twenty-six people were killed, most by rifle shots from state police and the National Guard, according to a state commission. Two victims were white, twenty-four were African American. Although twenty-three of the deaths were classified as homicides, there were no indictments. Property damage exceeded $10 million, a wound that remained open for decades. "Our nation is moving toward two societies, one black, one white—separate and unequal," concluded the National Advisory Commission on Civil Disorders.

In 1967, Governor Richard Hughes appointed a commission to investigate the causes of the riots. Its report stated, of urban renewal, "In the scramble for money, the poor, who were to be the chief beneficiaries of the programs, tended to be overlooked." And, because of "ghetto schools," most poor and black children "have no hope in the present situation. A few may succeed in spite of the barriers. The majority will not. Society cannot afford to have such human potential go to waste."

The report quoted the testimony of school board president Harold Ashby, the first African American in the job: "I think somewhere along the line, someone has to say, 'Stop.' . . . Until such time as these reading levels and arithmetic levels come up, there isn't anyone who can say in the city of Newark, professional or otherwise, we are doing a good job because these children just can't read and do arithmetic."

The legislature rejected a bid by Hughes to take over the schools, and the cycle of neglect and corruption continued.

In the next election, black voters and the growing Puerto Rican population united to elect Kenneth Gibson, a city engineer running on a reform platform, the first black mayor of a major northeastern city. He defeated Addonizio, then on trial for extortion. True to his words about the riches he expected to reap as mayor, Addonizio was convicted, along with four compatriots, of extorting $1.4 million from city contractors. Both Gibson and Sharpe James, his successor, also became convicted felons. Booker was the first Newark mayor in forty-four years not to be indicted.

In 1994, state Department of Education investigators cited gross mismanagement, corruption, and instructional failure throughout the Newark district, even as school board members treated themselves to public cars, tropical junkets, and expensive meals. The investigators found rat infestation, asbestos, and high levels of lead paint in a rented building being used as an elementary school. The school board was negotiating to buy the building, worth about $120,000, for $2.7 million. It turned out to be owned, through a sham company, by two school principals prominent in Italian American politics. They were indicted on multiple charges and later acquitted.

In a series of rulings in the nineties, the state supreme court found that funding disparities among school districts violated the state constitutional right to an education for children in New Jersey's poorest communities. The court ordered the legislature to spend billions of dollars to equalize funding, portending a windfall for Newark. In 1995, the state seized control of the Newark district, just as money was beginning to flow.

Money had always been at the center of struggles for control of the Newark schools. "That's the prize that every mayor has been trying to get back control of," said Junius Williams, a longtime education activist who came to Newark in 1967, just out of Yale Law School. When a reform mayor was elected in the 1950s on a pledge to purge city hall of corruption, purveyors of patronage simply relocated to the school district. In the early 1980s, with Gibson in the mayor's office, a grassroots campaign of parents, teachers, and many political organizations came together to wrest control of the schools from the mayor and give it to an elected school board. The shift was touted as a victory for democracy, but school board elections were held when there were no other races on the ballot, and turnout was minimal. The board came under the control of those who got the most followers to the polls — unions and the city's most powerful political boss. For decades, education seemed incidental to the purpose of the school district.

"The Newark schools are like a candy store that's a front for a gambling operation," Ross Danis, president of the nonprofit Newark Trust for Education, said. "When a threat materializes, everyone takes his position and sells candy. When it recedes, they go back to gambling."

Early in the summer of 2010, months after their nighttime ride, Booker presented Christie with a proposal, stamped "Confidential Draft," titled "Newark Public Schools—A Reform Plan." It called for imposing reform from the top down, warning that a more open political process could be taken captive by unions and machine politicians. "Real change has casualties and those who prospered under the pre-existing order will fight loudly and viciously," the proposal said. Seeking consensus would undercut real reform. One of the goals was to "make Newark the charter school capital of the nation." The plan called for an "infusion of philanthropic support" to recruit teachers and principals through national school-reform organizations, build sophisticated data and accountability systems, and weaken tenure and seniority protections. Philanthropy, unlike government funding, required no public review of priorities or spending. Christie approved the plan, and Booker began pitching it to major donors.

In those pitches, Booker portrayed the Newark schools as a prize of a very different sort: a laboratory where the education reform movement could apply its strategies to one of the nation's most troubled school districts. He predicted that Newark would be transformed into "a hemisphere of hope," catalyzing the spread of reform throughout urban America.

2

Seduction in Sun Valley

July–September 2010

A FEW WEEKS LATER, in July of 2010, Cory Booker found himself in the company of billionaires and multimillionaires at the posh and secluded Sun Valley Resort, in the mountains of central Idaho, for a ritual mixing of big business and pleasure. The invitation-only extravaganza of deal-making and schmoozing for media moguls and investors, hosted by New York banker Herbert Allen, drew the richest and most famous people in the business. That year's guest list for the first time included twenty-six-year-old Mark Zuckerberg, founder of Facebook. Booker had his sights set on Zuckerberg to fund his and Christie's plans for the Newark schools. As it turned out, Zuckerberg wanted to meet him, too.

The Newark mayor had an extraordinary social network of his own, but for this particular connection, Booker once again had his Yale Law School classmate Ed Nicoll to thank.

When Booker was still a city councilman, Nicoll introduced him to one of his investors, a venture capitalist named Marc Bodnick. Booker remembered Nicoll briefing him: "This guy's a diehard Democrat and also hates the failures in education and heard that you believed in everything from vouchers to charter schools, whatever, and wants to meet you." They clicked in the first meeting.

In what turned into a networking trifecta for Booker, Bodnick later married Michelle Sandberg, whose sister Sheryl became chief operating officer of Facebook in 2008. In mid-2010, according to Booker, Bodnick tipped him that the Facebook founder was planning a significant philanthropic move, "something big" in education. Then Bodnick learned that Sandberg, Zuckerberg, and Booker all would be at Allen's annual Sun Valley mixer, and Booker got another alert. "He said, 'Make sure you connect with Sheryl and her husband out there, because they want to connect you with Mark,'" Booker said.

As always at the Sun Valley event, the panel discussions featured some of the most interesting and compelling people in the country and the world. It was not surprising that a discussion on the future of cities included leaders from centers of commerce, culture, and influence, like Michael Bloomberg, mayor of New York, and Richard Daley, mayor of Chicago. The third panelist, whose city had long ago lost its wealth and influence, was Booker. Like Zuckerberg, Booker was a first-timer at Sun Valley, and he poked fun at the incongruity of his presence. He felt, he said, like a community college sitting beside the Harvard and Yale of mayors.

But the incongruity was what made Booker intriguing. He was in fact completely at ease among the rich and powerful. For years, he had been a regularly featured guest at Manhattan celebrity galas and Hollywood premieres, a sought-after speaker around the country at political fundraisers, charity events, and college commencements, a frequent chatting partner on late-night talk shows. Wherever he traveled, he made rich people want to write checks for causes in Newark: Brad Pitt financed housing for low-income veterans, Jon Bon Jovi for HIV/AIDS patients, Oprah Winfrey for battered women. Shaquille O'Neal was developing a twelve-screen movie complex and high-rise apartments. Even United States senators marveled at the way this mayor of an impoverished city coaxed money from the wealthiest donors.

Booker and Zuckerberg met at a buffet dinner one night on the deck of Herbert Allen's Sun Valley townhouse, overlooking a golf course and a stream. They shared a table with Amazon's Jeff Bezos and media executive Michael Eisner, among others. Afterward, Zuckerberg invited Booker on a walk and explained that he was looking for a city poised to upend the forces impeding urban education, where his money could make the difference and create a national model. Booker responded with a pitch that showcased what made him such a dazzling fundraiser.

The mayor of Newark understood well that venture philanthropists were looking for a "proof point," a city where they could deploy multiple initiatives and demonstrate measurable improvement in poor children's achievement. He already had pitched Newark to many of them as fertile ground for charter growth, emphasizing its proximity to a huge teaching talent pool across the Hudson River and its manageable size in contrast to New York, where then chancellor Joel Klein, a hero of reformers, had shaken the school system's foundations but hadn't begun to reach all 1.2 million students. In raising $20 million for the Newark Charter School Fund in 2008, Booker had emphasized the success of some of Newark's earliest charter schools and New Jersey's generous school-funding formula—more than twice the amount per pupil as in California, for example. Now, he was pitching Zuckerberg on the next stage of the vision—Newark as a proof point for turning around an entire school district.

Walking side by side with Zuckerberg, Booker began, "The question facing cities is not 'Can we deal with our most difficult problems—recidivism, health care, education?' The real question is 'Do we have the will?'" Why not, he went on, take the best models in the country for success in education and bring them all to Newark? "There's no way we can't count to forty-five thousand [Newark children of school age] and get all of them into high-performing environments," the mayor later recalled. The former Stanford football player, big of build, with shaved head, hazel eyes, and overpowering optimism, added, with the confidence of a born winner: "You could flip a whole city!"

"I just thought, this is the guy I want to invest in," Zuckerberg would later tell reporters. "This is a person who can create change."

Zuckerberg was disarmingly open about how little he knew at the time about philanthropy. He recently had joined Bill Gates and Warren Buffett in pledging to give away half of his fortune in his lifetime, but unlike older billionaires, he had little time to devote to a foundation. "Running a company is a full-time job," he explained, somewhat unnecessarily. He said his goal, in addition to helping the Newark schools, was to learn from his experience and become a better philanthropist in the process.

While his personal experience in public education was limited — he'd started out in public schools, graduated from the elite prep school Phillips Exeter Academy, and dropped out of Harvard as a sophomore — Zuckerberg was drawn to the cause by the experiences of his wife, Priscilla Chan, then his girlfriend, and her passion for children. They decided to embark on philanthropy as a couple, and when they began talking about it, early in 2010, she was in medical school, preparing to become a pediatrician in community medicine to care for underserved children. She had no more time for active philanthropy than he did.

Sitting beside Zuckerberg in his glass-walled meeting room at Facebook, Chan said her own life experiences drew her to the challenges facing inner-city children. She came from a "disadvantaged" family, as she described it, in which her Chinese-Vietnamese immigrant parents worked eighteen hours a day to build a better life for their three daughters, her father running a Chinese restaurant, her mother working two jobs. Her grandparents lived with them and helped care for her. Two of her public school teachers, to whom she remains close,

saw her potential and helped put her on a path that eventually led to
Harvard. Chan was the first in her extended family to go to college,
followed soon by her two younger sisters.

She recalled her first days at Harvard as overwhelming, but she
found an anchor by volunteering in an after-school program for children in two housing projects in the low-income Dorchester section
of Boston. "I was like, 'Oh my God, these kids are me, except I got
a lucky break somewhere along the way and things turned out really
well. I should help these kids because this is me and maybe one or two
small things can sort of change their trajectory.'"

She teared up and stopped to compose herself. "I always cry talking about this," she said. Silently, Zuckerberg got up and fetched her
a box of Kleenex. "Just power through it," he said under his breath,
pumping his fist like a cross between an athletic trainer and a comic.
She laughed, pressed a tissue to her eyes, and continued the story.

Chan worked all four years of college in the program, running it
for the last three. More than academics, it involved helping children
navigate the day-in, day-out challenges of growing up in poverty,
from neighborhood rivalries to health issues.

In medical school, she became active in Pediatric Leaders for the
Underserved, and as a resident she cared for foster children at the
county safety-net hospital in San Francisco. Again she felt a personal
connection. "All these Hispanic immigrant families in my clinic in the
hospital—I'm like, 'You are like me, except we have completely different lives,'" she said. As for her own "completely different lives"—
her childhood versus life as a billionaire—she said, "Anyone would be
shocked. You don't have to have quite the same background I did."

A different experience of Chan's influenced Zuckerberg's view of
education and Newark. She spent a year between college and medical school teaching science in a private school in San Jose, and "when
she went to be a teacher, coming out of Harvard, a lot of people acted
like she was going to do charity," Zuckerberg said. "My own view
was you're going to have more of an impact than a lot of these other
people who are going into jobs that are paying a lot more. And that's

kind of a basic economic inefficiency. Society should value these roles more, and what are the things that are getting in the way of that?"

His hope was to make teaching in an urban school—one of the most important jobs in America, as he saw it—as attractive to the most talented college graduates as working at Facebook. He couldn't succeed without having his pick of the best people in the business. Why would it be different for public schools?

"Economically, I think it's probably the most important problem in the world," Zuckerberg said of the state of public education for the poorest children.

Chan cast a questioning look his way, smiling as if in amusement. "We're different," she explained. He saw the problem as systemic and economic, while she viewed it from the ground level, through the needs of individual children. In her view, investing in children had value for its own sake. "It's the coolest thing, because you never know what they're going to do later on and you can't really follow up on it. You just sort of have this idea, 'Who knows what that kid's going to do?'"

In emails and documents Booker and Zuckerberg sent back and forth after their talks in Sun Valley, their stated goal was not simply to re-pair education in Newark but to develop a model for saving it in all of urban America—and to do it in five years. Booker argued that by succeeding in a district as challenging as Newark, Zuckerberg would emerge with a model that he could take to one city after another.

In August, Booker sent Zuckerberg a proposal, prepared with the pro bono help of McKinsey consultants. It was titled "Creating a National Model of Educational Transformation." On the cover was a color photograph of Booker surrounded by African American chil-dren, all reaching skyward, as was the mayor. The document referred repeatedly to Newark's potential as a national model. "Our youth population is manageable in size, making Newark an ideal laboratory for community change," it said. Newark would "coordinate a critical mass of local and national partners with proven models of excellence to deliver high impact programs and best practices." The last page listed four criteria for success, only one in boldface: "Blueprint for national replication across America's urban centers to transform the lives of its youth." The language of national models left little room for attention to the unique problems of Newark, its schools, or its children.

A few weeks later, Zuckerberg invited Booker to Palo Alto to talk more, and they continued the conversation by phone, in secret (the name on Booker's private schedule was "Mr. Z."). No one in the Newark schools or local politics was to know what was afoot. The talks went late into the night, with Sheryl Sandberg on the line as well as Booker's chief education adviser, De'Shawn Wright. "The mayor, Sheryl, Mark, and I were on the phone at two or three o'clock in the morning, talking about education reform and what are the levers of change and how do you do it systemically and what are the hurdles with politics, policy, and legislation that would get us to this utopia of education," Wright said. Zuckerberg made clear that his primary goal was to find a way to attract, nurture, and handsomely reward top teachers. Like almost every school district in the country, Newark paid teachers based on how long they had held their jobs and how many graduate degrees they had earned, although neither correlated with increased effectiveness. In other words, teachers who transformed students' lives received the same pay as the deadwood. "Who would want to work in a system like that?" Zuckerberg wondered aloud about circumstances that applied to almost all of America's 3.3 million public school teachers.

The world Zuckerberg worked in could not have provided a sharper contrast to the Newark public schools. At Facebook, he sat in a gymnasium-sized room filled with coders in their twenties, many of them pursued by tech companies around the world with offers of signing bonuses that dwarfed the annual salaries of experienced Newark teachers. Around the workstations were red-lettered motivational signs: STAY FOCUSED AND KEEP SHIPPING. MOVE FAST AND BREAK THINGS. DONE IS BETTER THAN PERFECT. WHAT WOULD YOU DO IF YOU WEREN'T AFRAID? In the Newark schools, which

Zuckerberg had never visited, nothing moved fast, much was already broken, and most people were afraid of change.

A month after their conversations in Sun Valley, Booker gave Zuckerberg a six-point agenda drawn from the McKinsey document, which in turn was based on the original plan Booker had devised for Christie. It called for a data system to track student progress and hold everyone accountable for it; new school models, including charters, single-sex schools, and schools for students at risk of dropping out; recruitment and training of top-quality educators for future openings; a community awareness program to build public support and services for disaffected youth. The top agenda item for Zuckerberg was a new labor contract that would significantly reward Newark teachers who improved their students' performance, a shift he believed would raise the status of the profession. "Over the long term, that's the only way they're going to get the very best people, a *lot* of the very best people," he concluded.

Booker asked Zuckerberg for $100 million over five years. The mayor conceded, however, that he did not know at the time what the initiatives would cost. He chose the number largely for its size and the public attention it would draw to the effort. "We knew it had to be big, we both thought it had to be bold, eye-catching," said Booker. Zuckerberg agreed, with the caveat that Booker would have to match it with another $100 million from other donors. Booker didn't blink, although this meant raising a king-sized amount of money in an economy still reeling from the financial crisis of 2008.

In late summer 2010, Booker called Christie with the $100 million news. "I didn't believe it," Christie recalled. "I said, 'Come on, *really?*' He said, 'Governor, I believe I can close this deal. I really do. I need you, though.'"

Booker asked Christie to grant him control of the schools by fiat, but the governor demurred, offering him instead a role as unofficial partner in all decisions and policies, beginning with their joint selection of a "superstar" superintendent to lead the charge. Booker's first choice was John King, then deputy New York State education commissioner, who had led some of the top-performing charter schools in New York City and Boston and who credited public school teachers with inspiring him to persevere after he was orphaned as a young boy in Brooklyn. Zuckerberg and Chan flew King to Palo Alto for a weekend with them and Sandberg; Christie hosted him at the governor's beach retreat on the Jersey Shore; and Booker led King and his wife, Melissa, on a tour of Newark, with stops at parks and businesses that hadn't existed before his mayoralty. But after much thought, King turned them down. Zuckerberg, Christie, and Booker expected to arrive at their national model within five years. King believed it could take almost that long to change the system's fundamental procedures and to raise expectations across the city for children and schools. "John's view was that no one has achieved what they're trying to achieve: build an urban school district serving high-poverty kids that gets uniformly strong outcomes," said an acquaintance who talked with King about the offer. "You'd have to invest not only a long period of time but tremendous political capital to get it done." King had questions about a five-year plan overseen by politicians who were likely to seek higher office.

Zuckerberg had questions, too, about politics—particularly about the power-sharing plan between Booker and Christie. He asked to meet Christie face to face. He and Chan flew to Newark in August 2010 and met the governor and mayor in a secluded area of the airport's Continental Airlines Presidents Club. The couple was struck by the personal chemistry between two prominent politicians of different parties. It dated to Booker's unsuccessful 2002 mayoral campaign, when Christie, as United States attorney in Newark, deployed volunteers from his office to act as election-day monitors following reports of violence and intimidation against Booker's supporters. (He found none.) Another important moment in their relationship occurred in 2006, when aides to the newly elected mayor came upon suspicious-looking records from a credit card account registered to the police department but used by Booker's five-term predecessor, Sharpe James. Booker delivered the records to Christie, who found in them the gift of a lifetime—the break in a case that sent James to jail, one of the biggest convictions of Christie's career as a prosecutor.

A rising Republican star after only nine months as governor, Christie was now waging political war on the state teachers' union as he slashed his way through a bloated budget. More than one million people had watched him on YouTube as he shamed—critics said "bullied"—a teacher for attacking him and his education cuts at a town hall meeting. This knack for playing a Republican everyman aggrieved by protections of public sector workers was winning him mentions as GOP presidential material.

Given the polarized state of national politics, Zuckerberg was impressed that a Democrat and a Republican were uniting in the interest of New Jersey's poorest children. But would this last? He asked Booker and Christie what would happen if they ran against each other for governor in three years. Both men said they were in complete agreement on education and would not allow politics to interfere, according to participants. John King had raised the question also, asking Christie how the superintendent would be affected if Booker ran against him in 2013. "In that case," Christie responded, "the superintendent would spend the year hiding under his desk."

A maestro at leveraging publicity, Booker wanted to announce the $100 million gift on *The Oprah Winfrey Show,* timed to coincide with the September 24 debut of the movie *Waiting for Superman.* The film, whose marketing campaign was aided by a $2 million grant from the Gates Foundation, focused on five families who desperately wanted their children to attend a charter school. The charters featured in the movie each had a dedicated team of teachers and leaders, along with a record of putting the poorest children on a path to college. Four of the five families lived in inner cities, and their children's only other option was to attend a dysfunctional public school that was little more than a dropout factory. There was a mention in a voice-over that only one in five charters then outperformed traditional public schools, but overall, the film belted out a thunderous cheer for charter schools as the answer to the crisis in urban education.

There was a complication, however. Another movie was scheduled to debut the same weekend: *The Social Network,* Aaron Sorkin's fictionalized account of the founding of Facebook in which, it was already well known, Zuckerberg came off as an arrogant boy genius who betrayed a trusting friend on his way to fame and fortune. There was plenty of anxiety at Facebook headquarters about the potential of the movie, sure to be a box office blowout, to tarnish the company's brand. Facebook's communications team flatly advised Zuckerberg not to make such an attention-grabbing gesture of generosity just when *The Social Network* hit theaters. It would probably be criticized as a $100 million damage-control stunt, not seen as a bold and selfless commitment to a better tomorrow for children, senior advisers told him. Zuckerberg asked Booker, Christie, and Winfrey for a postponement, but they were determined to go ahead, largely because Booker wanted to use the marketing campaign for *Waiting for Superman* as a catalyst for raising the second $100 million. Zuckerberg said he then proposed making the gift anonymously. But again Booker, Christie, and Winfrey pushed back, saying they needed his name and cachet to attract donors. Zuckerberg said he did a rough calculation in his head and concluded that the number of people likely to see *The Social Network* was about two percent of the number who then logged on to Facebook every day. Let's go ahead, he said.

Although Facebook insisted the gift was unrelated to the movie, there was no question that it would create a splashy and favorable narrative about the young billionaire at the very moment he was being bludgeoned on the big screen. Christie and Booker also had much to gain from the timing. Booker faced an epic fiscal crisis and was preparing to lay off almost a quarter of the city's workforce. And Christie was under heavy fire for a botched state bid for $400 million in Race to the Top funds.

As the day of the announcement approached—with Newark residents still in the dark about the revolution coming to their schools

—teams around Booker and Zuckerberg anticipated it would trigger a nationwide flood of matching contributions from the richest as well as ordinary Americans. "A national provocation, really provoking people to get involved, to get engaged," as Booker put it. Sandberg emailed updates to Booker's chief fundraiser, Bari Mattes, regarding billionaires she and Zuckerberg were soliciting: "Mark is following up with Gates this week. I will call David Einhorn (my cousin). Mark is scheduling dinner with Broad . . . AMAZING if Oprah will donate herself? Will she? I am following up with John Doerr/NewSchools Venture Fund." The references were to Bill Gates, hedge fund manager David Einhorn, real estate and insurance magnate Eli Broad, and Silicon Valley venture capitalist John Doerr. Einhorn and Winfrey did not contribute, and Sandberg reported that Broad first wanted to know who would be named superintendent. Gates gave $3 million through his and his wife's foundation—Zuckerberg had hoped for between $10 and $15 million—and Doerr's fund gave $10 million, to be used to expand networks of high-quality charter schools.

Ray Chambers, a Newark native who had made a fortune in private equity and for decades had donated generously to education and the city's children, offered to coordinate a $1 million gift from local philanthropies as a show of community support. But Mattes was unimpressed. "I think that commitment is way too small and I wouldn't bother," she wrote the mayor in an email, concluding: "$1 million as a collective gift over five years is just too insignificant for this group."

Because the reforms would focus on systemic changes, Mattes wrote in one email, "Mark's money is not going into classrooms." This aspect of the gift alone was sure to pose a public relations challenge in a city where teachers and schools desperately needed support for children who were years behind their grade level. But it was Sandberg, not Booker or his fundraiser Mattes, who expressed concern about the reaction in Newark, whose residents would soon learn from national television that there was a grand design to transform their schools. She asked in an email about plans for a "community awareness piece," deeming it "so critical." Sandberg also critiqued Booker's proposed press release for placing too much emphasis on the initiative's national import, rather than on what was in it for Newark. "My one question is whether for local purposes there is too much 'national' language in here," she wrote. "I wonder if we should basically make this focused on Newark with just a touch of 'and this will be a national model.'"

Calling from the flight to Chicago for the *Oprah* show, Booker solicited one of his most loyal supporters, New York City hedge fund manager and billionaire philanthropist William Ackman. The two had met when Booker was a city councilman running for mayor, and a decade later, Ackman still vividly recalled his stunned reaction. "It was the first time I ever met a politician where I had this moving, unbelievable life experience: This guy can change the world. I want be part of what he's doing," Ackman said. Over the years, he helped Booker raise millions of dollars in political and philanthropic campaigns and personally donated $1 million to update Newark's police equipment. This time, the mayor's ask was steeper: $50 million. Ackman offered $25 million, and Booker accepted. It was more than he intended to give — more than he had ever given to a single philanthropic cause — but when Booker set the bar so high, Ackman said he felt sheepish about holding back. "It's a good fundraising strategy — ask for a really, really big number," he said with a laugh.

Earlier that month, Booker had presented the board of Ackman's Pershing Square Foundation with his six-point proposal to Zuckerberg for reforming the Newark schools. Unlike most venture philanthropists, Ackman said he didn't grill Booker on exactly how he would spend his money or dictate timetables and metrics for measuring results. "The idea was to fix education," he said. "How they were going to do it, that was just the detail. I was just confident he'd approve the best team, the best people, and it would end up in the right place."

It was just as Booker's law school pal Ed Nicoll had said all those years ago. Investors bet on people, not on business plans.

On September 24, 2010, Zuckerberg, Booker, and Christie ended up in matching black leather chairs on the stage of *The Oprah Winfrey*

Show. Christie recalled that Zuckerberg, who until that point had kept a low public profile, confided to him as they walked onstage that he was nervous. Christie said he promised the young magnate that it was actually going to be fun. With the cameras rolling, Booker and Christie went first, describing their bipartisan pact to transform the Newark schools.

"So, Mr. Zuckerberg, what role are you playing in all of this?" Winfrey asked, feigning cluelessness.

"I've committed to starting the Startup: Education Foundation," he said. "The first project will be a $100 million challenge grant—"

He was not able to complete the sentence, as Winfrey exclaimed, slowly, as if in amazement, "ONE. HUNDRED. MILLION. DOLLARS?" The audience broke into applause. "YO! YO! YO! YO! YO!" Winfrey whooped, and she, Booker, Christie, and the studio audience gave Zuckerberg an explosive standing ovation. The world's youngest billionaire philanthropist remained seated, blushing, appearing uncomfortable amid the adulation.

Asked by Winfrey why he picked Newark, out of all the cities in the country, the T-shirted entrepreneur in open blazer and running shoes gestured toward the dark-suited politicians and said, "Newark is really just because I believe in these guys. Running a company, the main thing that I have to do is find people who are going to be really great leaders and invest in them, and that's what we're doing here. We're setting up a $100 million challenge grant so that Mayor Booker and Governor Christie can have the flexibility they need to . . . turn Newark into a symbol of educational excellence for the whole nation."

3

The View from Avon Avenue

September 2010

F AR FROM THE set of the *Oprah* show, a young teacher from
Newark named Princess Williams had embarked on a profoundly different approach to repairing public education. For
eighteen months, Williams had worked with school leaders Dominique Lee, Charity Haygood, and three other teachers and administrators preparing to take the helm of Avon Avenue School, one of the
very worst in the state, in one of Newark's poorest neighborhoods.
Booker was right, they agreed, that the district urgently needed a systemic overhaul. But as teachers, they knew that transforming education would require far more than strict accountability, performance
incentives, and heightened emphasis on data. They were intimately
familiar with the challenges Newark children brought to the classroom, and they knew of no model for addressing them other than
child by child, teacher by teacher, school by school, from the bottom
up. As Booker, Zuckerberg, and Christie vowed on television to create
a national model for turning around failing districts within five years,
Williams, Lee, and Haygood resolved to commit their entire careers
to Newark's schools. They considered themselves reformers too, hav-

ing arrived in the Newark school district initially through Teach for America. Princess Williams, who signed on as Avon's lead kindergarten teacher, felt a sense of destiny about teaching Newark children.

Lee referred to Room 112, Williams's kindergarten classroom, as "the future." The door opened onto a room appointed with simple, homemade learning activities — a large calendar highlighting the date and day of the week, a chart displaying the day's weather (clouds), Post-it notes in a repeating color pattern enumerating the days since school started. A clothesline stretched across the room, with student work hanging at child's-eye level. On this day, the line displayed colored paper on which children had represented the numbers zero through ten in dots, stars, or blocks. Williams had written an enthusiastic remark on each.

Looking younger than her twenty-seven years, the small, pretty teacher wearing a rose-colored blouse over brown cropped pants commanded complete attention from twenty-three children seated before her on an alphabet rug. "We have a special visitor who would like to show you two new letters," she announced with excitement. "Drumroll, please!"

The children rapidly and rhythmically slapped their legs, eyes focused with anticipation on Williams. The teacher reached dramatically behind a whiteboard and slowly, her dark eyes widening, revealed a white stuffed owl with brown speckles, holding a card bearing the letter O in its beak. There were oohs, ahhs, and wriggles of excitement.

"I want you to meet Echo," said Williams, cuddling the fluffy toy in her lap. "What letter did he bring for us?" The class answered in unison. She then turned the card over and showed them a picture of an octopus. "O. Octopus. Aw," everyone chanted. Then Williams made Echo disappear behind the whiteboard and emerge with a card displaying a G and a picture of a board game. "G. Game. Gih," everyone said.

Williams noticed one girl not looking at Echo. Without raising her voice or breaking the mood, she said, "Sah'Jaidah, our eyes are looking at the letters so our brains all remember them and make a connection to the sound." Sah'Jaidah looked immediately at Echo, who now was showing the class a K and a kite, followed by an H and a hat. Williams had the children hold their hands in front of their mouths to feel the hot air as they made the "h" sound.

It all appeared to unfold effortlessly, with the grace and pacing of ballet. But everything Williams did that day and every day was the result of serious thought, preparation, and even love. She knew from experience that learning represented a lifeline for every child seated before her. Her calling was to ensure that they loved it and craved it, starting now, at the beginning of kindergarten. She treated every moment of every class as an opportunity to infuse the ordinary with wonder—a special visit from Echo to light up a phonics lesson, a pause to create a sensory connection to the rush of air in the "h" sound. It was no coincidence that Echo was within arm's reach. Williams placed him there when plotting out the day's lesson to guard against any interruption in the action, which could allow young minds to wander, breaking the spell of learning. As if to illustrate the risk, squeals and shrieks arose from the kindergarten class next door. "Yes, I'm wearing fishnets!" the teacher could be heard screaming above the clamor, which went on for several minutes as Williams's class moved to their tables where phonics workbooks awaited them for a writing activity. "Look for the O page in the workbook," she said, as if sending them off on a treasure hunt. "Oooh! Lanice found it! Let's see quiet thumbs-up if you found the O page." She moved among the tables, giving encouragement and help to those who hadn't found the right page. When the noise died down next door, Williams's students were busy at work, writing O's and circling pictures of an orange, an ocean, an octopus, an owl.

She seemed to have endless ways to make learning playful. When calling on students to spell sight words—those they were supposed to recognize instantly, without sounding out—she offered them a choice: play it (as if strumming a banjo with each letter), shoot it (as if throwing a basketball), kick it, or punch it. A girl named Shaniyah, her braids clasped with colorful barrettes, loved kickboxing, so she kicked out each letter of c-a-n.

Explaining the difference between a square and a rectangle one day, Williams summoned the two smallest and two tallest children and asked the class if the four of them could form a square with their bodies as its sides. "NOOOO!" chorused about half the students. Since not everyone got it, she instructed the short and tall students to lie down in a four-sided figure. "Are these sides all the same or are two shorter and two longer?" she asked. Some children still weren't sure. She reached for some masking tape, running a strip alongside each student, then asked the four to stand so that everyone could see the resulting four-sided figure. Clearly the sides were unequal. "OOOOH!" everyone exclaimed. So what is it, Williams asked. "A RECTANGLE!" they all said with excitement.

At the beginning of school, few of her students could distinguish between the front and back cover of a book. Nor did most know that words moved from left to right in a sentence, although New Jersey provided free preschool led by certified teachers for children in the poorest school districts. Williams used a literacy program called STEP, developed at the University of Chicago to measure each child's pre-reading skills and target instruction to their individual needs.

But beyond tools and teaching skill, what made Williams powerful as a teacher was her connection to her students. She was one of them, and they could feel it. One day, teaching a lesson on the importance of vivid details in storytelling, Williams sat down at a whiteboard and said she wanted to draw a picture of her family's recent barbecue. What details should be in the picture? Everyone had ideas: a grill, hamburgers, hot dogs, grass, the sun, the sky, her baby cousin, her mother, her aunt. As Williams drew the pictures, one boy asked, "Where's your daddy?" A girl who never had known her own father cast an annoyed look at the boy and declared, as if stating the obvious, "Miss Williams ain't got no daddy!" Williams responded that she did have a father, but he wasn't there.

"The children know I'm from Newark. They'll tell me a parent is in jail or parents were fighting. They blurt it out during a lesson," Williams said one day after school, sitting in a child-sized chair under the clothesline of her students' latest work. Once, a little girl confided that she had seen her mother's boyfriend beat up her father the night before. With no time to think about what to say, the response rolled out from her life experience: "Miss Williams has seen things like that. One day you'll be able to choose not to be in situations where people treat each other that way. I'm going to help you do that."

Knowing well that poverty cramped children's horizons, Williams talked to them of "excellence," striving to surpass their best. At the end of each day, she singled out the students who had done so. Some of those who missed the cut were invariably disappointed, but Williams reminded them that they knew how to handle it. "Don't pout! Blow it out!" they said along with her, taking a deep breath and exhaling. "I push them to be more excellent, never to accept mediocrity, otherwise they hit a ceiling," she said. She sometimes lay in bed at night thinking of ways to raise their expectations of themselves. If a child liked to braid hair, Williams would say, "That's a great skill for a surgeon." Those who talked a little too much in class heard, "You should think about becoming a debater."

"I think a lot about what distinguished me from my friends who became statistics," she said. "Yes, I saw people get shot. Yes, I saw people get arrested in my own family. But I never had a teacher say, 'I'm going to expect less of you because of what you're going through.' We have to say, 'We understand this is very hard for you, but we're not going to use that as an excuse to hold you to a lower standard, and you can't allow it to make you lower your own standards for yourself.'"

Williams came by this understanding the hard way, beginning at age seven, when she, her mother, and two brothers fled their Newark apartment—and Williams's stepfather—for a battered-women's shelter. From then on, there were periods of stability alternating with homelessness. But through it all, Williams's mother, Samantha Lucien, focused her children on learning as the surest path to a better life.

Lucien told her children that her own childhood was troubled, as was her education, and now she wanted—expected—only the best for them.

Williams took her mother's expectations as her own, as did her brothers. When money ran short and their electricity was turned off, she would gather her books and go into the hallway of their apartment building to do her homework under the fluorescent lights. It didn't occur to her to ask her teacher or mother for a reprieve. She was valedictorian of her middle school and won a scholarship to Kent Place, an all-girls private school in upscale Summit, New Jersey, through a national program for students of color with leadership potential, A Better Chance. She excelled as a student and a dancer, even when the family became homeless again and she commuted by bus from a Newark shelter to attend classes with daughters of privilege. As holidays approached, her classmates talked of traveling overseas —"like something that happened every day: you got on a plane and went to Madrid. I was going to Six Flags." It was the mid-1990s, and urban styles hadn't made it to Summit, so when Williams arrived at Kent Place one day with braids and extensions, she recalled drawing a crowd. "It felt like a cultural barrier," she remembered. "They said, 'Your hair grew!'"

Halfway through her junior year, she was suffering from depression and transferred to West Side High School back home in Newark. There Williams met students she considered as bright as she was— students she was sure would have excelled, as she did, if given opportunities—and yet the school system appeared to treat them as if they weren't worth the effort. While some of her own teachers were excellent, Williams felt that, overall, she had gone from a level of rigor that challenged her every day to no rigor at all—no advanced placement classes, no anatomy and physiology. "The mindset at West Side was 'These kids can't do AP. They're nowhere near ready for it. They're incapable,'" she said. Worse still, most of the students appeared to have the same expectations of themselves. "They mostly didn't do homework until the period before it was due," she said. By contrast, she and her group of friends were always studying. She'd sit in the cafeteria reading and taking notes while other kids talked. Inevitably, someone would ask why she was studying at lunchtime, why she carried a book bag full of books, why she carried books at all, she recalled. What made her normal at Kent Place—a drive for knowledge and excellence—made her an outlier among most kids back home.

In her senior year at West Side, Williams's family became homeless again and wound up living in a family friend's basement, in a single room lit by one lamp. She remembered sitting under it filling out her college applications, telling herself, "This is going to get me out of here." She got into New York University, where she studied and graduated alongside the academic elite from around the country.

While there, she did a work-study program in the New York City public schools, tutoring struggling elementary school readers under the supervision of teachers she considered exceptional—experienced, nurturing, demanding of themselves and the children. She found herself imagining what her friends and classmates at West Side would have become with teachers like that all along the way.

"That's when I said I want to teach, and I want to teach in Newark," she said. "I want to help cultivate those brilliant minds. I want to deposit in my hometown what people deposited into me. I want to teach in Newark because I love my city. I love it because there's so much promise here. I want to invest my life's work in the city, because I believe in it."

Avon Avenue School, where Princess Williams saw so much promise, was 105 years old, an immense hulk of red brick rising three stories and filling almost a full square block. The grand scale reflected the school's aspirations—very much akin to Williams's—when in the early 1900s Newark and public education were passageways to opportunity for hundreds of thousands of working-class immigrants and their children. The city was a national leader in manufacturing and retail. It had visionary civic leaders who built public institutions —the library, the museum—into engines of democracy that spread culture and literacy to the masses. In heavily poor, immigrant communities like Avon's, public schools remained open all summer to "continue the process of Americanization" of disadvantaged children and "give the opportunity for a large number to advance rapidly," in the words of Addison B. Poland, Newark's turn-of-the-century superintendent.

The Avon area in the early 1900s was mostly German immigrants, living in three- and four-family homes, working in factories, and sending their children to the neighborhood school. A century later, after economic decline, riots, and white flight, it was almost all black and poor. Nearly half of the children came from families who lived in what the government classified as "extreme poverty," or fifty percent of the federal poverty level, approximately $11,000 a year for a family of four. The school had suffered along with the neighborhood. Nothing inside worked as it was supposed to, even the clocks, which each told a different time, all of them wrong. Barely one in six students in third through seventh grade had passed the most recent state literacy test, and the math results were even worse, especially in the middle school, where only four percent of seventh graders passed.

"A generous description of Avon Avenue students would be 'semi-literate,'" wrote Gordon MacInnes, a policy analyst, summarizing the years leading up to the turnaround effort that drew Williams there. "The results on the math test raise this question: was there any intentional effort to teach mathematics to Avon Avenue students?"

MacInnes emphasized that poverty posed an enormous barrier to learning in Newark and nationally. The pattern was consistent across the country: the poorer the children, the lower the test scores. Yet worse than the damage from poverty at Avon, he found, was the district's unconscionable and systematic neglect of the children's needs. MacInnes wrote with outrage and astonishment, hurling aside the detached tone of most policy papers: "There is no helpful explanation how the Avon results could be overlooked for so many years without triggering intensive attention from NPS," the Newark Public Schools administration.

During the summer of 2010, the newly appointed leaders of Avon, Dominique Lee and Charity Haygood, along with Williams and other teachers, were intently studying the school's academic results and developing a reform strategy rooted in supporting and strengthening the teaching staff. All of them had a personal journey that led them to teach in Newark. Lee, just twenty-five years old at the time, had spent most of his childhood in low-income housing developments in Pontiac, Michigan, with a single mother who was periodically on welfare. Then, as if by magic—in Lee's view, by God's grace—his father, who had been living in Texas, reappeared to care for him as he entered his teens. Having risen into management at Exxon, his father took a position in the Detroit area with ExxonMobil after the two oil giants merged. Lee moved in with his dad in suburban Bloomfield Hills but remained at his urban Pontiac high school. Accustomed to making B's and C's, he faced a new standard with his father: nothing below an A would do. Lee graduated at the top of his class, was admitted to the University of Michigan, and graduated with honors. He liked pointing out that he was a third-generation college graduate on his father's side, first generation on his mother's. "I should be a statistic," he said. "I'm a black male with an uneducated single mother. 'Amazing grace!' God 'saved a wretch like me.'"

After college, when Lee arrived at Newark's Malcolm X Shabazz High School to teach social studies and English, many of his students reminded him of his younger self—except that no one had saved them. They were often reading four or more years below grade level, couldn't name the continents, and didn't know the difference between a governor and a mayor. Angular and high-energy, a towering six feet five inches tall, Lee was irrepressibly positive, pushing his students and himself. After struggling for three years to teach basic skills in tandem with the Civil War, he felt compelled to confront the larger problem: four lower schools, all serving Newark's poorest children, fed into Shabazz, and barely a quarter of their graduates were proficient in reading and math. His idea was to recruit a small group of highly motivated Newark teachers for each of those schools, to build a culture of excellence in which newcomers and veterans together would raise the quality of teaching and learning. He called his idea "a kind of naïve little dream to meet the neediest children's needs."

His first call was to Charity Haygood, then a district assistant principal who had come to Newark thirteen years earlier with Teach for America and made it her home. They connected instantly. Haygood grew up in Denver, with a single mother who never finished high school but inspired her to work her hardest. She attended chronically low-performing Manual High School, which was closed soon after she graduated — later to be reopened — but she credited teachers and classmates in her college-bound classes with pushing her to aim high. She was admitted to Colorado College and, based on her family's poverty, received a full scholarship.

She also shared Lee's religious conviction. For years, Haygood and her husband, a civil rights attorney, had led a weekly church youth group and had taken into their home children whose parents struggled with addiction and illness. "If you live in Newark and you're going to do what needs to be done, you have to be brave enough to act in faith," she said. "It's not about being the boss, but being the servant willing to wash other people's feet. More than anything, it's about understanding you don't have all the answers. This is so much bigger than me. It's bigger than Cory Booker. It's bigger than Barack Obama. It's recognizing that you've got to be humble."

They began planning in earnest in 2009, recruiting four colleagues from other Newark schools. Princess Williams was the only one of them to have been born and raised in the city. At dinner one night, they brainstormed a name for their organization and came up with Building Responsible, Intelligent, Creative Kids, or BRICK — an allusion to Brick City, Newark's nickname from the 1940s, when brick housing projects stood at the heart of the city.

They spent eighteen months reviewing research, consulting educators, and visiting high-achieving urban schools, including charter schools. The earliest charters were expected to serve as laboratories for innovative practices that district schools would adopt and spread. In fact, there had been little cross-pollination in Newark or elsewhere. The BRICK team, though, took it upon themselves to glean many lessons from the city's best charter schools, and found charter school leaders eager to help. They organized themselves as a nonprofit agency through which they raised private money to purchase the rigorous, early-literacy program, developed at the University of Chicago for kindergarten through third grade, that was used in the two leading charter networks—the TEAM schools of the national KIPP organization and North Star Academy, a subsidiary of Uncommon Schools. This was the STEP program Williams now used with her kindergarten class.

They envied the charters' freedom to hire the best teachers and to set their schedules based on student needs—unconstrained by union contracts, tenure law, and the district bureaucracy. But BRICK's founders resolved to work in district schools. They were convinced that charters didn't serve children from the most struggling families, with the greatest learning needs, the kind who came to Avon. They believed some charters deliberately avoided these students, or pushed them out. Even the TEAM schools, which went to great lengths to recruit the most disadvantaged children, faced a selection bias: the most motivated parents with the highest ambitions for children were applying in droves. The Avon teachers felt almost personally insulted by the notion that the district was too broken to fix. Princess Williams had turned away overtures to teach at TEAM and North Star, despite being impressed by their commitment to top-level instruction. "My calling is to fix the public schools," she said. "If something is broken and we have the power to fix it, why would we abandon it for something else? It's like saying, 'Because so much negative is happening in Newark, we should just totally level the town and bring in new people.'" That was the message many in Newark took from Governor Christie's call to "grab the system by the roots, pull it out and start over." With more than four out of five children in district schools at the time, that was where the BRICK teachers felt they belonged. "If you want to change public education, you have to attack the district buildings," Lee said.

Clifford Janey, then the Newark superintendent, encouraged the BRICK team to write a proposal for a school. They wanted to concentrate on the early school years to ensure students were reading proficiently by third grade. They proposed to open with only kindergarten, first, and second grades, and then to grow one grade a year. Most charters in Newark began with a single grade level, then added one a year as the founding class advanced. They also asked for a waiver from the union contract to hire teachers of their choice, another hallmark of charters. In April 2010, Janey named Dominique Lee and his team to lead Avon, but instead of only three grades, he gave them all nine, six hundred and fifty students, in kindergarten through eighth grade. He also assigned them the existing staff, under whom Avon students had failed for years.

If they had a choice, Lee said, they would have rejected about a third of Avon's forty teachers as subpar. But among the others they found capable teachers who they believed could become good with the right support, and good ones who could become exceptional. It was a mantra of the reform movement that children and their genius were trapped in failing schools, but the BRICK leaders found gifted teachers were trapped there as well. Since few Newark principals spent time observing teachers and supporting their growth, teachers throughout the district had languished for years with unrealized potential. Avon, for example, already had a star-quality third-grade team in Sharon Rappaport, Teresa Olivieria, and Regina Sherrod, who coaxed impressive gains from their students, only to see them lose ground in later years with less effective teachers. Because so few teachers had received meaningful support from principals, Lee and Haygood looked not for preexisting powerhouses but for teachers who knew their subjects, had strong relationships with students, and were willing to work on their practice with a goal of becoming more effective.

The BRICK leaders divided administrative responsibilities so Haygood could devote the bulk of her time to observing teachers and helping them improve. Dressed in the BRICK uniform of yellow shirt and navy pants, her dark hair bound in a curly ponytail, she radiated kindness, even when delivering harsh assessments. "Charity can tell you essentially, 'You suck,' and you walk out with a smile on your face," said Lee.

Rappaport said she and some other veterans resented the new leaders at first: "They came in saying we were going to work longer days, longer weeks, longer years, and I said, 'Who let them in here? This is *our* building.'" But she said she changed her mind because of one of the newcomers, Chris Perpich, who at half her age was her instructional coach and assistant principal. With modest suggestions, one at a time, she said, he made her a stronger teacher.

The new leaders also required all teachers to develop a "BRICK plan" for each student, an individualized improvement program with specific responsibilities for families as well as teachers. Federal law mandated such plans for students with disabilities, but the BRICK leaders felt all parents should know how their children performed in comparison to national standards in reading, writing, and math, and how to help each of them meet the bar. After so many years of failure as the norm, they said, parents often didn't know what to expect of children. The BRICK plan listed up to three tasks for families to perform with students every night, and three kinds of academic support activities that teachers would carry out with them every day.

One of the cruel ironies of Newark's schools was that throughout their long decline, the district often appeared on paper to be in perfect compliance with all requirements. A 2009 outside review of the Avon Avenue School found that the curriculum aligned well with state standards in math and literacy. And the district had a written policy requiring principals to observe teachers regularly, supplying feedback and coaching to ensure they were reaching all children.

But inside Avon, as in many schools across the district, reality bore little resemblance to the script. An application for federal aid, filed shortly after the outside review, reported that too many teachers displayed "an inability to captivate student interest and motivate them." And there was "minimal use of higher order questioning." The quality of the curriculum had little relevance without effective instruction. Numerous students recalled that in earlier years, while they sat in class trying to learn, other children routinely ran, yelled, or fought in the halls. Principals and teachers appeared powerless to stop them. Avon was mentioned in the police blotter almost as often as in the *Star-Ledger's* education coverage. In 1996, an Avon kindergarten teacher was indicted on charges of official misconduct for ordering her five-year-old students to line up and punch a classmate in the back for tearing up her lesson plan. In 1998, two men were charged with selling heroin and cocaine from an apartment next door.

The disconnect between rules and reality was hardly limited to education. Down the hill from the Avon school, a city sign for years had warned, "No Littering $1,000 Fine." No one in the neighborhood had $1,000 to spare, so the seemingly harsh consequence was a joke, as the broken liquor bottles, crushed beer cans, and candy wrappers strewn in all directions made clear. As school board member Marques-Aquil Lewis once put it: "This is Newark. Rules were made to be broken."

Against this backdrop, the new leaders of Avon fanned across the neighborhood in the summer of 2010 to knock on every door and talk to parents about working together to change the school. They gained credibility when they persuaded the district to light Avon's playground, which led to a blossoming of nighttime hoops. And Dominique Lee successfully fought the district to have the aging school's interior repainted with a trim of bold, primary colors, as opposed to the default hues of beige and brown. In late summer, four hundred men, women, and children from the neighborhood turned out for a barbecue—the best attendance anyone could recall at a school event.

Yet doubts kept surfacing in the form of a recurring question: Are you turning Avon into a charter school? Charters had become a code word in parts of Newark for rich, white outsiders who hid self-interest behind a veil of altruism—a narrative of distrust going back to urban renewal days.

Lee patiently batted away the rumors, affirming BRICK's solid commitment to district schools. But the question rankled. Why vent so much anger and fear on charters while excusing the district for failing Avon students for so long? One day, in response to yet another question about the rumor, he blurted out: "No, we are not a charter school. But what is it about charters that's scarier than four percent proficiency in math?"

A life-sized casualty of the long decline arrived in sixth grade on the opening day of the rechristened BRICK Avon Academy, three weeks before the *Oprah* announcement. His name was Alif Beyah, and he had been promoted year after year despite failing basic subjects. He also was a discipline challenge, forever getting thrown out of class for refusing to do his work.

"He acted—excuse my French—like an ass to me in the hallway one day and I suspended him," said Melinda Weidman, the assistant principal for the middle school grades.

But the next morning, she said, Alif returned and apologized, pleading to be allowed to go back to class. Another time, she gave him detention and noticed that he arrived precisely on schedule to serve his time. When she called him out for being disrespectful, she said, he was quick to own up to it, showing genuine remorse.

Weidman, a former high school social studies teacher, was small, with blue eyes, long blond hair, and a voice like a drill sergeant's. The rowdiest eighth graders straightened up when they saw her coming, in part because they knew she'd risk her safety to protect them if a fight broke out. They'd seen her do it.

Weidman built a relationship with Alif's mother, Lakiesha Mills, who confided that she and her boys' father had recently split up. She worked from noon until midnight at concession stands at various arenas and rarely was home to make dinner or supervise homework and bedtime. She was terrified that Alif would fall increasingly behind and slip into a brutally familiar spiral: failure in school, leading to anger and eventually expulsion, with nowhere to turn but the streets. She was desperate for help.

Weidman began to conclude that this wiry stringbean of a trouble-maker with large, dark eyes and a shy smile was in fact a good boy. But somewhere along the line he had fallen far off the track, and now, on the verge of becoming a teenager, faced maximum peril.

"I just started looking out for him and wanting to figure out what had happened," Weidman said.

Part of the explanation was in Alif's cumulative record—known in the school district as a cume card—an oversized, vanilla-colored chart with handwritten notations added year by year, listing his teachers and grades beginning in kindergarten. Every year through third grade—years when he should have learned to read—he got mostly D's and F's. By his own admission, he was a hellion. "I was bad then," he said. "I used to just sit in class and do no work. I was not acting right." Looking back, he couldn't explain why, nor could his mother. Lakiesha Mills said she had assumed that Alif simply wasn't trying. A cousin who was an aide in Alif's third-grade classroom told Mills that he refused to pay attention or do his work. Mills said it didn't occur to her that his teachers could have been responsible.

But it is hard to separate a discipline problem from a teaching problem, especially in a classroom of young children. The BRICK team took the view that effective teachers were a powerful antidote to most misbehavior—teachers who captured and held children's attention through a combination of strong pedagogy, empathy, and leadership. Even reluctant learners tended to get caught up in the positive flow. As it turned out, Haygood and Lee determined that Alif had almost uniformly weak teachers in those years. Asked what he thought of the teachers, Alif said he liked most of them, but he recalled that his classes were full of disruptions, and he always joined in. "If other kids were talking, I always went along with them," he said.

In those years, Avon had four certified teachers on the payroll as full-time tutors to support struggling students, thanks to the New Jersey Supreme Court's landmark *Abbott v. Burke* decisions. In a series of rulings in the 1990s, the court ordered the legislature to equalize the funding of New Jersey's poorest and most affluent districts in the name of guaranteeing educational opportunity to the state's poorest children. But Alif and his mother said he never was offered tutoring.

Required to repeat third grade, he landed the second time around in the class of Sharon Rappaport, one of Avon's finest and firmest teachers. His reputation preceded him. "I saw his name on my class list, and I just took a deep breath and thought, 'We're going to work this out,'" Rappaport recalled.

A mother of five who demanded the same respect and cooperation from pupils that she got at her dinner table, Rappaport was meticulously organized about reaching all her students, from stars to strugglers. Raised in Williamsburg, Brooklyn, in the 1960s, she felt connected to them as a fellow child of what she called "the ghetto," who grabbed education as her ticket out. She immediately noticed that Alif had almost no foundation in reading. She also recognized that he needed tremendous emotional support just to bring himself to try to learn.

"You could tell he really wanted to do well, to be proud of himself," she said. "He would get this little glow if you praised him." She sat with him during independent-reading periods, reading aloud to him, asking questions about the texts and working on letter sounds. She praised every positive step he took—a word he spelled correctly, a neatly written sentence. She developed relationships with his mother and father, talking often about how he was doing at school and at home.

Rappaport also noticed that Alif was relatively strong in math and asked him to stay after school to help tutor students who were failing. His attitude changed dramatically, and his mother was stunned.

"That was one of his teachers that he really, really loved," his mother said. "She knew how to go about getting inside children that age. He'd come home and say, 'Mrs. Rappaport wants me to do this. She wants me to do that.' He loved staying after school and helping her. He began to believe that he could be good in math. Mrs. Rappaport embraced him, and for the first time he felt comfortable enough to try."

At the end of the year, Alif failed the state proficiency test in literacy, but he easily passed in math, falling only five points short of "advanced proficient." For the first time in his life, he made the honor roll, with all A's and B's, except for a C in reading and writing.

After his banner year with Rappaport, though, Alif returned to making D's and F's in fourth and fifth grade. On his cume card, under a category labeled "Demonstrates Evidence of Learning Through Completion of Class and Homework Assignments," he received an N, for "not evident." Yet both years, under the old Avon regime, he had been promoted to the next grade.

The idea behind every school reform effort taking shape in Newark —from the Booker-Christie-Zuckerberg plan to BRICK—was that in the future there would be no Alifs. Equipping five-year-olds from the poorest neighborhoods in Newark with a strong foundation in reading and math, along with a love of learning, represented an essential first step on a path toward a better life. For now, the odds were stacked perilously against poor children everywhere. Research had shown that children in the lowest-income families heard only a fraction of the words or conversations that were the daily bread of the more affluent. By age three, the difference was an astonishing twenty million words. They also had little exposure to books. After kindergarten, the gap grew wider and more treacherous every year. Children who entered first grade without basic literacy skills were unlikely to read proficiently by the end of third grade, which was equivalent to falling off a cognitive cliff. Elementary education boiled down to this: children learn to read by third grade; they read to learn from then on. After third grade, reading was the ball game—math moved into word problems, social studies and science into demanding texts, language arts into novels. A straight line ran from the poor reading skills of Avon third graders to the single-digit passing rate of its middle schoolers on state reading and math tests. Children who couldn't keep up in later grades became frustrated, alienated, and more likely to act out. According to a consultant's analysis of Newark district data, only four percent of students who arrived in high school significantly below grade level went on to pass the state proficiency test for graduation.

Every brand of education reformer shared the same end goal — to reverse the damaging tide of poverty that robbed the poorest children of their potential. The big difference lay in where they started: from the top down or the bottom up.

4

Engaging the Community

September 2010–February 2011

BOOKER CALCULATED CORRECTLY. Timing the Zucker-berg announcement to the premiere of *Waiting for Super-man* swept the young billionaire, the mayor, the governor, and Newark into an extravaganza of media attention. Every television network carried the story and, within three hours of the *Oprah* segment, so did 263 news outlets across the country and around the world. The following Monday, NBC began a week of heavily promoted television programming called *Education Nation,* sponsored in large part by the Gates and Broad foundations — an arrangement that drew some criticism because the coverage dovetailed closely with the venture philanthropists' views. NBC kicked off the week with Booker, Christie, and Education Secretary Arne Duncan as featured guests on MSNBC's *Morning Joe,* talking about Zuckerberg's $100 million gift and the threesome's commitment to turning around public education in Newark.

Although residents of Newark had to tune in to *Oprah* to learn that their mayor, their governor, and a billionaire planned to transform their schools, Booker vowed to the national television audience that this would be the people's project—driven by Newark parents and their demands for change.

"What I believe is that Newark, New Jersey, can help lead America back," Booker declared, "but we have to let Newark lead and not let people drop in from outside and point the way."

"What he is doing that is so smart," Duncan said, gesturing toward Booker. "He's trying to put in place a process to empower average parents, the parents of *Waiting for Superman* who have been disempowered for too long. He's going to put them in the driver's seat."

The testimonials to grassroots democracy came against the backdrop of a major political setback for the school reform movement. Less than two weeks earlier, a voter backlash over the record of Washington, D.C., schools chancellor Michelle Rhee had contributed to the ouster of Mayor Adrian Fenty, who had appointed and defended her. A heroine of reformers—and of the *Waiting for Superman* movie—Rhee had ridden like a crusader through the bureaucracy of the faltering school district, firing hundreds of teachers and dozens of principals and imposing strict accountability for student performance. As resistance rose among teachers, unions, and many parents, Rhee posed resolutely on the cover of *Time* with a broom, as if sweeping aside all who stood in her way. "Cooperation, collaboration and consensus-building are way overrated," she famously declared in a speech to the Aspen Institute.

No one doubted that urban education across the country needed a jolt. Schools were catastrophically failing children in the poorest neighborhoods, and there was little accountability—for teachers, principals, or the bureaucracy itself. Nor was there recourse through the ballot box. Democracy favored unions and powerful political bosses, whose loyalists tended to dominate turnout in school board elections and whose candidates often fought harder for adult jobs than for children's education. Only in districts run by reform-friendly mayors or governors rather than school boards—such as New Orleans, Washington, New York, and now Newark—did officials have a free hand to impose politically unpopular changes. But even Rhee's allies in the reform movement were critical of her autocratic approach, and the warnings loomed large over Newark.

"Education reform is not about its leaders and their prerogatives. It's about communities," Michael Lomax, president of the United Negro College Fund and an ardent reformer, wrote on *The Root,* an online magazine. "Education reform doesn't have to be—indeed, cannot be—force-fed to communities of color ... We can be equal partners in ensuring what is best for our children and all children. It won't work any other way."

What Booker, Christie, and Zuckerberg set out to achieve in Newark had not been accomplished in modern times—turning a failing urban school district into one of universally high achievement. In districts across the country, the education reform movement and the Obama administration had similarly been advocating strategies built on test-based accountability for teachers and rapid expansion of charter schools—strategies whose value was not grounded in scientific research but which advocates saw as remedies for the influence of unions and large bureaucracies. Results were mixed at best. New Orleans, where Hurricane Katrina destroyed all but a handful of district schools, was on its way to becoming a city of almost all charters—all of them non-union—and reformers pointed to it as an exemplar, citing a twenty-point rise in the percentage of third through eighth graders scoring at least "basic" on the state achievement tests. However, only twelve percent achieved the "mastery" level, defined as being "well prepared" for the next grade. And a number of scholars questioned whether the curriculum was aligned too narrowly to tests instead of fostering richer learning. In Washington, D.C., in the wake of Rhee's replacement by Kaya Henderson, who continued her policies, students would go on to post the largest gains of all urban districts on a national assessment of reading and math skills in 2013. Across the country, the results of the National Assessment of Education Progress showed improvement in urban districts over the previous decade, but proficiency remained dauntingly low, and the gap between poor and minority students and all others—in D.C. and elsewhere—was widening rather than closing. "The deep message here is that nobody knows how to educate large numbers of disadvantaged kids successfully," wrote Paul Hill, founder of the Center on Reinventing Public Education, which advocated the development of "portfolio" districts that combined traditional, charter, and contract schools. That verdict became even more ominous when a study revealed that in the 2012–13 school year, for the first time in fifty years, more than half of American public school children lived in low-income families. Hill said the national test results called for an urgent and extensive exploration of a variety of approaches to meet students' needs in each community—a more humble prescription than the rallying cry of Booker and many reformers: "We know what works."

In one of the first expenditures of his philanthropic bounty, Booker immediately launched a community engagement campaign. But the $1 million contract to manage it—which rose eventually to almost $2 million—went not to someone from the community, but rather to a consultant with strong credentials in the school reform movement, Bradley Tusk, of Tusk Strategies in New York City. There was no public disclosure of Tusk's hiring or his qualifications, which included no experience on the ground in Newark. Tusk had managed New York mayor Michael Bloomberg's reelection effort as well as a successful campaign to lift the New York State cap on charter school expansion. He also advised NBC's *Education Nation* team on what his website called the "often very politically-charged education reform landscape." And he advised Rhee, after she left Washington, on strategy for Students First, a national lobbying organization she launched as a political counterforce to teachers' unions.

In Newark, Tusk spent heavily on billboards, television, and radio, although local organizers warned that word of mouth from neighbors, friends, and family was far more powerful. Everyone he hired had connections to the education reform movement. He brought on a national communications firm, SKDKnickerbocker, whose principals included Anita Dunn, a former Obama White House communications director and adviser to Michelle Rhee when she was D.C. chancellor. Notably, he contracted with Education Reform Now, a mobilizing arm of Democrats for Education Reform, the political action committee that advocated for charter schools and was backed by hedge fund managers. The group had worked with Tusk in New York on the campaign to lift the cap on charter schools.

The public face of the engagement effort, announced by Booker in early November as a campaign of "relentless outreach," was a series of eleven forums for Newark residents. "We want bottom-up, teacher-driven reforms that will be sustained," the mayor said at one forum, although he missed most of them. "We can now access the resources —whatever we need—but we need a community vision for change and reform."

Booker's call for a community vision resonated with Tynesha McHarris. A rising star among Newark activists, she was respected for her commitment to the city's most vulnerable youth. At twenty-five, she already had founded and run reentry programs for young men returning from prison, an intensive summer literacy campaign for 150 elementary school students, and a leadership initiative for teenage girls on confronting sexual violence. While an undergraduate at Rutgers University's Newark campus, McHarris led a protest in front of Shabazz High School, demanding action to address abysmal student achievement. A stunning beauty with an untamed Afro, she stood out in the crowd most of all for her poster: "What Would Malcolm X think of Malcolm X Shabazz High School?"

Like many fellow local activists, she had grown skeptical of Booker and his heroic national reputation despite the expansive unfinished business in Newark. When a close friend, Jeremiah Grace, signed on to organize the ten community forums and a door-knocking campaign to mobilize participants, McHarris warned, "Be careful, dude. Nobody wants to get near that." But when Grace told her that Booker had given him the latitude to galvanize a citywide discussion about education and that he needed her help, she saw it as an opportunity. "I was tired of what I'd seen, tired of knowing when Newark kids got locked up exactly what schools they'd come from. I was frustrated that the schools were so bad. I still had in my mind a report on Newark by the Council of Great City Schools in 2007 — it said there is no shared vision for the city's schools. I wanted to be part of creating a shared vision for Newark."

McHarris, Grace, and other organizers hired dozens of hourly workers to knock on thousands of doors to recruit residents to forums, and they won endorsements from more than a hundred nonprofit organizations. A list of frequently asked questions given to canvassers included this noticeably pointed one: "Is this about Cory Booker?" The suggested answer was that it was about everyone in Newark, including Booker. The mayor joined the canvassers several times, including on a Saturday morning in the Stella Gardens housing project. "We don't want to pull people out of the public school system," he told residents. "We want to make it the best public school system in the country."

In truth, there was a palpable consensus in Newark that the city was failing its schoolchildren. Elected city officials, including the most outspoken defenders of district schools, had been sending their children to private and parochial academies for generations. So many district school parents were opting for charter schools that the best ones had waiting lists in the thousands. The failure of education was a subtext at vigils for murder victims, held with depressing weekly regularity by the Newark Anti-Violence Coalition. At one gathering at South Ninth Street and South Orange Avenue, where thirteen-year-old Dante Young was gunned down under a church archway, his sister cried out to the young men leaning against buildings watching from afar: "Y'all carry book bags but you don't carry books. Get back to school! Study! Get out of the streets!"

A similar message was reaching the young people of Newark through an unconventional but highly authoritative source: Akbar Pray, a notorious drug kingpin in the 1980s, who became an evangelist for education from prison, after losing three of his own sons to violence. "The game is dead," he said in audio messages and letters distributed online. Get an education, it's your way up and out, he admonished the next generation. "Each day here I run into a brother or homie that is barely literate, can scarcely read and is about to be released and has no idea as to what he is going to do when he gets out. How is he going to stay out of the institutional trap? I am bothered," he wrote.

Students in one Newark high school wrote back to Pray, to thank him for his guidance and concern. Interviewed in the visiting room at the Otisville, New York, federal prison, in his twenty-fifth year of a life sentence, the aging convict said the students' responses heartened him. He then leaned forward with a troubled expression, signaling that he wanted to share a private thought. "Some of them didn't write even one complete sentence," he said in a whisper. "What's wrong with these schools?"

The community engagement campaign was called Partnership for Education in Newark — known by the uncatchy shorthand PENewark — and McHarris kicked off most discussions by telling audiences with feeling, "It's our goal to collect the voices of *every* Newarker." Residents of all ages came to the forums, and many took seriously the offer to "have a voice of influence," as the outreach campaign's literature promised.

Perhaps the most consistent plea was for the district to treat the social and emotional health of children and families as essential to learning. The effect of poverty on student performance had been reduced to a war of sound bites in the politically polarized national conversation about education. Reformers said district schools used poverty as an excuse for failure rather than fixing the real problems — bad teachers, bloated and incompetent bureaucracies, and low expectations. Defenders of traditional schools said reformers willfully ignored the well-documented toll of poverty as part of a campaign to discredit public education and demonize unions. But among those who came to the forums, poverty was a glaring fact of life, not a debating point. Schools didn't need excuses; they needed help supporting children and families.

At one forum, young men and women who grew up amid the mayhem of the crack epidemic became emotional about gang wars shattering yet another generation of families. They wanted to volunteer to work with students one or both of whose parents couldn't, or simply didn't, support them academically.

"Don't lose those of us who came up and saw it was so horrible. No one can change it the way we can change it ourselves," said Calvin Souder, a lawyer who went to prep school and college on football scholarships. While in law school in the early 2000s, Souder had taught for five years at one of Newark's most challenging schools, Barringer High, and said some of his most difficult students were children of former classmates who turned to gangs and gave up on education. "Those of us who have had success need to get in our nice cars and drive into the neighborhood and park next to the drug dealer and say to the kids, 'I got an education and I succeeded, and the cops aren't going to come take my car, because I own it. And you know what? Mine is better than the dealer's,'" he said.

Souder's remarks set off a cascade of offers to help the hardest-to-reach students. "Teachers need to bring people like us to the classroom to talk to kids," said Crystal Anderson, herself a product of the Newark schools, now a coordinator for a large mentoring organization. "It can't just be 'I taught you how to read and write and now it's time to go home.' It's not just about passing the HSPA test," she said, referring to the state's high school proficiency exam.

"I have kids every day in my program, their homes are broken by drugs," said Shareef Austin, who supervised evening sports programs at Newark's Westside Park. "Tears come out of my eyes at night worrying about them. If you haven't been here and grown up through this, you can't help the way we can."

School counselors called for workshops to teach young parents what to do at home to help children succeed in school. One social worker offered to share a curriculum she had prepared, "How to Be a Parent of a Child Who Learns."

Despite the spirited participation at the forums, Tynesha McHarris kept finding confirmation of her initial doubts about the community engagement effort. She asked why her paycheck was coming from an organization called Education Reform Now, which was allied with charter schools and their supporters on Wall Street, and was told that Bradley Tusk had brought them on. "Who's Bradley Tusk?" she demanded. Only then did she learn that he was her boss, his firm making over $1 million while she was taking home less than $600 a week.

Shareef Austin, the recreation leader who pleaded for attention to the children of crack addicts, said no one called to follow up with him or his friends about their interest in mentoring students whose parents were absent. "I guess those ideas look little to the people at the top, but they're big to us, because we know what it can mean to the kids," he said.

A planned phase two of the community engagement campaign never happened. A senior aide to Booker privately deemed Tusk's work "a boondoggle." According to a board member of the Foundation for Newark's Future, which paid the bill, "It wasn't real community engagement. It was public relations."

McHarris and the other organizers did not know that Booker and Zuckerberg already had agreed on an agenda. Nor had anyone told them of the tough choices embedded in it, such as closing failing schools, expanding charters, and weakening teacher tenure. If they had known, the organizers said, they would have asked residents to weigh in on these tradeoffs, which could have led to important community conversations. Instead, discussions ranged widely. One Newark principal said a stricter policy on school uniforms would help, with clear consequences for those who failed to wear them. "Charter schools can send you home for that," she said. An assistant principal mentioned an initiative in Mississippi that integrated the arts into the curriculum. A Newark high school freshman said she wanted "an environment where everyone would want to learn. It's hard if everyone around you is playing around."

Some comments aligned with the Booker-Zuckerberg agenda, particularly its call for autonomy for individual schools and principals. At a forum held at BRICK Avon, teachers and leaders of the turn-around school said they wanted to be able to spend money where it was needed most, rather than having budgets dictated by the central office. Principal Charity Haygood told the room that Avon had only one social worker for 650 students who lived in neighborhoods racked by poverty and violence. "We'd allocate our money differently if we had the authority," she said. "We so desperately need help so we can move up." A BRICK Avon assistant principal said the school needed a waiver from state seniority protections to keep from losing a number of younger teachers in the next layoff. "These are valuable suggestions," Booker boomed from the back of the room.

Despite Booker's public promises of "bottom-up" reform led by the people of Newark, he quietly hired a team of education consultants—none from Newark—soon after the *Oprah* announcement, to create a "fact base" of the district's needs and to lay the groundwork for the changes he and Zuckerberg had agreed on over the summer. Booker raised $500,000 from a charitable arm of Goldman Sachs and $500,000 from the Broad Foundation to start paying the firm of Global Education Advisers, whose consultants charged $1,000 and more a day. The total bill for the firm and its consultants eventually reached $2.8 million, with the excess paid by Mark Zuckerberg's foundation, Startup: Education, and matching funds from William Ackman's Pershing Square Foundation. With no public money involved, no public notice was legally required, and as with Tusk's hiring, none was given.

The merging of public and private business only progressed from there. Also without public notice, Booker arranged for two of his top city hall aides to get paid with the philanthropic money for their efforts to secure the donations and set up a local foundation to oversee them. Bari Mattes, Booker's fundraiser, received $120,000 between October 2010 and June 2011, in addition to her city hall pay of $83,000 for the first ten months of 2010. Booker's education adviser, De'Shawn Wright, got $94,500, atop a 2010 salary of $140,000, which was paid by the Newark Charter School Fund. In other words, a substantial portion of the paycheck of the person who counseled Booker on policies affecting the district as well as the charter schools came not from taxpayers but from a privately funded charter school organization.

These arrangements were as philosophically and personally entwined as they were closely held. Even Shavar Jeffries, president of Newark's advisory school board—"advisory" because the state held all the power—who actually supported most of the reforms Booker and Zuckerberg sought, was in the dark about who was spending the Zuckerberg money, and on what. "This remains a black hole to me and thus I suspect everyone," Jeffries wrote in an email to Jen Holleran, the executive director of Zuckerberg's foundation. "I'd like to know how funding decisions are being made, who's at the table when they're being made and how all of this is tied into district decision-making and planning?"

Jeffries had put his finger on one of the thornier questions surrounding private philanthropy in public education. Almost all philanthropy is by definition undemocratic, its priorities set by wealthy donors and boards of trustees, who by extension can shape the direction of public policy in faraway communities. Representatives of Zuckerberg, Booker, and Christie spoke of their partnership as a "three-legged stool," in which the mayor, the governor, and philanthropists would jointly chart the direction of the district.

To exert hometown influence over how the private donations were spent, Booker insisted on creating a local foundation to handle the Zuckerberg gift and matching donations. But seats on the board of what was called the Foundation for Newark's Future went only to donors who gave at least $10 million (later reduced to $5 million), pricing all Newark residents and foundations out of contention. Only

Zuckerberg, billionaire financier Ackman, and Goldman Sachs met the threshold. Their representatives, along with Booker as an ex-officio member, made up the board, with the result that the donors decided how their own money would be spent. They paid their first CEO, Greg Taylor, $380,000 a year, but took so few of his recommendations that he left in frustration in less than two years for a job with the National Basketball Association.

The board convened monthly in a black, glass-walled office tower high above downtown Newark. On the day of its meeting in May 2011, two flat-screen televisions in the lobby carried the large headline WHO'S DUMPING GM STOCK? over photographs of Ackman and billionaire investor George Soros. Fourteen floors above, in a conference room with windows overlooking the Passaic River, the CEO of Ackman's foundation was chairing the FNF meeting, where it was reported that Soros's foundation was considering a donation to help match Zuckerberg's $100 million gift. Although Soros ended up not giving, it was no coincidence that two men moving the stock market on that day were also in positions to move the direction of school reform in one of America's poorest cities. In a twist, their private business concerns were public while their potential effect on the public's business was private. This was not what Shavar Jeffries had in mind regarding transparency.

The contrast between Booker's private actions and his public vow to involve Newark residents was in high relief one Sunday morning in early January 2011 when he convened representatives of seven billionaire donors to hear where the reform effort was headed—none of which was known to Newark residents.

The presentation was led by Christopher Cerf, founder of the Global Education Advisers consulting firm. In December, Christie had named Cerf his education commissioner, in charge of reforms across the state, and in particular in the Newark Public Schools, which he now would control on the governor's behalf.

Tall, fit, and exuding confidence, Cerf was in many ways an archetype of a school reformer. A Democrat who spoke with convincing passion of his concern for the poorest children in failing districts, he was highly educated, accomplished, and unwaveringly sure that his vision was right. He often invoked war metaphors in discussing the politics of education reform. A product of Amherst College and Columbia Law School, he had been a Supreme Court clerk to Justice Sandra Day O'Connor and associate White House counsel under Bill Clinton. Cerf had become a sort of central switching station for the education reform movement, with connections at all levels. For eight years he was general counsel and then president of the Edison Project, later Edison Schools, Inc., and now EdisonLearning—a for-profit operator of public schools and an early combatant in the campaign to disrupt the government-run, unionized model of education. The company ultimately failed to deliver promised profits or notable academic gains for students, but it was a training ground for several leaders of the education reform movement. While at Edison, Cerf attended the Broad Superintendents Academy, founded by Eli Broad, the Los Angeles billionaire whose philanthropy aimed to reshape school districts along the lines of high-performing businesses. Cerf then worked for four years at Joel Klein's side to redesign the New York City school system.

"I was asked to reorganize everything from the ground up—a $22-billion-a-year system, 1,500 schools, 1.1 million students," Cerf explained one day over coffee. "My specialty is system reform. I take on micropolitics, selfishness, corruption, old customs unmoored from any clear objectives."

Cerf said he'd met Booker at a fundraiser in his suburban town, near Newark, when Booker first ran for mayor. He recalled being thrilled by the young councilman's blistering critique of the Newark schools and enthusiasm for charters. Cerf was soon an unofficial education adviser to Booker, and when Booker became mayor in 2006, Cerf pressed him to demand control of the state-run district from Governor Jon Corzine, a fellow Democrat. Booker demurred, insisting that no Democrat would turn over urban schools to a mayor on the wrong side of the teachers' union. Exasperated that Booker wouldn't use his star power to try to pressure Corzine, Cerf let the relationship atrophy. "Cory was everyone's choice of a black man to put out there as a voice for choice, charters, and vouchers, but here was this billion-dollar district he wasn't touching," Cerf said.

When Christie won in 2009, Cerf tried again and hit pay dirt. "I kept shaming him until he gave up," Cerf said.

Gathered around a conference table to hear from Cerf in the city's public access television studio were representatives of more money than had ever been assembled in Newark, or perhaps most cities in the world. Jen Holleran, a former private school teacher and principal with a graduate business degree from Yale, was representing Zuckerberg. The directors of William Ackman's Pershing Square Foundation and Silicon Valley venture capitalist John Doerr's NewSchools Venture Fund were at the table, as was the CEO of the Newark Charter School Fund, whose donors included the Gates, Fisher, Walton, and Robertson foundations; Laurene Powell Jobs; and Newark's Prudential, Victoria, Gem, and MCJ Amelior foundations.

As Cerf rose to address the funders, he called Newark an important new front for education reform: "whole district reform—taking a whole district that's frozen in place, failing children, and turning it into something different." Newark, he said, was a perfect test: "It's manageable in size, it's led by an extraordinary mayor, and it's managed by the state. We still control all the levers."

Cerf was well known to the funders in his former role as Klein's top deputy in New York City in charge of innovation and strategy, a title he shorthanded as "chief of transformation." Transformation was a popular word among education reformers. Teach for America promised "transformational teachers"; New Leaders for New Schools, "transformational" principals; the Broad Center, superintendents "with transformational skill and will" who would enact "transformational, sustainable and replicable reforms." The NewSchools Venture Fund, which backed entrepreneurship, subtitled its tenth annual summit, "Education Entrepreneurs and the Transformation of Public Education."

"I'm very firmly of the view that when a system is as broken as this one, you cannot fix it by doing the same things you've always done, only better," Cerf told the funders. "There are those who will say, 'Gosh, we need literacy programs. We need reading tutors. We need more resources in the library.' We've tried all that. We want to get from good to great, but the bureaucracy drives everything. We have top-down, prescriptive policies and we've barely moved from awful to adequate."

The fifty-six-year-old Cerf, dressed in jeans and a gray sweater, with silvery hair and reading glasses perched low on his nose, stood at a whiteboard with a black marker and sketched out a blueprint for Newark that mirrored the one he and Klein had followed in New York. Indeed, Cerf said he and Booker recently had run it by Klein, who was now executive vice president of Rupert Murdoch's News Corp, in charge of a new education technology division, soon to be named Amplify. The plan was to drastically reduce the size of the centralized school district and create a "portfolio" of schools, including traditional public schools, charters, and programs tailored to student needs, such as single-sex schools and a school for returning dropouts. Business methodology would inform strategies in the transformed district: invest in best-in-class data systems to track student outcomes; treat principals like CEOs, giving them autonomy over school budgets, staffing, and instruction, and holding them accountable for results; and renegotiate union contracts to loosen tenure protections, allowing for dismissal of ineffective teachers and rewards for the best ones.

As part of the portfolio strategy, Zuckerberg and the other donors had already agreed to pay start-up costs for new charter schools as well as for a number of new district high schools modeled on programs from around the country. Newark's lame-duck superintendent, Clifford Janey, had pursued several new models in hopes of luring back dropouts and students leaving for charters and private schools. But Janey lacked the money and staff to get new schools up and running. The donors saw launching them as an "early win," delivering tangible benefits to parents and children.

None of these plans were aired at the recently concluded public forums, although each implied upheavals for Newark children and families—from job losses for hundreds of low-skilled workers at the district's headquarters to school reassignments for thousands of children.

Booker told the donors about another initiative still under wraps. He had secured commitments from the city's two largest charter networks to double in size, in return for his promise to arrange grants from Zuckerberg, Ackman, and other philanthropists to cover their start-up costs. This would increase the charter enrollment by ten thousand pupils, and reduce that of the district, over the next five to seven years. The mayor emphasized that charters also would need space in district schools to expand.

"You're going to announce co-location for free," Cerf declared, as if imposing by fiat another Klein policy on Newark.

"That's the happiest news of the week," Booker exclaimed. This meant that new charters would open inside existing, underpopulated district schools, rent-free—a policy that had provoked anger and tension in New York between parents of charter and traditional public schools because of the charters' visibly superior resources. Indeed, in Newark the charters would end up having to pay the cash-hungry district to use its space.

The funders around the conference table were struck by the easy rapport between the mayor and the commissioner. Booker, in a brown pullover sweater and black pants, leaned far back in his chair, listening intently as Cerf spoke, often nodding in assent, his big hands clasped behind his head.

The two talked about the importance of making Newark the most attractive destination for talented, mission-driven teachers from around the country.

"We need to be the sexiest city to teach in, not New Orleans and not D.C.," Booker said.

"We're going to have cabaret shows," Cerf said.

"You and I singing the blues," Booker said, throwing his head back for a full-throated laugh.

Cerf, Booker, and the funders also brainstormed about bringing in outside experts to lead various aspects of the district's transformation. They needed "the smartest person in the country" on school finance, a "brainiac" on teacher evaluation systems. Cerf suggested several members of the team that had worked closely with Klein. Everyone agreed with Cerf that they needed what he called "a communications strategy to soften the battlefield for the conflict to come, to create a counter-narrative to the status quo."

The experts being mustered—men and women who started out with Klein or Teach for America or McKinsey's education division and now were consultants to charter networks, school districts, state departments of education, and venture philanthropists, and many others—were representative of what Dominique Lee of BRICK Avon called the "school failure industry." They gravitated to districts rich in venture philanthropy or in Obama administration grants for failing schools, including New York's under Klein, Washington's under Rhee, and now Newark's under Booker and Cerf. They ran communications campaigns, built data systems, analyzed test scores, taught principals how to train and evaluate teachers, rewrote tenure laws, restructured districts' central offices, advised labor negotiations. Although children in these districts were mostly black and brown, the consultants were almost all white, setting up inevitable tension about the money they made even as public school budgets kept shrinking. The going rate for consultants in Newark and elsewhere on the East Coast was $1,000 a day, and their pay comprised more than $20 million of the $200 million in philanthropy spent or committed in Newark. "Everyone's getting paid, but Raheem still can't read," observed Vivian Cox Fraser, president of the Urban League of Essex County, where Newark is located.

While Chris Cerf helped colleagues get consulting jobs in Newark, he got none of the bounty for himself. Christie named him education commissioner before his consulting firm received its first check, and he severed all ties to the firm. Cerf said he had never intended to accept money for his efforts. A pedigreed lawyer with extensive political, business, and public policy experience, he likely would have commanded a seven-figure salary in the private sector. Instead, with two children in college and a third in private school, he took the commissioner's post, which paid a salary of $140,000.

It was easy to imagine, however, that Cerf would have a hard time explaining his role to Newark residents. Here was someone who railed against urban politicians for using public money to ply friends and allies with jobs and contracts. Now, with private money, he appeared to be doing the same. Cerf had no question that his own choices were meritorious, made purely in the interest of children, and that the old-style political patronage definitely was not. "I didn't see how it was anything but trying to be helpful," he said.

But that's not how it came across in the *Star-Ledger,* Newark's daily newspaper, in an article dominating the front page on February 23, 2011, reporting that a firm originally founded by the state's education commissioner had been hired to overhaul Newark schools. The newspaper obtained a confidential list created by the firm of options to close or consolidate up to a dozen of the lowest-performing district schools—displacing thousands of children—to make room for charters and new high schools. Despite the mayor's promise to engage them in every step of the reform process, this was news to the citizens of Newark, as was the role of a firm founded by Cerf and paid by billionaires.

As it happened, the advisory school board was scheduled to have its monthly meeting that night—usually a sleepy, sparsely attended af-

fair featuring votes on such items as a field-trip policy or supply contracts. By the time it began, more than six hundred parents and activists had converged, raging against what one after another saw as an
obvious conspiracy of rich outsiders to make a killing off the Newark
schools.

"We not having no wealthy white people coming in here destroy-
ing our kids!" an enraged mother shrieked. From aisles and balconies,
men and women screamed, "Where's Christie?" "Where's Booker?"

The meeting was held at Fifteenth Avenue School, a failing and
crumbling hulk with flickering lights and a faulty sound system. It
was one of the schools the consultants had proposed for closure, with
an overall student proficiency rate of only twenty percent. Its students
would be dispersed to surrounding schools, including some with a
similar failure rate. In the leaked document, Fifteenth Avenue was
designated as the new home of a high-performing Newark charter
school, which was in fact what eventually became of it.

School board members took the microphone, one by one, to say
they knew nothing of the plan and to declare themselves "insulted"
and "disrespected" by the governor, the mayor, and various outside
forces. But the sound system kept cutting in and out, chewing up
their words. From the jam-packed auditorium, parents and activists
looked up to the dais to see their elected board members soundlessly
tapping their microphones, straining over the din to complain that
they, like Newark residents, had no power.

Those who did have power—Booker, Cerf, the governor, Zuckerberg—were not there. It fell to Deborah Terrell, the interim superintendent, appearing at her first board meeting, to try to shift the
conversation to the underlying challenge. Clifford Janey had stepped
down the previous month, and Booker had told funders that Terrell
was only a figurehead; a deputy to Cerf would wield ultimate authority while Booker and Christie recruited a permanent superintendent.

"Our kids are not getting the education they deserve, and it's the
fault of the adults, and we have to recognize that," Terrell said with
feeling. "Public education as we know it no longer exists in Newark."

The raucous crowd quieted respectfully as she spoke. Tall and striking, always immaculately coiffed and dressed, she had a principal's knack for asserting authority over a room. She came by the respect honestly, having led two Newark elementary schools that both won the U.S. Department of Education's sought-after Blue Ribbon award for achievement or significant improvement. Just as important to everyone in the jam-packed auditorium, she was one of them, as she took care to point out when she rose to speak.

"I was born and raised in Newark. I live here, went to school here, my kids went to school here," she said.

But no one took up her point that the Newark district was failing its students. The main item on the agenda—a report by the facilities director on the dubious results of $150 million in state funds spent on school construction in Newark—seemed only to reinforce the crowd's conviction that someone they couldn't see was getting rich on the backs of their kids.

The state government had paid $14.5 million for plans to replace a school struck by lightning five years earlier, but now had decided not to rebuild it after all. (Cerf later reversed the decision, and construction went forward.) Three recently built schools had such serious flaws, from leaking roofs to unsafe handrails, that they still lacked occupancy certificates. Boilers in two schools were damaged beyond repair; unable to afford replacements and with no state repair funds available, the district was using mobile boilers mounted on trucks.

"Where'd the money go? Where'd the money go? Where'd the money go?" the crowd chanted, growing louder and louder.

Newark's most influential business and community leaders were bombarding the city hall switchboard, demanding explanations from the mayor. How would he calm the city? What was the way forward? After decades of efforts to improve education in Newark, they had been hopeful that the Zuckerberg gift and the alignment of Booker and Christie would at last catalyze sustainable and positive change. But already the whole effort seemed to be unraveling.

The mayor turned to Clement Price, the respected professor of African American history and leading historian of Newark, and asked him to assemble concerned civic leaders to help him regain trust. Booker had pressed Price into service so often as a behind-the-scenes peacemaker that Price had given himself an unofficial title: Newark's civic steward. Raised under segregation in Washington, D.C., the son of a federal civil servant and a teacher, the gentlemanly and distinguished scholar was known deferentially throughout Newark as "Dr. Price" — Clem, to friends. At sixty-six, he held one of the highest faculty honors at Rutgers, as a Board of Governors Distinguished Service Professor. Adding to his many academic and civic obligations, Price had recently been named vice chairman of President Obama's advisory council on historic preservation. His expanded workload and travel schedule left little time for stewardship. But when Booker called, he stifled a sigh and agreed to help.

Early on a Saturday morning, Price convened about twenty business and community organization leaders at Conklin Hall on the Rutgers Newark campus. It was an establishment crowd, including leaders of the Prudential Foundation, a coalition of major businesses, smaller local philanthropies, the city's oldest Puerto Rican community organization, revered religious leaders. Just as a clergyman would have opened with a blessing, Price opened with an invocation of Newark history. The very building where they were gathered, he said, was the site of a famous black student occupation in the 1960s, the era when Newark's black majority rose up against corrupt, white minority rule. The student sit-in led to the hiring of more black professors and administrators and the admission of more black students.

Booker brought Cerf along to explain to the group what he had done as a consultant as well as to lay out the vision for the district. Those around the table were quick to fault the two men for proceeding in a way that activated the city's deepest and most racialized fears.

"Your theory of change may be perfect, but this is the average Newarker's nightmare," one leader said of the report leaked to the *Star-Ledger*. "We believe in conspiracies, we were fed them growing up, with our milk. This was the making of the perfect Newark conspiracy."

"This is the DNA of the city," Price said. "Even if there's no evidence of conspiracy, there's the ability to imagine one."

The leaders in the room made clear their exasperation with Booker's missteps with the Zuckerberg gift.

"Where's the discipline in the process? What are the responsible roles, what's the plan to engage the community?" asked Al Koeppe, CEO of the Newark Alliance, a coalition of the state's biggest corporations.

"It's as if you guys are going out of your way to foment the most opposition possible to what you're doing," said Richard Cammarieri, a leader of a community development organization and one of the only consistent Booker critics invited by Price.

Cerf emphasized that his motives were altruistic. "Public education embodies the noble ideal of equal opportunity," he said. "It's the catalytic lever that executes on that myth. I know equal opportunity was a massive lie. It's a lie in Newark, in New York, in inner cities across the country. Call me a nut, but I am committing my life to try to fix that."

Cerf and Booker vowed to meet more regularly with community audiences and to solicit more feedback from parents and teachers. Booker, for his part, attributed any missteps to the urgency of the task. "Parents don't have time for around-the-edges reform," he said. "They need transformational reform." Besides, he added, within three years, he or Christie or both could be out of office. If Christie was defeated, a union-friendly Democrat would take office and likely return the Newark schools to local control. "We want to do as much as possible right away before someone else takes over," Booker said. "Entrenched forces are very invested in resisting choices we're making around a one-billion-dollar budget. There are *jobs* at stake." The notion of "fixing" a badly broken and impoverished district in three years seemed wildly unrealistic to men and women who had worked for decades with Newark's families, children, and schools. But Booker asked them to unite behind him and help rally public support to the reform effort.

Cerf warned that the process was sure to be rancorous. "Real change is inevitably hard and deeply unpopular," he said. "And change has casualties. You can't make real change through least-common-denominator, consensus solutions. One reason school reform has failed is the tremendous emphasis on consensus."

Cammarieri, a former school board member, bristled at the choice of words. "I get nervous when we're talking about schoolchildren and you say, 'Change is going to have casualties,'" he said. "I don't want to take risks with children. Please, plan carefully and comprehensively."

"Why not say, 'Change has beneficiaries'?" suggested Price, with a hint of a chuckle. "You don't want to sound like General Grant. Try to sound a little more like Abe Lincoln."

5

The Rise of the Anti-Booker Candidacy

November 2010–April 2012

O N T H E S E C O N D floor of Newark's Central High School, Milagros Harris worked hard to coax historical imagination out of eighteen sophomores and juniors arrayed around her in varying poses of classic teenage boredom. She was introducing her students to the Holocaust through a curriculum known as Facing History, and she asked them to contemplate the mindset of ordinary Germans at the time. Did everyone in Germany want to kill all the Jews?

A boy slouched so far down in his desk that he was almost supine said he felt sure they didn't. This is what Harris was hoping to hear. That should raise a question, she said with excitement. If people opposed the mass killing of Jews, why didn't they stop it?

No one answered.

"Were they getting accurate information about Jews?" Harris asked. "What's the word for a message being sent over and over and over again to influence how you think?"

"Publicity?" one boy asked more than answered.

"That's a kind of message, but the word I'm looking for is 'propaganda,'" she said. "Does anyone know the word 'propaganda'?" There was no answer from the students. She defined the word and explained how the Nazis used propaganda to blame Jews for Germany's ills.

She asked if they knew the word "stereotype." Again, no one answered. She explained that Hitler stereotyped Jews as less than human.

"Indifference is the enemy," she said. "There might have been Germans opposed to Hitler, but because it didn't affect them, or because they thought Jews' lives didn't matter, they didn't do anything." The students looked puzzled. Harris asked if they knew the word "indifference." They didn't. "Break it down," she encouraged them. "*In*-difference. You don't see a difference. It doesn't matter to you, so you don't get involved."

Several students became animated, eager to be heard on the subject of how decent people could have remained passive in the face of evil.

"Nobody in Newark is happy about gangs, but we don't try to stop them. You could get killed," said a boy in the back of the room.

"Ain't nobody always gonna put themselves in the middle of someone else's mess," a boy across the room responded. "That's a good way to get shot in Newark, New Jersey."

As often happened in Milagros Harris's classroom, a lesson about history and war veered inexorably forward, into Newark's permeating present of gangs and violence. Central was a comprehensive high school, meaning everyone got in, unlike at magnet schools and charters. Based on their eighth-grade standardized test scores, almost three-quarters of freshmen were at risk of never graduating from high school. Harris was a popular teacher at Central, a former hairdresser whose clients recognized how smart she was, persuaded her to go to college, and helped her get scholarships. She majored in history and became a teacher in her mid-forties. Puerto Rican, short and fiery, with ever-changing hairstyles, she had a daughter at Columbia University and another in fifth grade who was reading at a high school level. Her students told her everything—about baby daddies and baby mamas, shooting deaths of parents, dreams of leaving the ghetto. "It must be the hairdresser in me," she said. "Everybody talks to me." The students said she was one of the only teachers who made school interesting, who explained material until they understood it, who made them feel smart.

While Harris's students struggled with words like "stereotype" and "propaganda," they were brilliant at navigating life in a war zone, because many grew up in one. On a bulletin board behind them hung a recent class project. They had created Google Maps of the routes they all walked to school, with labels of everything they passed. One student identified a single commercial establishment—a Domino's Pizza—while all other labels said "Danger Zone," "Killing Zone," or "Robberies." Territory controlled by the Crips gang was colored blue; the turf of the Bloods gang was in red. There were danger ratings for each block, ranging from three to five stars. Atop the scene was a sun, half smiling, half frowning, and the warning "Watch Your Surroundings."

Ever prospecting for hope in dark places, Harris posed the questions, "What can you do to not fall victim to propaganda and stereotypes? What about activism?" On this November day in 2011, she had invited Central High's principal, Ras Baraka, as a guest speaker, because he had been an activist much of his life. Baraka, then forty-two, grew up in Newark, a son of the renowned poet and playwright Amiri Baraka, the most prominent radical voice in Newark's recent history. Amiri Baraka was known for declaring that black leadership in the city had failed the people, ultimately serving the same power structure as their white predecessors. "What we got was Black Dude Number One, Black Dude Number Two and Black Dude Number Three," said the senior Baraka, reflecting on Newark history one Saturday morning at an empowerment class for public school parents. In more hopeful times, Amiri Baraka led the unity movement of blacks and Puerto Ricans that elected Newark's first black mayor in 1970. Ras Baraka, bearing a striking resemblance to his father—the same deep-set eyes, penetrating gaze, and naturally furrowed brow—doubled as a first-term city councilman and was also a slam-poetry enthusiast whose verses were posted in the atrium at Central. He represented the South Ward, where he was born and raised; it now was the largest and poorest jurisdiction in Newark, with the highest concentration of black residents.

In his role as councilman, Baraka positioned himself as the anti-Booker, deeming the mayor, with his Stanford-Oxford-Yale pedigree, a servant of the rich. He delivered speeches in the style of a charismatic street preacher, rousing Newark's dispossessed as forcefully as Booker inspired more affluent audiences.

Baraka, like Booker, was born in 1969, in the aftermath of the civil rights revolution. While Booker was raised in the suburbs, acutely aware of his generation's promise and obligation to "give back," Baraka grew up focused on the movement's unfinished business. "I was in my mother's stomach during the eve of the election of Ken Gibson," he said of the man his father now called Black Dude Number One. "I was raised in the heat of transformation." On his visit to Milagros Harris's class, he told students about attending protests with his father in the 1980s against disparities between the jail sentences of white and black males. As a junior at Howard University, he recounted, he led a student occupation of the administration building that resulted in the resignation of Lee Atwater, a former adviser to President Ronald Reagan and chairman of the Republican National Committee, from Howard's board of trustees. He paused in midsentence to define "trustees," for those unfamiliar with the word, then went on, "We protested that he was racist."

Harris asked Baraka when he became an activist. "At about seventeen or eighteen, it began to trigger," he said. "People said something about my community, I spoke out."

"Boy, I don't feel I have a role in my community," a boy said to no one in particular, as if thinking out loud.

Harris asked the student if he knew of people who had made a positive impact on the community. After thinking a long time, he said he had a kind of role model in a cousin who was a gang leader. The boy said he knew gangs were bad for the community, but he admired his cousin because he discouraged younger children from gravitating to gangs. "When little kids try to hang out with him on corners, he'll say, 'Get out of this area. You don't want to be here.'"

Harris commended the boy for ingenuity: life hadn't handed him role models, so he was constructing a composite, finding admirable qualities in flawed people.

"We don't have anyone to look up to because the whole generation ahead of us is messed up," a girl in blue and white, one of the few wearing the school uniform, said matter-of-factly.

"Is not having great role models an excuse for bad behavior?" Harris countered, pacing the room, looking into her students' faces. A few of them shook their heads no. "Can we be a role model without having one ourselves? You need to set criteria for yourself. Do you know what that is? Keep your standards high, learn from your mistakes, keep it moving."

Baraka told the class that he turned to teaching as a form of activism. When he boarded a bus to attend college at Howard two decades earlier, he said, his best friend was on a bus to prison.

"I became a teacher to counter that conspiracy," Baraka told them. "I want to prevent more of my friends—to prevent many kids—from taking that bus ride. I want them going to college, not to jail." He had been a Newark teacher, coach, assistant principal, and principal for twenty years.

But the schools in Newark hadn't turned the tide. Harris asked how many students had friends or family members in prison. Half the class raised their hands. How many had friends or relatives who had fallen victim to violence? Again, half the students' hands went up. How did this make them feel, she asked.

"Thank God it's not me," said a boy in a red sweater and white baggy pants.

Harris announced an impromptu homework assignment: Google "indifference" and "Martin Luther King." She was hoping someone would return with King's ringing quote: "It may well be that we will have to repent in this generation. Not merely for the vitriolic words and the violent actions of the bad people, but for the appalling silence and indifference of the good people who sit around and say, 'Wait on time.'" Just then, strains of instrumental music filtered through the classroom speakers, signaling the end of the period. This hour's offering was "Didn't We Almost Have It All?" made famous by Newark's own Whitney Houston.

Ras Baraka was a cult figure at Central High. Students called him B-Rak, as if he were a rap star. They said he understood where they came from, what they faced. They knew that he had a famous father — Nina Simone played the piano in his boyhood home and Maya Angelou read poetry there. But they knew, too, that his tirades against violence and poverty were personal, that his father was brutally beaten by white police officers in the 1960s, a sister was murdered, and a brother was shot in the head and permanently disabled. He was invariably late for public events, often explaining that he was attending to grieving families — at a wake for a former student, a vigil in memory of the latest murder victim.

Before his arrival in 2008, Central was infamous for raucous fights; Harris's students remembered racing there from elementary and middle school every afternoon to watch the slugfests. A former principal once publicly declared the violence unstoppable, spillover from the larger society. Baraka called in gang members and declared Central High a sacred space, off-limits to rivalries. If your anger feels uncontrollable, he told them, report to my office and I'll find a place for you to cool off. In time, he prevailed. He met regularly with a group of fatherless boys, giving them books to read, hosting discussions over pizza (his treat), insisting they keep pushing to make it to college. Every day after school, dressed in his dark blue Central High School sweater or windbreaker and, in winter, his wool-knit Central hat, he led students through gang-ruled territory around the building, chest thrust forward, face in a scowl, to help them get home safely.

Shortly after Baraka became principal, a sixteen-year-old junior named Hakir Greene was shot and critically injured near Central in a street fight over a jacket, one of five drive-by shootings in Newark that day. A distraught Baraka called everyone to the gym and let loose a primal scream against the "sickness" life was teaching children. "This is not normal. I want you to know it's not normal," he cried out, pacing the floor with tears in his eyes. "You living this life like it's normal. It is *ab*-normal." He reeled off a litany of abnormalities—"to go to school, to talk about your friends dying, to not be able to walk home safely from school, to be jumped every other day, to fail everything, to live in squalor, to have people's parents coming outside fighting with them in the middle of the street. This is not normal—to be going to the hospital every other week, to be wearing T-shirts that say 'Rest in Peace,' to be writing 'Rest in Peace' on the wall. This is not normal. It's not normal. Nobody else's children do this . . . And don't take it like because it's happening, that mean you tough. It only mean you oppressed." He ended with a grim aside about the burden on inner-city schools: "And our job? Override oppression? Huh!"

Central High's students sat in the bleachers, looking more depressed and shamed than galvanized. A camera crew from *Brick City*, the popular Sundance Channel reality show featuring Cory Booker, arrived just in time to capture the speech. It was one of the most talked-about scenes of the program's first season.

"I made him famous, you know," Booker said ruefully of Baraka's star turn.

The undisputed star of *Brick City* was Booker, who to the outside world was the heroic, crime-fighting mayor of Newark, although at home his reputation was decidedly mixed. Unmentioned on the *Oprah* show or any of the follow-up national coverage of the Zuckerberg gift, the "rock star mayor," as Winfrey introduced him, was facing a catastrophic financial crisis. It was evident to anyone who entered the monumentally bedraggled Beaux Arts city hall, a remnant of Newark's glory days. A huge net stretched from wall to wall under the building's gold dome, visible from all three floors of the rotunda, to catch falling plaster and flaking paint the local government couldn't afford to repair. At the time, Booker was laying off almost a quarter of the city's four thousand employees, and the government was now closed one day a week, when lights and heat were turned off in much of the building to save money. Skeleton crews of essential workers shivered at their desks, some in jackets and scarves. A sign posted beside the main elevator announced that all employees were subject to transfers as budget cuts shredded the workforce.

Atop all that, six months after he was reelected in May 2010, with sixty percent of the vote, Booker was in political trouble. The city council was in open revolt, accusing him of having hidden the epic fiscal crisis from them and the voters in his recent reelection campaign. Following a nationally heralded drop in violent crime in his first term—showcased on *Brick City*—murder and mayhem were again on the rise. The summer of 2010 was the bloodiest in twenty years, with thirty-four homicides, many carried out execution-style by gangs. Making matters worse, on this day, November 9, 2010, Booker was about to lay off 167 police officers, including every recruit hired during his first term, as union leaders stiffed his demand for concessions. Grabbing one of his three BlackBerrys, he speed-dialed his chief labor negotiator from the back seat of his Chevy Tahoe SUV and shouted what seemed obvious: "We have a crisis on our hands!"

At that moment, Booker and his security detail were speeding out of Newark toward the Four Seasons Hotel in midtown Manhattan, where he would deliver a lunchtime fundraising appeal for HELP USA, a provider of housing and services for abused mothers in Newark and nationally. He often spoke to wealthy, well-connected audiences at luncheons and dinners, for fees of as much as $30,000 a talk. This day he spoke for free at the invitation of his friend and HELP USA board chair Maria Cuomo Cole—sister of New York governor Andrew Cuomo, daughter of former governor Mario Cuomo, and wife of fashion designer Kenneth Cole.

A remarkable transformation occurred as Booker's driver pulled the well-traveled Tahoe to a stop in New York City. The embattled mayor disappeared down a private passageway of the hotel, emerging into a packed ballroom as Cory Booker, Urban Superman. Heads turned as everyone recognized the strapping, six-foot-three-inch figure with shaved pate and dazzling smile. "I get to introduce one of my favorite men on the planet," Cuomo Cole crooned from the podium. "Just over the river there's a remarkable, dynamic star on the horizon who is making revolutionary change in education." People raised their smartphones and snapped pictures as applause rose and rose.

Booker delivered almost the same speech wherever he went, calling with heartfelt emotion on his audiences—"we who drink deeply from wells of freedom we did not dig, who eat lavishly from banquet tables prepared for us by our ancestors"—to work to perfect America. "From Newark to Oakland, the children are calling to our conscience every day with the same five words: liberty and justice for all. But we are failing in that," he said often. No matter how many times he repeated those phrases, he sounded passionate and spontaneous, and invariably he received standing ovations. Never relying on notes, he seemed to erupt with eloquence and inspiration.

Booker's audiences were disproportionately white, but there was no suggestion of racial distance between him and them. A white Democratic operative who knew Booker growing up said the relationship was similar to those Booker had as a boy—"he was the black kid who made every white kid feel comfortable." With his tan skin and suburban and Ivy League lineage, Booker did not evoke the blackness of riots or rage. Raised in almost all-white Harrington Park, New Jersey, he presented himself as postracial, fluent in lingos from business-speak to hip-hop, from English to Spanish and even a bit of Yiddish. He talked less about anger than love: "crazy love . . . unreasonable, irrational, impractical love that sustained African Americans through slavery, inequality, and the civil rights movement," as he once put it.

During the monster blizzard of December 2010, widely dubbed the "snowpocalypse," Booker set off a national media sensation by riding snowplows, BlackBerry in hand, using his prolific Twitter feed to respond to constituents in distress. A man tweeted that his snowbound sister, a new mother, had run out of diapers. "I'm on it," Booker tweeted back, and soon was at her door, diapers in hand. A picture of the diaper-bearing mayor soon appeared on his Twitter feed. A woman scheduled for a medical procedure couldn't get her car out of the ice. Booker posted her plea and his reply: "I just doug out ur car. All the best." Network news teams were not far behind, filming and airing stories about the Twitter-savvy mayor in action. VanityFair.com posted "The 10 Most Valiant Snow-Rescue Tweets from Cory Booker, Twitter's mayor." Time.com crowned him a "Blizzard Superhero." ABC News correspondent Jake Tapper tweeted, "How do we draft you to be Mayor of DC."

Meanwhile, back in Newark, large sections of the most populous wards—the South and West—remained snowbound. The *Star-Ledger* quoted residents complaining of the mayor's "snow job," citing unplowed thoroughfares throughout the city that the out-of-town coverage missed. Reverend William Howard, a civic leader who headed Booker's transition team in 2006, asked in exasperation: "What is the mayor doing riding snowplows? He should be at his desk drinking hot chocolate and solving our frightening fiscal crisis."

Booker was popular in the Twitterverse for posting inspirational quotes two to four times a day, each drawing thousands of "retweets." A *Star-Ledger* video-reporter read one of them—a quote from Vincent van Gogh—to sanitation workers demonstrating in front of city hall against Booker's threat to outsource their jobs. "If you hear a voice within you say you cannot paint, then by all means paint, and that voice will be silenced," the reporter read to one worker after another. They reacted as if hearing something from another planet. "I ain't got time for no Vincent van Gogh," said one. "We trying to keep our jobs."

It was hardly surprising that Booker had problems at home. What urban mayor didn't, with the flight of jobs and state aid forcing layoffs of cops, teachers, code enforcers, street sweepers? Economic distress was on the rise in Newark, particularly for children, with 43.5 percent living below the poverty line in 2011, the highest proportion in almost a decade and twice the national average. For most of Booker's years as mayor, municipal budgets relied on multimillion-dollar state bailouts to close deficits. In 2010, as Christie cut municipal aid and the recession savaged the nation's poorest cities, Booker sold and leased back sixteen city-owned buildings, raised property taxes sixteen percent, and eliminated one out of four jobs on the payroll.

But in a communications age when even local news traveled across the globe in an instant, what happened in Newark stayed in Newark—unless Booker tweeted it. Flooding the media universe with his tales of heroism and hope—he posted them on Facebook and Twitter, recounted them on television talk shows, recycled them in speeches delivered around the country—he effectively washed away downbeat news. Outside Newark, no matter where people looked, they found only the narrative according to Booker.

Nothing captured the disconnect between the outside and inside more acutely than *Brick City*, in which Booker was portrayed as a ubiquitous presence on the streets and in neighborhoods—"an outspoken and charismatic mayor" fighting alongside residents "to raise the city out of a half century of violence, poverty and corruption," according to the promotional materials. Civic leaders complained that the show, which along with Booker costarred a couple who belonged to warring gangs, depicted Newark—except for Booker—as a city whose people were "drugged out and thugged out," in the words of Councilwoman Mildred Crump. *Brick City*'s film crew showed up at a 2011 school board meeting where a mother of a Newark first grader was delivering an impassioned plea for parents to demand better schools. "In the inner city, we're of the mentality that the government should take care of us, and when they don't, we yell and get mad and go home and think we've done our job," said Keyeatta Hendricks, a New York City public school teacher and single mother who recently had bought a home in Newark. "No! It's not like that now. We need to get together and do for ourselves. I heard Al Sharpton say, 'The government is done with us.' I believe that. We need to take care of ourselves." It was a brave and stirring speech, one mother taking on the anger and rancor that passed for public discourse in Newark. But the only person to approach her afterward was a *Brick City* camera crew member, asking her to sign a release in case she appeared on the air. It felt as if public life in Newark had become a reality show, while outside of Newark, the reality show had become reality.

Touring hot Silicon Valley ventures like LinkedIn and Twitter in 2011, Booker was welcomed as the politician of the future at meetings with CEOs and tech workers that were streamed live over the Internet. In April of that year, *Time* named Booker one of the world's one hundred most influential people. A year later, he appeared on nine television programs in one day after having rescued a neighbor from her burning house and tweeting about it within seconds of emerging from the flames. He told the story in exactly 140 characters, the maximum Twitter could accommodate: "Thanks 2 all who are concerned. Just suffering smoke inhalation. We got the woman out of the house. We are both off to hospital. I will b ok . . ." Two weeks later he flew to Los Angeles to appear on *The Ellen DeGeneres Show,* where the talk-show host welcomed him this way: "Hello, your honor, your highness, your excellency. What do I call you?" She also presented him with a Superman costume. DeGeneres introduced Booker with a biographical video riddled with factual inaccuracies and exaggerations about his mayoralty amid photos of him rubbing shoulders with residents—sitting on their stoops, shooting hoops, shoveling their sidewalks. A narrator said Booker "lives in the housing projects Newark residents call home," although he lived in a rented, market-rate, free-standing house; reduced crime rates "almost fifty percent," although FBI data at the time showed that overall crime was down only eleven percent and violent crime had increased; and announced that "schools are being transformed," although there was no data to support the claim.

In speeches and on national television, the mayor described a Newark of struggling, yet optimistic, men and women, fired up by his leadership. But at school board meetings, activists routinely called him "Mayor Hollywood," insisting he was more devoted to national celebrity than to his constituents. With his omnipresence on social media and his frequent absences from Newark, Amiri Baraka dubbed him "the Virtual One."

Baraka the younger was at the same time emerging as the leader of the opposition to Booker—deriding not only his glamorous political style but specifically his education reform agenda. The Booker-Christie-Zuckerberg strategy was doomed, he said, because it included no systemic assault on poverty, the real enemy of achievement. In addition to raising legitimate questions—such as why reformers focused disproportionately on changing systems, barely addressing the daunting effects of poverty on schools and classrooms—Baraka masterfully stoked residents' fears of rich outsiders. He cast Booker, Christie, and Zuckerberg as part of a monied conspiracy to seize control of the district's $1 billion budget, its prize. "The wolf is at the door, and there's a couple of insiders about to make a deal with the wolf for your children," he said of Booker and Christie. "If we don't have a strategy, they gonna take it all from us." He likened school closings in poor neighborhoods to class warfare. "The banks fail and they give 'em eight hundred million dollars. You can't close the damn banks. They're too big to fail. Why aren't the Newark public schools too big to fail?" he demanded.

The reformers, on the other hand, cast Ras Baraka as the symbol of all that ailed urban schooling. In public, he blamed poor student performance on oppression and poverty, assigning no responsibility to teachers and principals. In a rich New Jersey tradition, he held two public jobs, paying him more than $200,000 a year—an arrangement he brashly defended. He also put his brother, Amiri Jr., on his city hall payroll. "They beat me up for having two jobs," Baraka said at a rally. "They don't know I've got more than two jobs. Councilman, principal, other people's father, father of my own children, police officer, conflict resolutionist, social worker, basketball coach, cheerleader at games. Yeah, I got a buncha jobs. Problem is I'm not getting paid for them." His supporters cheered loudly.

But inside Central High School, Baraka was more pragmatic educator than strident politician. In his first two years as principal, Central had such abysmal scores on the state proficiency exam given annually to juniors that it was in danger of being closed under the federal No Child Left Behind law. Baraka mounted an aggressive turnaround strategy, using some of the instructional techniques pioneered by the reform movement. He said he was particularly influenced by a superintendent in a high-poverty district in Colorado who was trained by philanthropist Eli Broad's leadership academy—an arm of the "conspiracy" Baraka the politician inveighed against. "I stole ideas from everywhere," he said. With a federal school-improvement grant, he extended the school day, introduced small learning academies, integrated art and drama into academic classes, greatly intensified test preparation, and hired consultants to coach teachers in literacy instruction.

In addition to English and math, the test-prep classes at Central High included a heavy dose of motivation. Teachers told students over and over: You *can* pass this test. You *must* pass it—for yourself, your school, your community. Baraka scheduled a school-wide pep rally on the day before testing at which teachers, administrators, clerks, and fellow students love-bombed the junior class. In past years, many students had slept during the state test. Asked why, one teacher who proctored the test many times—and who said she used to spend much of it pulling students up from a sleeping position—gave this explanation: "They were tired, they were bored, they figured they'd fail, everyone always told them they'd fail, all of the above." But in 2011, for the first time, everyone worked until the final bell and no one slept, the English department chair announced triumphantly at a sparsely attended parents' meeting. When the scores came back in April, seventy-two students had passed both the math and the literacy tests, more than a fivefold increase from the year before. Baraka summoned everyone to the gym for an impromptu assembly and told his students through tears what had just occurred. One by one, he called the passing students to center court, and each received a standing ovation worthy of a football team MVP. Later that week, Cerf made a special trip to Central to commend the students, and Baraka called another assembly for the occasion. The state Department of Education invited him to deliver the keynote speech at a workshop that summer on how to turn around failing schools.

Some of the improved performance surely was due to better preparation, but there was no question that some also resulted from persuading students to believe in themselves enough to try. The experience at Central begged the question: How much of the achievement gap was actually a hope gap?

Baraka and his students seemed to live in a different Newark from Booker. The mayor was a born optimist, "a prisoner of hope," he called himself.

For many students at Central, hope wasn't so easily conjured. A freshman English teacher named David Ganz devised a daily poetry exercise in which he wrote a word on his whiteboard and gave students several minutes to write whatever came to mind. As they composed, he played rap music to pump them up. One day, to the background of Eminem's "Till I Collapse," Ganz wrote the word "hope."

Fourteen-year-old Tyler read his poem to the class:

> *We hope to live,*
> *Live long enough to have kids*
> *We hope to make it home every day*
> *We hope we're not the next target to get sprayed . . .*
> *We hope never to end up in Newark's dead pool*
> *I hope, you hope, we all hope.*

A boy named Mark wrote, "My mother has hope that I won't fall victim to the streets. / I hope that hope finds me."

Khalif: "I hope to make it to an older age than I am."

Nick: "Living in Newark taught me to hope to get home safe."

Tariq: "Hope—that's one thing I don't have."

One day, while observing teachers and writing feedback for them, Baraka mentioned that he agreed with some of the more controversial changes Booker and Christie had proposed. In more than twenty years as a teacher and administrator, he said, he often had found tenure a headache, saddling students with weak teachers. He said he was comfortable with a recent Colorado law—celebrated throughout the reform movement—that revoked tenure for teachers with two consecutive years of the lowest ratings. He also thought teachers should receive raises for performance, not longevity, as enshrined in the current union contract—exactly what Zuckerberg was then advocating. He vehemently opposed charter schools, however, calling them an attempt to privatize education, although he later would soften that view as well.

"Quietly, a lot of people agree with a lot of this stuff," he said one afternoon after school in his conference room, its walls papered with student performance data. "This dictatorial bullying is a surefire way to get people to say 'No, get out of here.' It becomes my crew versus your crew, and it's disrespectful to the people of Newark. People have a thing about someone coming into our house and saying it's theirs, coming to our town and saying 'I'm going to fix you.'"

He laughed. "They talk about *Waiting for Superman*. Well, Superman is not real. Did you know that? And neither is his enemy."

In his other job, as a politician, Baraka, along with other African American city council members, were assembling a slate of candidates to challenge the dominance of the school board by the city's premier power broker, Stephen Adubato Sr., better known as Big Steve. Adubato, nearing eighty, ran the largest and most powerful community organization in Newark, along with highly regarded social service programs, preschools, and a charter school. He oversaw the region's most formidable voter-turnout operations, making him as indispensable to politicians as they were to the effectiveness of his organization, the

North Ward Center, which relied heavily on government contracts. A Democrat, he was close to both Booker and Christie—on the morning after his election, Christie's first stop was at Adubato's Newark charter school, Robert Treat Academy. Adubato was a key player in a Democratic political machine that had delivered crucial legislative votes to pass Christie's budget cuts and pension and benefit reforms. Thus Big Steve played an important, unseen role in the governor's growing national reputation as a Republican who could sell red-state values to a blue state. Adubato also supported Christie and Booker's education agenda. For all these reasons, the board election was shaping up as historic, a unity slate of African Americans seeking to break the grip of an aging Italian American boss on Newark politics. Although the board was advisory and had no real power, the election provided an opportunity for Ras Baraka to begin building a citywide base for an eventual run for mayor.

Despite the comfort Baraka expressed in private with tenure reform and performance-based pay for teachers, the council members' slate vowed to fight everything Booker and Christie had proposed. The teachers' and principals' unions signed on, as did all unions representing school district employees. At a rally of organized labor outside city hall, Councilwoman Crump urged the crowd to elect the slate that was "about labor." She didn't mention the stakes for Newark children and their education. "We have a clear choice between those who will do nothing for labor and those who will do everything for labor," she said, chanting along with the crowd, "Jobs, jobs, jobs! Jobs that are safe and secure." The slate called itself Children First.

City Council President Donald Payne Jr., who also supported Baraka's slate, publicly likened education reform to the so-called Tuskegee Experiment, in which black sharecroppers with syphilis unknowingly were deprived of treatment for forty years while government doctors used them to study the unchecked progress of the disease. Booker called the remark "unconscionable." Like most elected officials in Newark, Payne had sent his own children to private school (Catholic school, in his case)—a point Booker raised often, asking why the "connected and the elected" considered the public schools fine for all children except theirs.

The election would be held at the end of April 2011. In the weeks before the vote, the furor over the leaked consultants' report in February had died down, but grassroots suspicions about the overall motive behind the reform effort had not.

In March, Booker delivered a ringing call for radical reform in his State of the City speech. "Bold action and change are difficult and take great sacrifice, but we must move forward for our children," he said. As the school board election heated up, however, he fell noticeably silent. Endorsing and campaigning for Adubato's slate, he said, would only help the Baraka forces by giving them a bigger target—the mayor—to mobilize against. By his own acknowledgment, the "rock star mayor" of the national stage couldn't mobilize Newark voters for a school board election, except to vote against his slate. Booker apparently didn't even make phone calls on behalf of Adubato's candidates. On election day, one of his district leaders was handing out fliers for Baraka's slate at a polling place. Asked why, she replied, "I didn't hear anything from the mayor about this election, so I can support whoever I want."

Shavar Jeffries, the school board president who supported Booker's agenda of expanding charter schools and aggressively reforming the district, was furious. "How do we close schools that have been failing for decades, fire people who are terrible teachers, when the mayor can't even get behind a school board slate?" he asked. "At the grassroots level, there doesn't seem to be the structure to actually win the fight."

The school board elections were held the last Wednesday in April, an unusual day for an election in most cities, and no other races were on the ballot. It was always this way, and turnout was predictably marginal, a situation that favored unions and powerful political organizations that could mobilize thousands of foot soldiers. In a city of 150,000 registered voters, candidates needed fewer than 5,000 votes to win one of the three board seats up for grabs. In a historic upset, the Baraka slate won two of the three races, one of them by just 48 votes. A jubilant crowd overflowed the Children's First headquarters, spilling out the door and more than a block down Bergen Street until well after midnight. Amid the celebration, Councilman Ron Rice Jr. shared the winning message: "We went door to door telling people, 'If you're against what Mayor Booker and Governor Christie are doing to our schools, this is your team.'" Sitting behind a desk, Baraka's chief of staff, Amiri Jr., wrote $75 checks to hundreds of men and women who had knocked on doors all day, dragging people out to vote. "Anything that's against Cory Booker and Chris Christie, I'd work for it — for free," said one man, nonetheless accepting his check.

6

Searching for Newark's Superman

January–May 2011

WAITING FOR SUPERMAN had its own social action strategy, in which education reformers around the country hosted showings of the movie to recruit supporters. Mark Zuckerberg cohosted one in October 2010 with four hundred guests at a theater in Palo Alto, a few blocks from what was then Facebook headquarters. His fellow hosts included venture capitalist John Doerr and his wife, Ann, and Sheryl Sandberg and her husband, Dave Goldberg, the chief executive of Survey Monkey. The theater was packed with Silicon Valley's leading venture capitalists and executives of the hottest start-ups and tech companies and private equity investors. After the movie, the crowd massed around a table where charter school networks and other reform organizations were accepting donations—"a check-writing party," a participant called it.

A guest congratulated Zuckerberg on the Newark gift and asked who would be the superintendent.

"Anyone we want," he replied with a smile.

Zuckerberg could be forgiven for believing this. After all, he had the backing of Christie and Booker, who held all the cards in Newark — or at least appeared to. And they had agreed with him that their first order of business was recruiting a credentialed reformer as superintendent to carry out their ambitious agenda.

But politicians had agendas and timetables that Zuckerberg wasn't prepared for. After John King had turned down the job, Booker had no plan B. When Chris Cerf became New Jersey's education commissioner in January, the superintendent search intensified. In March 2011, with the school board elections looming, Cerf and Booker became enthusiastic about Jean-Claude Brizard, superintendent of schools in Rochester, New York, yet another former deputy to Klein in New York City and a graduate of the Broad Academy. He was smart, passionate, and politically astute, and he had the kind of battle scars that Cerf considered a badge of honor, including a vote of ninety-five percent no confidence from Rochester's teachers' union. He also was a seasoned educator, having risen through the ranks in New York City beginning as a teacher of incarcerated students on Rikers Island.

Cerf and Booker told Brizard in March that the job was his in principle, pending the governor's okay. They were in the process of arranging for him to meet with Zuckerberg in Palo Alto and with a community task force in Newark when Christie suddenly announced on March 17 that there would be no decision on the superintendent until May. This came as a shock to Zuckerberg, who had expected a decision months earlier and had made clear his impatience. He heard the news from Jen Holleran, executive director of his foundation, who learned it from a reporter.

Christie offered no public explanation, but he and Booker privately acknowledged that they were acting at Adubato's behest. The Newark boss was a linchpin of the powerful Essex County political machine, which had helped deliver pivotal Democratic legislative support for Christie's budget cuts and his pension and benefit reforms in the face of stiff union pushback. This made him an essential, if unsung, factor in Christie's national celebrity as a Republican who could sell a conservative agenda to a liberal state.

The delay had to do with the upcoming school board elections in which Adubato's slate would face Ras Baraka's. Adubato warned Christie and Booker that naming a superintendent before the election could provide a focal point for opponents of reform, increasing turnout for the Baraka slate.

Anyone unfamiliar with the byzantine politics of education in Newark—Zuckerberg, for example—would be understandably puzzled that the take-no-prisoners governor would make this concession to Adubato. Since the state ran the schools, Christie could veto any school board decision that went against his wishes. So why worry? The board exercised huge symbolic power in the racial shadowboxing of Newark politics. The spectacle of a white Republican governor continually overruling the elected representatives of a black and brown school district—and doing so in the name of saving its children—would make it hard for any state-appointed superintendent to win the public's trust. Christie and Booker both were content to let Adubato work his magic, hoping he would deliver them a board that backed their agenda. "It was a good decision," Christie said later, defending his curtsy to the Democratic boss, even though the strategy failed.

It was becoming clear that Christie's purported omnipotence over the Newark schools was not exactly as advertised. One of the consultants on the ground described how the realization dawned on him: "The mayor seemed indecisive on the superintendent search, so I thought, 'Why not go straight to the governor, since he's not afraid to pull the trigger?' But then it turns out Adubato pulls the governor's trigger. Maybe we should've just cut the deal with him."

Cerf explained the delay to Brizard, who agreed to wait. Soon afterward, however, former White House chief of staff Rahm Emanuel was elected mayor of Chicago and asked Brizard to come for a chat. "I met with him and told him I'm actually heading to Newark," Brizard recalled. "He asked if I had an offer in writing, and I said no. He said, 'Then you're available.'" Brizard went to Chicago, leaving Newark without a candidate. "It was like a bomb dropping," said Cerf. (Emanuel would let Brizard go seventeen months later.)

It was hardly surprising that Brizard chose the nation's third-largest school district over one with one-tenth the enrollment. But another attraction was the clarity of the lines of authority in Chicago: all of them led to Emanuel. In Newark, they were indecipherable, a hazard for a superintendent. "You can have complete control on paper, but a lot of people can come back with daggers and you're buried," Brizard said.

A striking feature of the Newark reform effort, from the beginning, was that no one was in charge. Cerf's concept of a "three-legged stool" implied that Zuckerberg, the governor (through the state-appointed superintendent), and the mayor would call the shots together. To those trying to carry out reforms, this arrangement was opaque and baffling. One of the consultants tasked with redesigning the district said in a private conversation, "I'm not sure who our client is. The contract came through Bari Mattes's office [Booker's chief fundraiser], so that suggests Booker is the client, but he has no constitutional authority over education. The funding is from Broad, Goldman Sachs, and Zuckerberg, but they have no legal authority. I think Cerf is the client, because the state runs the district. But I'm not positive." In other words, the consultants worked for the person who originally founded the consulting firm.

Although Booker, Christie, and Cerf were emphatic about the need to impose accountability on a notoriously unaccountable bureaucracy, it was becoming apparent that no one of them was ultimately accountable for making it happen.

From three thousand miles away, Zuckerberg and Sandberg were alarmed. Six months had passed since the *Oprah* announcement, and the quest for a model of transformational urban education appeared

in real danger of coming apart amid leaks, political deals, public rancor, and mismanagement. Jen Holleran had been traveling to Newark week after week, spending one to three days at a time, asking hard
questions about how Booker was implementing the vision they had
agreed on. A product of Harvard College, Harvard Graduate School
of Education, and Yale School of Management, Holleran had credentials that no one in Booker's circle could question. She had been an
executive of a national education reform organization and also packed
considerable soft power through a long-standing friendship with
Sheryl Sandberg. The two were in the same book club in San Francisco when Sandberg was vice president of Google and Holleran was
working in the Oakland school superintendent's Office of School Reform. Now, Holleran's dispatches from the ground in Newark were
raising concern. In early 2011, Sandberg began discreetly calling people who had worked with Booker, asking if he had the ability to concentrate on his and Zuckerberg's reform venture.

It was Booker's operating style to launch multiple missions at once,
assuming some would crash on takeoff, some would fall by the way-
side, and some would go the distance. "I'm thinking, 'Do everything
you can right now, instead of worrying what tomorrow will be like
or the next day,'" Booker said. "Right now, if TEAM [the charter net-
work] expands another school, if you add another school model, if
you expand the school day, if you change the life of one kid, today you
can do something — right now. People allow their inability to control
everything to undermine their determination to do something."

Had the young Internet entrepreneur gone online for a cursory
search of local news coverage, he would have known at the time he
made his gift that Booker already had more challenges than he could
count: the surge in violence, the fiscal crisis, the political rebellion on
the council, his heavy travel schedule. The *Star-Ledger* reported that
Booker spent more than one in five days out of the city in 2011. Sandberg had taken charge of vetting the $100 million arrangement, which
specified in writing that Christie would delegate "strategic and opera-

tional" leadership of the state-controlled schools to Booker. But despite her widely respected business acumen, she too was apparently caught off guard.

As Booker traveled the country making speeches and moved from crisis to crisis, the Facebook duo stumbled upon an open secret in Newark. Clement Price, the Rutgers historian, summed it up this way: "There's no such thing as a rock-star mayor. You're either a rock star or a mayor. You can't be both." In a pique of frustration one night over Booker's rapidly shifting attention, a city hall aide put it more crudely: "Everybody who comes to work here arrives with a hard-on or a crush, and then at some point you say, 'WTF?'"

Zuckerberg and Sandberg summoned the mayor to a meeting at Facebook headquarters on Saturday afternoon, April 2, where they made it clear they considered the pace of progress unacceptable. There was no superstar superintendent, no comprehensive reform plan, no progress toward a game-changing teachers' contract. If these are the wrong metrics for measuring progress, they asked, what are the right ones? They were holding Booker accountable for performance—as they did their own employees, and as Booker, Christie, and the reform movement vowed to do with teachers and principals.

Zuckerberg and Sandberg said firmly that they saw no way the overall effort could succeed without a strong superintendent in place, *and soon.* Zuckerberg, who had an unassuming habit of referring to Facebook simply as "a company"—as if he ran a shoe store or car repair shop—remarked, "I've only run one company, but in my experience, a company needs a leader."

Booker was contrite. "Guilty as charged," he remembered saying.

After three hours of talk, Zuckerberg and Chan invited Booker, who was accompanied by Cerf and two other advisers, to their home in Palo Alto for pizza and salads. The main topic of conversation was not education but the couple's adorable new puppy, a fluffy white Hungarian sheepdog named Beast, who had his own Facebook page that already had 97,000 "likes." Zuckerberg posted on Facebook a picture of Booker cuddling Beast.

Within days, hundreds of people had commented adoringly—most about Beast, but plenty about the celebrity mayor.

"Isn't it nice to cuddle the world famous, Mr. Booker?"

"Beast is cute, but Cory is the catch!"

"So ♥ Beast & Cory Booker!!!"

"SO jealous! LOVE Cory!"

Back home, angry overflow crowds became a regular feature of public hearings on the schools, where a core group of union and grassroots activists denounced every proposed reform as a conspiracy of the mayor and governor against the interests of Newark's children. One Saturday morning, Cerf gamely agreed to meet with concerned residents and found himself facing more than four hundred parents, grandparents, and teachers in the auditorium of Louise A. Spencer School. Charter schools had organized parents of their students for the occasion, providing free busing, and the auditorium was divided down the middle, charter parents on the right, public school parents on the left. The charter parents wore their schools' branded T-shirts, with slogans—navy blue for TEAM schools ("Be the Change"), a division of the national KIPP network; forest green for North Star Academy schools ("Change History"), a division of Uncommon Schools; bright red for Lady Liberty Academy, a Newark-only charter.

The divide only sharpened when several charter parents took the microphone to say the public schools had failed their children. One parent, Bendue James, said her daughter had been beaten up at Mount Vernon School but was now thriving at RISE Academy, a TEAM charter. Crystal Williams, with two children at North Star, had to compete with hecklers from the public school side. "Your teachers and principals are not educating your child," she yelled over their jeers.

A North Star father, a substitute teacher in the public schools for ten years, said with disdain that he saw too many district school parents "absolve themselves of any responsibility" for their children. As boos rose from the left side of the room, he faced the public school cheering section and thundered derisively, "When we talk about children, the apple never falls very far from the tree."

From the podium, board president Shavar Jeffries banged his gavel, demanding order but also peace. "We're acting like Bloods versus Crips, charters versus district. That's a gangster mentality," he said gravely. "We need to educate our children. It is not productive to fight each other *all* the time."

Cerf, nursing a cough and lingering bronchitis, appeared to be flagging as the meeting entered its third hour and Wilhelmina Holder, a grandmother and veteran public school activist, approached the microphone. "Oh, I am tired," he said under his breath, although loud enough for Holder to hear. Before Cerf realized it, she was teeing him up like a golf ball.

"Mr. Cerf, you're no more tired than I am," Holder scolded, recalling the decades she had spent advocating for Newark's schoolchildren. The left side of the room roared approval, and she went on. Was he more tired than single mothers in the room who worked two or three jobs to provide for their children? More roars from the left side. Was he more tired than . . . ? A chastened Cerf held up a hand in surrender, urging Holder and everyone in the room to ask whatever they wished. They did—for another hour and a half.

"You haven't begun to address resources for students whose schools will close," she said. "What's the message to their parents? Is it, 'We don't care about your child, we're going to close your school and destroy the community'?" she asked. And what's with all those consultants in Room 914 at the district headquarters? "Put some *color* in that room!" she said to whistles and cheers from the left side. "*And* some intelligence."

Nonetheless, Booker and Cerf's agenda lurched forward, thanks to the round-the-clock work of the consultants. They quietly revised the earlier proposal to close or consolidate failing district schools; those with the most vociferous community support were no longer on the list. The advisory school board, at the time still dominated by Adubato's forces, approved the plan in April and voted to lease the freed-up space to charter schools, over jeers and hoots from an audience stocked with union and grassroots activists. Marques-Aquil Lewis, a rehabilitated former gang member elected to the board in 2009, warned that hundreds of district school students would be uprooted from familiar teachers and buildings in order to accommodate the new or expanding charter schools. Meanwhile, the district students were being reassigned to schools that also were failing.

"We talking about inviting back what happened in 1967 — chaos," Lewis said. "We giving a child an invitation to join a gang, to carjack a car, to commit a murder by creating chaos."

He didn't mention that the reshuffling was also designed to benefit district students seeking alternatives to large, comprehensive high schools. Among the new options Zuckerberg was helping to finance was Bard High School Early College, a respected and rigorous academic program whose students in New York City, many from disadvantaged backgrounds, graduated with a diploma and two years of college credit. Another was YouthBuild, through which failing, unemployed, formerly incarcerated students in forty-six states finished high school while learning construction trades and other skills. A third, Diploma Plus, offered programs tailored to reengage dropouts and students on the verge of flunking out of high school. More than six hundred students from across the city had signed up for six proposed new schools at an open house.

"Newark must get in front of the death spiral of Detroit and so many cities," said Dan Gohl, then director of innovation and change for the district. "We are faced with the fight for the very life of public education." He argued that the new schools held out a survival strategy for urban districts losing students — and state funds — to charters. They could counter those losses, he said, enrolling students who previously had dropped out and luring highly motivated students who might have gone to charters or private schools.

Gohl had to compete with an increasingly restive audience angered by the earlier votes. Although the new programs were to be district schools with unionized teachers and principals, Donna Jackson, a full-time activist who rarely missed a board meeting, heckled him throughout his presentation, encouraging students to join in. "Don't let him talk, kids. Just boo him. Boo his ass," she yelled. "You know what this is all leading to—it's privatization." Now the audience was booing all new schools, whether public or charter, ignoring all the facts. Unlike for the session with Cerf, charter schools hadn't mobilized parents to attend the board meeting.

A majority of board members proceeded to vote down all the new schools. Down went Bard, YouthBuild, Diploma Plus, all of them. After each vote, Jackson led the crowd in a chant of "Cory fails! Cory fails!"

"The only thing we should be concerned about is whether our kids succeed or fail," board president Jeffries, who voted for most of the schools, said sadly.

Richard Cammarieri, the former board member who for years had demanded attention to disastrous student performance, watched in dismay. "These are potentially very good opportunities, but the process is poisoning the well for them," he said.

Dominique Lee of BRICK Avon Academy sat in a back row, his head buried in his hands. He had hoped the Zuckerberg gift would spur support for efforts like BRICK's to change Newark schools from within. "It's turned into a thing against Cory, not what's good for the kids," he said.

The final word was Cerf's, not the board's, and the next day he overruled all the no votes, clearing the way for the new schools to open. Reached that afternoon by phone, he was furiously resolute.

"I can't have any more talks about 'respecting the community.' Who is the community?" he asked. "Is it the generation of students, now voiceless, who dropped out? Is it the last five people who had a mic? Is it the parents who are lining up for charters, or is it the loudmouths? There's a level of ignorance and basic conspiracy-mongering and micropolitical decision-making that inevitably dominates any decision on education. This is exactly a poster child for why education reform doesn't happen. It's all a detriment to educating kids. They're literally not entitled to have their voice taken seriously. At the end of the day, I have to do what is right." There was a long pause, and then this: "Just wait until we name a white superintendent."

Soon after Booker returned from his meeting at Facebook headquarters, with renewed urgency about finding a superintendent, Zuckerberg sent one of the company's motivational posters for emphasis: DONE IS BETTER THAN PERFECT.

Cami Anderson had been in the mix from the beginning. At age thirty-nine, she had spent her entire career in reform circles. She'd taught in Teach for America, gotten a master's degree in education at Harvard, then joined TFA's executive team in New York for five years. She later helped run New Leaders for New Schools, whose mission was to train principals as agents of reform; one of its founders, Jon Schnur, became an architect of Obama's Race to the Top. She'd been a senior strategist for Booker's 2002 mayoral campaign and had been superintendent of alternative high schools in New York under Joel Klein.

Anderson had two apparent marks against her. First, she was white. Since 1973, Newark had had only African American superintendents, and ninety-five percent of district students were black and brown. Booker clearly had hoped to name a minority, beginning with his first choice, John King, whose black and Puerto Rican heritage spanned Newark's two largest demographic groups. Some of the mayor's advisers had even raised concerns about Jean-Claude Brizard, on grounds that he was Afro-Caribbean, not African American. At one point, Cerf said he was considering corporate leaders, but the only one he mentioned was black. "If Dick Parsons said 'I'd like to give a year of service,' I think I'd look at that," he said, referring to the retired chairman and CEO of Time Warner.

But Anderson had an interesting backstory. She often mentioned that she had grown up with nine adopted siblings who were black and brown. Her domestic partner, Jared Robinson, was African American, and they had a biracial son named Sampson Douglass, in honor of Frederick Douglass.

But there was another mark against Anderson: she was known for having an insular and uncompromising management style. "She has her own vision and she won't stop at anything to realize it," said Rebecca Donner, a friend since childhood, now a novelist. "If you're faint of heart, if you're easily cowed, if you disagree with her, you're going to feel intimidated." Cerf and Booker were well aware of this trait, but came to see it as a virtue. As Cerf put it, "Nobody gets anywhere in this business unless you're willing to get the shit absolutely kicked out of you and keep going. That's Cami."

Booker named a community task force to interview superintendent candidates, although in the end its members said there was only one viable candidate. He turned to Clement Price, the overworked civic steward, to chair it, and Price again agreed. Anderson was interviewed in late April, and word trickled out that the task force was impressed. They asked extremely tough questions, and she seemed ready for all of them. They told her that her New York position as head of alternative education—prominently including incarcerated students on Rikers Island—could make it appear that Newark had hired a prison warden to run its schools. She replied that every student deserves a quality education, including the formerly incarcerated. Asked if she knew that angry crowds were packing school board meetings, she replied, "One thousand parents are showing up for meetings? That's the kind of place I want to work." They asked point-blank if she had orders from Christie and Booker to privatize public schools. "She was clear that she would not take orders from anyone," Price said. "She told us she believed in listening to the community, giving principals significant authority, bringing in talented education leaders. She did not sound like an ideologue." Afterward, Price said he was surprised that even stern skeptics of Booker and Christie seemed impressed. "I hate to admit this, Clem, but I like her" was the reaction from longtime activist and advisory panel member Junius Williams. So did Robert

Curvin, a revered Newark native who was a civil rights leader in the 1960s, a Princeton-trained PhD, and a lecturer in political science at Rutgers. "The imperative for Newark now is to have the best superintendent we can find," Curvin wrote in support of Anderson in the *Star-Ledger*. "I wish there could have been more minority choices in the pool, but there were not."

The announcement took place on May 4, 2011, at Science Park High School, Newark's most selective magnet school, which sent more than ninety percent of its students to colleges, including the Ivy League. Christie, Cerf, and Booker were all on hand, beaming with satisfaction, in a room jammed with reporters, camera crews, and about thirty Newark civic leaders and politicians.

The plan was for Christie, Booker, and Cerf to comment briefly, giving center stage to Anderson and the important work of improving schools. Christie and Cerf followed the script, but Booker waxed poetic for half an hour. He veered into rhetorical flights, such as: "The thing that distinguishes her most to me is one simple aspect about her, and that is her love. It's not the kind of love that her life partner gets to enjoy in that individual-focused kind of way. This is the kind of love King called us to do. *Agape* love. She will weep for a child that's not her own when she sees a child whose potential is being squandered. She has a level of love in her spirit that is like her mother's, where I may not have a biological attachment to that child but every single one of them is mine, is my kid, and my destiny is intricately and intimately wrapped up with theirs." By the time he finished and Anderson took the microphone, the audience of school board members, civic leaders, parent activists, and journalists had been standing for more than forty-five minutes. Many were now leaning against walls and window ledges.

There was considerable speculation early that morning about whether Anderson would bring her son and domestic partner to her debut press conference, as a signal to Newark that she was no garden-variety white superintendent. Would she seem to be using them as props? Or would it look stilted for her *not* to be surrounded by family at such an important moment? The speculation ended when cars carrying Anderson and her family pulled up in front of Science Park High. The stroller came out first, then Jared Robinson, and then Anderson, carrying fourteen-month-old Sampson Douglass Anderson Robinson. Baby Sampson and father Jared Robinson received a very positive reception. At one point, Myra Jacobs, a grandmother who led the PTA at Central High School and was usually suspicious of outsiders, approached Robinson and suggested under her breath that he accompany Anderson to meetings whenever possible.

"It's a strong force you'll bring to this community, and I think you have a sense of what I mean," Jacobs said, raising her eyebrows for effect.

"I do indeed," Robinson responded with a smile.

When her turn came to speak, Anderson got right down to business. "Every single child, regardless of circumstances, should have a skill they can attain to make the choice they want, whether it's career or college. All kids, all choices," she said. Her strategy for getting there was straightforward: put excellent teachers and excellent leaders in every school and classroom. "Period. Full stop," she added for emphasis. "I'm more interested in results than fads."

She also called on her family experience. "My family is multiracial, and many of my siblings joined us because of unthinkable challenges that made it really hard for them to be placed in a home setting," Anderson said. ". . . My belief in the potential of every Newark student is based on those life lessons." In Newark's daunting dropout and failure rates, she said, "I literally see the faces of my brothers and sisters who've overcome so many challenges in their own lives.

"As one example, we're all too aware of the challenging statistics facing African American men in everything from incarceration rate to graduation rate," she went on. "And it's part of my personal passion to work alongside all the great leaders here to change those facts, because quite literally, those are my brothers, my life partner and soul mate, and now my son, who by the way just learned to walk."

She received a heartfelt ovation, which would have been a poignant ending to her introduction to Newark.

But the newsmakers then took questions. Asked why he felt so strongly about the Newark schools, Christie launched into his story, which had played well on the campaign trail, of having been born in the city, although his parents moved the family to the suburbs in search of better schools. "You know," he went on, "I don't think I'd be governor if I went to school in Newark." There were audible gasps. Most men and women in the audience had been born, raised, and educated in Newark. Conversation after the press conference focused almost exclusively on Christie's remark, not on a new era in Newark schools. Students at Science Park High, the top achievers in the city, heard of the comment within minutes and asked teachers how the governor could have said that.

"How does that inspire students to become governor, to become president?" asked Alturrick Kenney, one of the newly elected school board members on Baraka's slate. "We need to talk differently because children are listening."

7

Hi, I'm Cami

May 2011–September 2011

THE NEWARK PUBLIC SCHOOLS has its headquarters in a drab, ten-story downtown office building occupied mostly by state agencies. The school district fills the top three floors, crowned by the superintendent's suite and a photo gallery of its many occupants stretching back to 1855. The early leaders sport high collars, bushy mustaches, and wire-rimmed glasses. Over time, styles change, but through 118 years and eleven superintendents, two things remain constant: everyone in the photographs is white, and everyone is male. Then, in 1973, comes a line of demarcation—when Newark's first black mayor, Kenneth Gibson, appointed his first superintendent—and for the next thirty-eight years, everyone is black—five men and two women.

Then, in 2011, comes Cami Anderson—white, blond, and much younger than the others—jarringly out of sync with everyone before her. And while every superintendent for 156 years gazes out from a formal portrait, Anderson stands against a blank wall, smiling, her hair slightly mussed, as if she had paused momentarily for a snapshot while attending to something else. The camera angle is tight, so her face fills the frame, exaggerating the anomalies.

Anderson had arrived in Newark as a life-sized challenge to the status quo. She made this clear when, early on, she refused to hire the girlfriend of one city councilman and fired the cousin of another one. "The trading post is closed," as she put it. Her image as an agent of change was evident even in the way she introduced herself. "Hi, I'm Cami," she said to parents, principals, and teachers, even to students, displaying a lack of deference to local custom. All adults in the schools —from janitors to superintendents—addressed each other as Mr. or Mrs. or Dr., a veneer of respectfulness undisturbed by the district's tarnished history.

"Hi, I'm Cami," Anderson greeted a middle-aged African American male teacher in a summer school classroom early in her tenure. "Okay if I just walk around?" He nodded assent.

Dressed in khaki slacks and a peach-colored blouse, peace symbols swinging from her earrings, her blond hair in a ponytail, Anderson headed like a bullet train for the very back of the room, where several young men were laughing loudly, basically ignoring three plastic boxes of dirt on a lab table in front of them. They were attending summer school at Science Park High School, the elite magnet school during the rest of the year. The state-of-the-art science lab was crowded and cacophonous, with thirty-five students squeezed around lab tables. All had failed freshman earth science and had to pass it in order to get back on track to graduate. On the whiteboard, the subject of the unit was identified as wetlands.

"Hi, I'm Cami," Anderson said to the students at the back table. "Can you guys tell me what you're doing?"

They clearly had no idea who she was or what she was doing there.

"No," one boy shot back, as if telling her to bug off. Anderson squared her shoulders, authority figure–style, and turned to the boy next to him, who snapped to attention. With a nod toward the plastic containers, he said respectfully, "This is a wetland."

"Why are you making a wetland?" she asked.

"I don't know," he said.

"What did you guys do before today?"

He thought for a while. "This," he answered, again nodding at the dirt.

Just then another boy wandered by, wearing a T-shirt that said on the front, "How to Keep an Idiot Busy. (See back.)" The back had the same message, ending, "See front."

Anderson asked the teacher how he determined if students were grasping what he taught and how he adjusted his approach to reach those who didn't. He gave a rambling answer, mentioning quizzes and interim assessments, then blamed the students. "It's tough to do environmental science in urban districts," he said. She told him that the boys at the back table didn't understand the lesson. In their case, he had another excuse: "They're special ed."

Needless to say, these were the wrong answers, signs of a mentality Anderson had been crusading to purge from education since witnessing its crushing effect on her adopted siblings. Anderson understood only too well that it was hard to teach kids who were accustomed to failing, who lived in poverty, who lost friends to violence, whose fathers abandoned them, who burned with anger, who struggled with learning disabilities — but that's what made teachers so vitally important. If a teacher didn't *expect* his students to succeed, if he saw them as losers and gave up on them, what chance did they have to break the mindset of failure that had landed them in summer school in the first place?

Next, Anderson went into a geometry class. There were only eighteen students, almost all girls. They were working intently in groups, calculating the altitude of a rhombus. Their teacher, a young African American woman with six years of experience, radiated competence and purpose, moving throughout the room, checking everyone's progress. These students had not failed anything — ever. Rather, they were in summer school to get ahead. "I wanted to spend my summer doing something useful," a girl who attended Arts High School, a selective magnet, told Anderson. "I didn't want to have zero period," said a girl from Technology High, another magnet, referring to classes scheduled before the regular school day began. "So I decided to knock it out of the box right now." Anderson asked the teacher where she taught during the school year. She named one of the most troubled high schools in Newark, adding quickly that she hoped to transfer soon to a selective magnet. This was another factor in the failure equation. Teaching the best students was a reward, sought by almost everyone in education. Talented teachers won the honor, and struggling students got the leftovers.

"Well, that was instructive!" Anderson declared as she walked back to the school office with Edwin Mendez, a vice principal during the school year who supervised multiple summer school sites. She asked for a candid explanation of how the system worked: How did these students and teachers end up here? Mendez outlined a bizarre bureaucratic procedure in which all Newark schools sent lists of failing students to the district at the end of the regular school year, only three days before summer school began. The roster sent to each summer school site was invariably inaccurate—Science Park High had 2,400 students on its summer roster, of whom only 1,176 actually enrolled. Another high school had 1,860, but only 900 showed up. Moreover, he said, many students were incorrectly assigned to classes they had passed, not those they had failed. The reason? "Somebody didn't do their job," said Mendez, using a generic explanation in Newark for why systems failed.

As for the teachers, Mendez explained, the district office conducted a "mass posting" of all available summer school jobs, everyone applied at once, and the best teachers got the advanced classes, because those required a higher level of academic rigor. The weak teachers got the classes—and the students—no one else wanted.

"That's totally backwards," Anderson declared. "The kids who failed the first time around need *more* rigor. We need the strongest teachers with the weakest students."

She took notes on everything Mendez said, thanked him for his candor, then headed off to observe kindergarten through eighth grade at Speedway School, about two miles away.

"Hi, I'm Cami," she said jauntily to the Speedway security guard.

The older African American woman looked over her glasses at Anderson and responded without expression, "I'm Ms. Grimsley."

Cami Anderson grew up in "lily white" Manhattan Beach, California, as her mother described it, and attended the University of California at Berkeley. But nothing about her upbringing was conventional.

She was the second child of Sheila and Parker Anderson, a child welfare advocate and the community development director for Los Angeles mayor Tom Bradley. Sheila Anderson managed a large child welfare agency in Los Angeles and occasionally brought into her home severely abused and neglected children who were difficult to place. In some cases, they stayed. Beginning when Cami was a year old, her parents adopted nine children in ten years, later having another biological child, bringing the total to twelve. Cami's place in the birth order changed seven times, her mother said.

The Andersons raised their large family in a three-bedroom, one-bathroom house. One adopted child was born addicted to heroin and struggled with physical and emotional pain. Another had been hospitalized from severe physical, sexual, and chemical abuse. Two were orphans from Vietnam, each born to an African American GI and a Vietnamese woman. Everyone had laundry duty, dinner duty, and other jobs, all assigned at Sunday family meetings. Those with after-school activities were responsible for arranging their own rides. Cami Anderson said she never felt put upon. "It was just who we were."

All of the children went together to school, where the adopted siblings were among the only students of color. Anderson recalled being upset as early as elementary school that teachers found some of her siblings unmanageable and punished them. At home, her mother tapped their strengths, she said, by breaking tasks down to size and setting clear expectations. From an early age, her mother recalled,

Cami was her siblings' defender. "Cami understood them and wanted to explain to the rest of the world how much they'd been through," Sheila Anderson said. "She became the interpreter."

Her distinctive personality emerged in middle school. Anderson became passionate about acting and theater through classes at Santa Monica Playhouse, where its founder and director, Evelyn Rudie, used improvisational exercises to push children to tap their inner selves. Rudie then created characters in plays and musicals that allowed young actors to express onstage who they really were. "Cami was always cast as the hardass," recalled Rebecca Donner, her writer friend, who met Anderson at the playhouse the summer after sixth grade and has remained close ever since. "She played the person from the wrong side of the tracks, very assertive and tough, who wouldn't let anyone push her around."

Anderson's breakout role came at age eleven, when she starred in a musical as a fearless cowgirl defending her town against three rough, leering bad guys. While belting out a song, "You've Got Another Think Coming," swinging the microphone cord like a lasso, she slugged her way across the stage, leaving all three bullies unconscious —one draped over a ladder, another stuffed in a whiskey barrel, the third sprawled on the floor. The curtain fell with the loudmouthed little blonde standing alone and triumphant in her shiny red cowboy boots, having single-handedly saved the day. It was, Donner recalled, "a show-stopper."

As an educator, Anderson similarly styled herself as lone champion of the defenseless, speaker of inconvenient truths. In New York City, under Klein, she was senior superintendent for five years, responsible for 30,000 students in alternative high schools and 60,000 more in prison, drug treatment and teen pregnancy programs, suspension centers, GED programs, career and technical training, and adult education centers. The position gave her critical distance on aspects of Klein's reform agenda, particularly charter schools. As Klein championed the expansion of charters, Anderson saw no benefits reaching her own students. She told of trying in vain to find a charter school that would serve incarcerated students, blending social services and no-excuses academics.

In Newark, it quickly emerged that while Anderson had all the credentials valued by the reform movement, she differed with her bosses on the role of charter schools in urban districts. She pointed out that charters in Newark served a smaller proportion than the district schools of children who lived in extreme poverty, had learning disabilities, or struggled to speak English. Moreover, she had the same concerns Dominique Lee of BRICK Avon expressed about charters disproportionately attracting parents she called the "choosers"—those with time to navigate the charter lotteries and to foster a striving attitude at home. Charters were under the control of Cerf, not Anderson. They drew from the same student population as the school district, but the state alone decided whether and how much they would expand and whether to close those that performed poorly. The local superintendent's only role was to react. In cities like Newark, where the overall student population was static, growth for charters meant shrinkage for the district. Newark charters now were growing at a pace to enroll forty percent of children in five years, leaving the district with sixty percent—the neediest sixty percent, according to Anderson. Booker, Christie, and Zuckerberg had searched the country for a leader of education reform in Newark, but in practice, Newark had two school systems and she governed only one of them. Anderson pointed out that she was expected to turn Newark's public schools into a national model, yet as children left for charters—and state funds followed them—she would be continually closing schools and dismissing teachers, social workers, and guidance counselors. And because of the state's seniority rules, the most junior teachers would go first, without regard to merit. Anderson called this "the lifeboat theory of education reform," arguing that it could leave a majority of children to sink on the big ship. "Your theories of change are on a collision course," she told Cerf and Booker. "I told the governor I did not come here to shuffle the deck chairs on the *Titanic*," she said. "I did not come here to phase the district out."

Surprisingly, Cerf, Booker, and Christie had no plan for ensuring a stable learning environment for children in district schools as they advocated aggressive expansion of charters. They couldn't answer Anderson's questions: How many district schools will have to close? Where will displaced children go if there is no longer a school within walking distance? (With its long history of neighborhood schools, Newark did not provide school busing.) How will district teachers address an increasing concentration of children with emotional and learning challenges? Had anyone calculated a sustainable size for a diminished Newark district? In shaking up the bureaucracy, reformers said often that they were prioritizing children's education over adult jobs. But in their zeal to disrupt the old, failed system, many of them neglected to acknowledge the disruption they were going to cause in the lives of tens of thousands of children.

Anderson's gale-force advocacy for her point of view was a major asset, given the baffling lines of authority among Booker, Christie, and the philanthropists. But it also became a liability, alienating everyone who tried to suggest changes in her approach. Even among fellow reformers, she developed a reputation as "not playing well in the sandbox with others," as several of them put it.

Before Anderson was hired, Zuckerberg and other donors anticipated a much faster expansion of charters. But they put the plans on hold in the face of Anderson's resistance. Although Anderson had to answer to Christie and Cerf, they often gave in to her demands, as did the board of the Foundation for Newark's Future. She insisted that she, not the politicians or philanthropists, was the education expert. Talking privately with aides, she would say, "I'm the supe!" She regularly pointed out that she had more money than the FNF: "I've got a billion dollars and they've got only a hundred million," she told the aides. Early and often, she threatened to quit and throw the reform effort into even more disarray. Cerf, Holleran, and others privately told colleagues that Anderson was, in effect, their horse to ride; like it or not, they were committed to her success, because as Anderson fared, so fared all of them—and education reform in Newark.

In her first summer on the job, Anderson aired her concerns about charters at a conference of the KIPP schools network in Nashville, attended by some of the nation's wealthiest donors to charter schools. Many of those in attendance were alarmed, and said so, which made Anderson livid. "There were meetings all over the country about me after that speech at KIPP, reformers framing me as anti-charter, anti-innovation, defender of the status quo. Seriously?" She said she simply was challenging her allies to join her in seeking a strategy that would benefit district as well as charter students.

But back in Newark, the middle ground seemed more elusive than ever. Many grassroots activists regarded Anderson from the day of her arrival as an occupying force—an agent of Booker, Christie, and Zuckerberg. In her first month on the job, she went to city hall to pledge open and candid communication with the city council, laying out her belief in principals as the prime agents of change in schools and the district. "To me," she said, "great leadership is everything—putting a great principal in every school, helping them set student achievement targets and come up with a game plan, and then frankly staying out of their way. Not bogging them down." This strategy—to give principals more autonomy while at the same time making them accountable for results—was patterned on Klein's and Cerf's work in New York, and Anderson believed in it passionately. She didn't say a word at city hall about charter schools.

The council members were cordial and thanked her for coming. But at the end, Council President Donald Payne Jr. suggested that nothing Anderson accomplished would matter as much as the fact that she was imposed on Newark by the state. "What is your perspective on local control?" he asked. "Because if we get back local control, it puts you out of business."

• • •

Anderson moved swiftly on her strategy to vest principals with much of the responsibility for reforming the district. She hired seventeen new ones in her first summer, recruiting from around the country, and within three years had replaced well over half of the seventy she inherited. She eliminated binders full of monthly paperwork they had been required to complete, telling principals to spend the time as instructional leaders, observing and coaching teachers to higher and higher levels of effectiveness. Every month, she led training sessions with all seventy principals in various aspects of her reform strategy, terming the sessions "the West Point" of principal training.

In the past, the district's central office had filled teacher vacancies with little input from principals, often saddling them with men and women ill suited to the school or its students. The priority had been to ensure that every teacher had an assignment, not to maximize the level of instruction. From now on, Anderson said, when vacancies occurred, principals should select the highest-quality applicant and best fit for their school team — an approach common in most workplaces, although unfamiliar in Newark public schools and many other districts.

The policy change had an immediate impact. The previous year's school closings left about a hundred teachers without jobs. In her first months in Newark, Anderson hired consultants to create a staffing system called Talent Match, in which principals would post all vacancies online, and any interested teacher could apply. Cerf and many reformers saw this system — which they called "mutual consent," meaning teachers and principals chose each other — as essential to education reform. Flexing their new autonomy, principals throughout the district filled vacancies with teachers they considered the best, leaving about eighty without placements. Not all the leftovers were inferior, however; some taught subjects for which there were no vacancies.

The idea had one major flaw: the district had no way of shedding the leftover teachers. New Jersey's tenure law included strict seniority protections. If Anderson laid off all eighty excess teachers, those with the longest tenure could "bump" junior ones in any school, without regard to merit, undoing many principals' choices. Anderson said this would lead to "catastrophic" consequences. "Kids have only one year in third grade," she said. With Cerf's encouragement, again following his and Klein's New York playbook, she decided to keep all excess teachers on the payroll as a temporary solution while Booker, Cerf, and Christie worked to change the state tenure and seniority laws. The cost in the first year was $8 million. Anderson assigned the excess teachers to support duties in schools, emphasizing that Newark had no "rubber room," in which unassigned teachers sat idle and collected pay.

Every Monday, Anderson gathered with her leadership team in her tenth-floor conference room, where the agenda often involved replacing dysfunctional district practices with management systems that emphasized accountability for each desired result. On the walls around them were aging posters and plaques created by past superintendents, under whom much of the dysfunction originated. The most prominent poster featured a smiling, bright-eyed girl sitting extra-tall at her desk, chin tilted up in expectation. "There are no sad faces when education works," read the caption. It was signed by Eugene Campbell and Charles Bell, the superintendent and school board chair during the era of self-dealing and neglect that led to the state takeover.

One morning, the topic of the leadership meeting was Newark's abominable high school graduation rate of fifty-four percent. An analyst had discovered that a significant number of students dropped out because they didn't learn until it was too late that they had failed too many courses to graduate. Anderson and her team were adopting a computerized system they called Grad Tracker to alert district leaders and high school principals as soon as a student failed a required class; principals would be responsible for taking immediate steps to ensure the student made up the credits and got back on track.

Only one person at these meetings had taught or worked as a principal in the Newark schools — Roger Leon, acting director of academic affairs, who grew up in Newark and graduated from Science High. A Newark teacher or administrator for almost thirty years, Leon doubled as an unofficial anthropologist for Anderson, called upon regularly to explain the origins of policies and customs that made no sense to the systems-minded newcomers.

"Roger, I call you an encyclopedia, so don't disappoint me," Anderson said during a discussion about Grad Tracker. "What was the system before?"

Leon, a small, bespectacled man respected throughout Newark for his twin skills as educator and political survivor, explained that when a student failed a required class, there was a point person in one of the district's regional offices who alerted the school's director of guidance, who in turn was responsible for ensuring that the student recovered the missing credits. Anderson asked why that didn't work. "The point person retired and the director of guidance position no longer exists," Leon said.

"Oh! *That's* sustainable," Anderson said, slapping the table in exasperation. Although Leon's anthropology lessons were invariably disconcerting, Anderson relished their gory details: "I feel as if a hundred mysteries have just been solved. Or revealed."

Later, in an interview, Leon said the old approach drew on research suggesting that struggling students often made progress when they got one-on-one attention from an interested staff member. "If you failed a class, there was supposed to be a plan in place for you to recover credits, and someone who cared about you was supposed to monitor it," he said. "It would've been a good system, but no one followed through. No one was accountable." Once again: somebody didn't do their job.

If Anderson needed an anthropologist in Leon to understand the strange workings of the Newark district, many longtime employees viewed her and her leadership team as equally foreign. At times, they seemed to the veterans to speak a language all their own. For example, education reformers referred to high-risk decisions made in the name of progress as "building the airplane while we're flying it." Anderson, Booker, and Cerf invoked the phrase at various times to connote that the urgency of their task required them to act first and deal with consequences later. Their decision to keep excess teachers on the payroll in hopes of eventually changing seniority protections was a classic illustration. Principals with disproportionately younger staffs were grateful to avoid the upheavals that had occurred in the past when these teachers were bumped to make way for more senior teachers in need of a position. But what if the legislature refused to change the seniority law, causing the pool of excess teachers to balloon as Anderson closed more and more schools? She, Booker, and Cerf had no plan for this costly—and likely—eventuality.

Often employing the lingo of business, Anderson presented herself as a skilled manager in her monthly training sessions with principals, telling them in the first such session to run their schools as if they were CEOs. She told them to create a document listing three to five goals for raising student achievement and to assign everyone in the building specific responsibilities for reaching them. "Every good and high-performing coach and CEO has a game plan—a lean, focused, clear plan," she said. "They're setting goals and going after them like their life depended on it."

As part of this process, she said, principals should articulate something she called a BHAG ("*Bee-hag*"). When no one appeared familiar with the term, Anderson explained that it stood for a Big Hairy Audacious Goal. This, she said, was a clear and seemingly impossible objective around which everyone in a school could organize to achieve previously unthinkable progress. She credited the term to best-selling business author Jim Collins, whose many analyses of successful companies were treated as scripture across the school reform movement.

Several staff members said they felt that the district had been overtaken by a cadre of technocrats, most of them white and commuting from New York, whose vocabulary was rich in education reform buzzwords. Besides "transformational"—never incremental—change, they also made it a priority to "move the needle," which meant to achieve measurable progress, usually in test scores. To do this, they had to "pull the right levers," like allowing principals to choose their teachers. They would "drill deep" or "take a deep dive" into complex issues. They divided strategies into "buckets," such as the accountability bucket, the teacher-evaluation bucket. They took liberties with parts of speech, changing nouns into verbs—as in, "Bucket those two ideas together"—and adverbs into nouns, as when Anderson referred to her expertise in "behindedness," or students who were several years behind their grade level. Data had to be "robust." They worried about "optics," or how things would look to the public. The reasoning of critics was invariably "fatally flawed." The district desperately needed more "bandwidth," or highly skilled people at every level, necessitating the hiring of consultants to fill the gap until permanent hires were recruited through a "robust talent pipeline." And paraphrasing Collins, the prolific business writer, you had to get "the right people on the bus and in the right seats."

Anderson shared the reform movement's faith in business-style management and accountability. The goal, she said, was to mobilize the bureaucracy around high performance rather than mere compliance with rules. She hired the Parthenon Group, consultants in international business strategy who had worked for Joel Klein in New York, to upgrade the district's data and accountability systems. They eventually were paid more than $3 million, mostly from philanthropy. Among Parthenon's early assignments was the creation of "data dashboards" for principals—another practice adopted from Klein, who had taken it from the business world. Corporate leaders used dashboards to see a company's vital statistics at a glance, like drivers surveying a car's gauges. But unlike the dashboards of corporate executives, which were updated continuously, the principals' dashboards—displaying the passing rate of students by race and income on standardized tests, attendance and dropout rates, and other metrics—were updated only once a year, when new test score data arrived. Several principals said privately that they could have assembled the data themselves.

Anderson violated one of her own principles of management by going more than a year without recruiting a permanent leadership team. Instead, she relied heavily on consultants, many of them paid $1,000 a day, and she persuaded Zuckerberg, Ackman, and the other philanthropists to foot the bill. After pressing Anderson without result to submit a grant request specifying which consultants she intended to hire for which tasks and at what price, the board of the Foundation for Newark's Future—Booker and representatives of Zuckerberg, Ackman, and Goldman Sachs—gave in and awarded her $4 million to spend mostly at her discretion on what it designated on the foundation's website as "technical assistance." The goal of the grant was "to transform Newark Public Schools into a service-oriented organization, primarily focused on talent management and human capital, finance and operations, and innovation."

Two of the highest-paid consultants were friends and former colleagues of Anderson, Alison Avera and Tracy Breslin, both senior officials in New York under Klein and Cerf and both fellows at the Broad Academy. Both had worked for the Global Education Advisers consulting firm originally founded by Cerf, and Anderson asked them to stay on for about a year in two of her most strategic positions—Avera as interim chief of staff and Breslin, who had extensive experience in human resources, as interim director of a new Office of Talent. Breslin would oversee three of Anderson's top initiatives: negotiating a new teachers' contract; supervising the new staffing system through which principals rather than district bureaucrats selected teachers; and implementing a new teacher evaluation system, developed by the nonprofit consulting firm The New Teacher Project.

The arrangement was unusual on several levels. Avera and Breslin were married to each other; had they been public employees, nepotism rules would have prohibited one from supervising the other. A number of other officials complained that they could not get a hearing from Avera or Anderson on concerns related to Breslin's high-stakes initiatives, seeding frustration in the ranks. There was also considerable contention about their pay. Avera and Breslin had joined

Global Education Advisers at $1,200 and $1,000 a day, respectively, and they continued at those rates for Anderson; Breslin charged overtime on days when she worked more than eight hours, even though her contract specified that she be paid by the day, not the hour. The staff of the Foundation for Newark's Future ultimately barred the practice, according to officials familiar with Breslin's compensation. In less than eighteen months working for Anderson, FNF's tax records showed, their combined pay exceeded $740,000. The FNF staff repeatedly pressed Anderson to negotiate lower rates, arguing that their long-term assignments didn't conform to traditionally shorter-term consulting work. But Anderson said she needed their help and expertise as she sought a permanent team while simultaneously learning the workings of the district and moving to reform it. "I had to fix the plane, fly the plane, figure out who should be on the plane, and make sure we didn't crash the plane," she said. After appealing to the FNF board, she got her way.

Anderson herself was paid $247,500 a year, plus a potential bonus of $50,000, for a total of just under $300,000 if she achieved goals that she and Cerf, as commissioner, were to negotiate at the outset of each school year. Tying extra pay to the achievement of specific goals was typical of performance-based contracts in the private sector. But Cerf and Anderson waited until the school year was almost over to finalize the goals — akin to tailoring an answer sheet to a test taker's responses. Each year, she received almost all of the available bonus money.

There was an advantage to taking the helm of a school system as troubled as Newark's: you could make a major impression by doing some basic things right. Jen Holleran had observed early in her time there, "The scariest thing and the most hopeful thing is that so little works."

It was long accepted in Newark that student registration took up much of the first week of school, with lines of children and parents snaking out the entranceway and often around blocks. As a result, many children lost up to a week of instruction, and lessons were constantly interrupted by the arrival of new students. The Global Education Advisers consulting team had reported with alarm shortly before Anderson's arrival that the district had no action plan to achieve a smooth opening of schools in the fall.

Anderson made it a signature project to have a successful opening day. She put longtime school business administrator Valerie Wilson in charge, and Wilson deployed a team of project managers—the Successful School Opening Team—who worked all summer to ensure principals in all seventy buildings had a teacher for every classroom, a desk for every child, clean bathrooms and floors, security guards assigned, walls painted, light bulbs in every socket, leaks patched. Wilson's team arranged for student registration to begin an unheard-of two weeks before school opened, so that all students were on a class roster on day one.

On the first day of classes, as children streamed into BRICK Avon Academy, Patricia Hargrove, the school's secretary, sat at her desk looking in disbelief and wonder at the front counter, where lines of children and parents used to clamor for her attention. No one was there. "I've been here twenty-seven years," she said, "and I don't think I've ever seen this happen."

Anderson spent the morning visiting schools and observing classrooms. One of her stops was George Washington Carver Elementary, a struggling school in a neighborhood racked by violence and home foreclosures. Carver had been losing population, and over the summer, a KIPP charter school, SPARK Academy, had moved onto its third floor, forcing a reorganization of classrooms and causing considerable anger in the neighborhood. Carver principal Winston Jackson had taken the lead in calming the community, saying that he and the SPARK principal were committed to all the children in the building. His message, essentially, was: Keep your eyes on the prize—the children, that is.

Anderson sent word that Jackson should take her to observe three teachers in action—his newest teacher, a veteran teacher, and a third whom he was free to choose. Only forty-five minutes into the first day of school, the newest teacher and the veteran had everyone enthusiastically engaged and on task. The third, a tenured fifth-grade math teacher, appeared hopelessly flustered, stumbling through a lesson on the area of a square. Afterward, huddling with Jackson in the school lobby, Anderson delivered withering feedback, not mentioning the energy and student participation evident in two of the three classrooms. According to Anderson, all three teachers had unclear objectives, particularly the math teacher, who seemed to confuse geometry and algebra.

Then she turned to the class of the veteran teacher, whose eighth-grade class had been discussing a short story. Why, Anderson asked, would she assign eighth graders to work in groups on the first day of school? "You've got to set up the group. Who's the recorder? On day one, you can't be a group and expect kids to talk," she said. But Carver was a neighborhood school, and most of its eighth graders had been talking to each other all their lives, both in and out of school. The class discussion had, in fact, been lively. Jackson, appearing somewhat stunned, listened deferentially.

"But still, it's great to see learning on day one," Anderson declared, bullish on the orderliness of her opening day. And off she went to continue inspecting the troops.

8

District School, Charter School

August 2011–June 2012

I T WAS A week before the first day of school at SPARK Academy, the charter elementary school that shared space with Carver Elementary, in one of Newark's most impoverished and violent neighborhoods. SPARK principal Joanna Belcher was leading her teachers in a workshop on the "growth mindset," which called for viewing setbacks—for children as well as themselves—as opportunities to learn. The thirty-year-old Belcher hardly looked the part of an inner-city principal—she was white, with long, thick golden-brown hair—but she had won the affection of Carver as well as SPARK teachers with her respectful attitude and passion for excellence and justice. She had worked in inner-city district schools for six years in Washington, D.C., and in California, and had resisted working for charter schools until KIPP leaders promised her a school that enrolled, in her words, "kids most charters don't serve." On the back of all the teachers' chairs, she had taped a statistic for them to contemplate. For example: "Only 1/10 students growing up in poverty will graduate from college."

In midsession, who should arrive but Cory Booker. He was escort-

ing Cari Tuna, then the girlfriend, later the wife, of Dustin Moskovitz, who had become a billionaire by virtue of cofounding Facebook
with Mark Zuckerberg, his Harvard roommate. Hoping Moskovitz
and Tuna would help match Zuckerberg's $100 million gift, Booker
took her to see two of the city's highest-performing charter schools.

Booker vowed to do anything to help SPARK succeed. He told the
teachers that Belcher had his cell-phone number, that he expected her
to call or text him with any problems. "Hit me up on Facebook. Tweet
me. I will respond and take care of it," he promised.

Most of SPARK's teachers had begun their careers as recruits to
Teach for America. Unlike many of their TFA peers, who left the
classroom after two years, they had continued to teach in inner cities,
becoming fiercely committed to addressing the needs of underserved
children, whether in district or charter schools. They had moved over
the summer onto the third floor of George Washington Carver, which
had lost forty percent of its enrollment in nine years. Belcher and
her team were impressed by the dedication and passion that Winston
Jackson, Carver's principal, had for the school and its community.
But they were alarmed to learn that the district had for years treated
Carver as a dumping ground for teachers no other principal wanted.
The result was that some of the weakest teachers had charge of some
of the city's most challenging children. By contrast, Belcher recruited
nationally for teachers she deemed best suited to meet her students'
needs.

The SPARK teachers took Booker up on his offer to help them. One
problem, they said, was a row of burned-out and abandoned houses
across the street from the school, dangerous havens for crime and
criminals that Carver and SPARK children passed daily. "If kids have
to go through a pathway of hazards, that's reprehensible," Booker replied. "Tweet me and I'll put my director of neighborhood services
on it." The houses had stood vacant for years without triggering city
attention. The same was true of the environs of most schools in the
South Ward.

The teachers asked Booker what his plan was to support the Carver students, who occupied the other floors of the building. Fewer than thirty percent of them were reading at their grade level. "I'll be very frank," Booker answered. "I want you to expand as fast as you can. But when schools are failing, I don't think pouring new wine into old skins is the way. We need to close them and start new ones."

One of twenty-three schools in Newark in danger of being closed for rock-bottom test performance under the No Child Left Behind law, Carver indeed was failing. But why? The district had systematically neglected it. So had the police. For years, gangs routinely held violent nighttime initiation rites in the school's play area, and sometimes Jackson arrived early in the morning to find blood pooled on school steps. He reported this at community meetings with police and pleaded for extra security, but never got a response.

Within a month of SPARK's arrival, there was another initiation, with blood splattered on school steps and bloody handprints on the sidewalk. A security camera recorded grainy images of nine young men mauling another at 9:30 at night, while some SPARK teachers remained at work on the third floor. The next morning, Jackson immediately emailed two school district officials, asking them to arrange a meeting with Anderson and the police. No one responded. Belcher wrote to the same officials six days later, asking, "Please let us know what the next steps are." Still no response. Jackson then asked Belcher to email the mayor, which she did, attaching three pictures of the trail of blood on "the steps our K–2 scholars use to enter the building." Within twenty minutes, Booker responded: "Joanna, your email greatly concerned me. I have copied this email to the police director who will contact you as soon as possible. Cory." Police director Samuel DeMaio called the next day, the police captain for the precinct visited the day after that, and the gang unit soon afterward. Police stepped up their after-hours presence around the school, and a detective assured Belcher and Jackson that the gang members would congregate elsewhere when they realized the area was being watched. The gang indeed moved on.

• • •

As Booker had suggested, the reform movement's prescription for failing schools was to close them and replace them with charter schools
or schools based on models that had succeeded in other cities and
states. But if charters or new models could succeed, why couldn't a
failing district school be revived, thereby sparing children the dislocation of having to leave teachers and classmates they had come to
know and trust?

That was the question posed by Dominique Lee and Charity Haygood, the founders of BRICK Avon. Their vision was to support and
coach district school teachers—not only to make them better instruc-
tors, but also to kindle motivation as more and more staff members
recognized untapped potential in themselves and colleagues. They
saw it as the equivalent of a grassroots movement, catching fire among
staff, students, and families. They pushed teachers hard to work on
their practice, to raise their expectations of students and lead them
to mastery. They also secured a federal school improvement grant to
extend the school day by ninety minutes. The pressure was not universally welcome; by the end of the year about a dozen teachers asked
for transfers to other schools, including most of those the new leaders
considered the weakest.

But there was a more troubling exodus. A third of Avon's students
left each year, their parents forced out of the neighborhood by evic-
tions, family strife, or fears of violence. With no school busing in
Newark, and many Avon families unable to afford a car, the children
had to transfer schools. From the start, BRICK Avon made its biggest
bet on raising the performance of the youngest children, from kindergarten through second grade, in hopes of escorting them to the all-
important threshold of success—reading proficiently by grade three
—and from there to higher performance in all subjects. "We think
it's a realistic goal that if a child is with us three years, he should be
at grade level," said Chris Perpich, the BRICK Avon assistant principal who had won over veteran teacher Sharon Rappaport with the
quality of his coaching. But the school leaders hadn't factored in the
toll of transience and poverty in Avon's catchment area—the poorest

in Newark. By the time their first kindergarten cohort reached third grade, barely thirty percent remained at Avon. Rather than welcoming a reading-ready class, third-grade teachers were almost starting from scratch.

"The ethos when I went through Teach for America was that good teaching and good leadership could solve the problems of poverty," said Dominique Lee. "That's part of the pie, but that's not all of the pie. Our most dynamic teachers were burning out—the need and anger in the children, the mental health issues, the absenteeism, the transience."

They were witnessing the effect of what researchers call adverse childhood experiences, multiple traumas that, studies have shown, significantly interfere with learning and focus in children in the most disadvantaged communities. One year, state child-welfare workers were monitoring fifteen of twenty-six children in Princess Williams's kindergarten class for alleged neglect or exposure to domestic violence. Children with more than one traumatic experience—violence, severe poverty, family breakup, or substance abuse in the home— were more than twice as likely as others to fail at least one grade. And trauma was hard to avoid in the South Ward of Newark, where violent crime rose seventy percent from 2010 to 2013.

"Our children's nervous systems are designed from birth to be in trauma mode," said Haygood, the Avon principal who had worked in Newark schools for more than a decade. "I don't think we understood that at first. We were like, 'If you just work hard enough, we can fix it.'"

Still, the new leaders were improving the school, although not at the pace they expected. In their first three years at Avon, school-wide scores on state tests in math showed the third-steepest increase in the district, although almost sixty percent of students still were below grade level—in literacy, almost seventy-five percent. In New Jersey, there is no standardized testing before third grade, so the only yardstick for early grades came from STEP, the research-based literacy program Avon had adopted on the advice of charter school leaders.

When BRICK arrived, STEP testing showed that only seven of fifty-five first graders were on track to read proficiently by grade three. Two years later, thirty-four out of seventy-two were on track, an increase from thirteen to forty-seven percent. This was a dramatic and positive change, but it still left more than half the class off track. The results in Williams's class were much more encouraging. When her twenty-three students arrived in 2011, for example, all but one failed the STEP readiness test for kindergarten; they couldn't spell their names, count to twenty, distinguish between a letter and a word, or recognize that words progressed from left to right across a page. At the end of the year, eleven of them met STEP's rigorous national benchmark for first grade, with another seven missing it by one question. Those eighteen children all met the district's standard for promotion, however. But only five of them would still be at Avon for third grade in the fall of 2014.

The unanimous conclusion of teachers and leaders at Avon was that they needed more resources, to support children not only in the classroom but also outside it. But how could resources be a problem in a district with a billion-dollar budget?

In decrying the failure of the Newark schools, Christie regularly highlighted the vast amount of money spent on them, three-quarters of it provided by the state's taxpayers. The governor put the figure at $24,000 per student; in fact, it was closer to $20,000, still an extraordinary sum in national terms. California spent $9,139 per student in 2011, Texas spent $8,671, and almost half of all states spent under $10,000. Newark's bounty was a direct result of a series of state supreme court rulings in the 1980s and 1990s in the landmark case of *Abbott v. Burke,* directing extra resources to the lowest-income districts.

Christie had not funded the full formula since taking office, citing the state fiscal crisis, but the allocation was still equivalent to about $20,000 per student. Less than half of this, though, reached district schools to pay teachers, social workers, counselors, classroom aides, secretaries, and administrators—the people who actually delivered education to children. The rest went into the central bureaucracy, which technically served students but at huge cost. For example, the district calculated that it spent $1,200 a year per student on Avon's janitorial services; BRICK founder Dominique Lee researched the cost on the private market and found it was close to $400 per student. The difference could have paid salaries for up to ten additional teachers and counselors, he said. The central office also paid for specialists who diagnosed learning disabilities, and math and literacy experts who helped teachers adapt to the newly demanding Common Core State Standards.

But district money gushed and oozed in myriad directions. Saddled with dilapidated school buildings, some dating to the Civil War, the district spent $10 million to $15 million a year on structural emergencies like crumbling façades and caving roofs—money that was supposed to help educate children. It spent another $4 million in rent for its headquarters in a drab, aging downtown office building owned by the real estate giant Hartz Mountain Industries, a large contributor to state and local politicians' campaigns. When district officials tried unsuccessfully to break the lease years earlier to move to less expensive quarters, the rival landlord filed a lawsuit alleging political shenanigans, which Hartz Mountain emphatically denied. In 2012, the district facilities director discovered that high school football stadium lights were bizarrely being left to burn all night, costing $300,000 a year.

More than eighty percent of the Newark Public Schools budget went to salaries and benefits, which was typical for a school district. Still, many positions were unnecessary, created years earlier and still locked in by state civil service rules and seniority laws. These jobs were mostly near the bottom of the pay scale, bestowing income and benefits on low-skilled workers for whom no similar opportunities existed in Newark. Unlike in the private sector, where one clerk served multiple managers, NPS assigned multiple clerks to individual managers.

All of this reflected the district's history of operating as both a patronage mill and an educational institution, controlled by whatever political machine happened to be in office—Irish American, Italian American, African American. After fifteen years in charge, the state had done little to ensure that money reached the underserved children who desperately needed it.

Although Anderson laid off hundreds of workers—clerks, security guards, custodians, attendance counselors—the schools saw no increase in resources, largely because overall district revenue was shrinking as students left for charters. Meanwhile, the excess teacher pool ballooned to consume more than $60 million in Anderson's first three years, leading her to cut school budgets in order to pay teachers who had no classroom—all in the name of school reform.

Under state law, charters received only ninety percent of the allotment for district school students, on the assumption that districts had some administrative costs related to charters. But they had none of the legacy costs that came from decades of serving as an employer of last resort for a struggling city. Even starting out with less, well-run charter networks got more money to their schools than the district did, fueling a perception that the state favored them over traditional public schools.

SPARK Academy, the KIPP charter school that Booker had visited with philanthropist Cari Tuna, provided a striking illustration of what the district's money and staff could have been doing for children. According to financial documents from Newark's KIPP schools, the charter network sent $12,664 per child to SPARK Academy, while the Newark Public Schools sent only $7,597 per child to BRICK Avon. The KIPP schools also raised large sums of philanthropy to cover start-up costs for new schools, but once they reached full enrollment, SPARK and the others operated fully on public funds.

In addition to having more money at the school level, Joanna Belcher, the SPARK principal, had wide latitude to use it to address the particular needs of her students. Because SPARK, like all charters in Newark and the great majority nationally, was non-union, she and her leadership team also were free to adjust teachers' schedules and responsibilities. "We designed the school and the budget purposely based on what kids are going through and what they need," she said.

To support students who struggled, Belcher placed two certified teachers in each kindergarten, as well as in every math and English class in grades one through three. Students who fell behind got small-group instruction from one teacher while the other led the lesson for those on grade level. For children who still couldn't keep up, a full-time learning specialist — one for each grade — provided tutoring and other interventions. By contrast, Avon and all district schools had one teacher in each classroom. In kindergarten, there was also a classroom aide, who was not required to have graduated from college. Most district schools shared one to two specialists among all grades, if they had any at all. Nor were district classes necessarily smaller. Williams had twenty-three kindergarteners in her class, versus SPARK's twenty-six. It was mind-boggling to contemplate what Avon kindergarteners could have learned had there been two Princess Williamses in Room 112 instead of one.

While all charters had equal flexibility with staff and resources, there was wide variation in their results and in the makeup of their student bodies. North Star had by far the highest student test scores in Newark, followed by a number of individual charter schools. TEAM's schools ranked sixth among charters in a 2012 analysis by district consultants. A Stanford University study in the same year found that Newark children in charter schools gained an extra seven and a half months of reading skills and nine months in math. However, some Newark charters failed dramatically — the state shut down one for financial improprieties and another for such poor instruction and classroom management that children were deemed unsafe. And in other New Jersey cities, charter students learned "significantly less" in reading and about the same in math as their district peers, according to the Stanford study.

All Newark schools, charter and district, served a low-income population, but some considerably more than others. Of the high-performing charter networks, KIPP had the largest proportion of children in poverty and those who had behavior and learning disabilities, although still not as large as the district's. Seventy-three percent of KIPP students qualified for a free lunch, meaning they lived on no more than $30,000 per family of four. At BRICK Avon, eighty-three percent qualified, compared to seventy-nine percent on average across the district. At top-scoring North Star, sixty-eight percent qualified. The KIPP network invested time and money combating the selection bias for charters. It was the only Newark charter to provide school busing, opening access to the large number of children whose families didn't own cars or couldn't arrange to take them to and from school on public transit.

Belcher considered great teaching and leadership crucial, but not sufficient for a quality education in a city as troubled as Newark. She knew that not all children had an adult at home who could consistently treat their education as a priority. Rather than leave such issues to individual teachers to overcome, Belcher made them a responsibility of the school by creating a dean of student and family engagement, a position that didn't exist in any district school. Belcher conceived of it after observing Diane Adams, a tall and lanky kindergarten teacher who walked with the perfect posture of a dancer, her frizzy ponytail swinging with each step. With a fun and spirited teaching style that all but camouflaged how demanding she was, Adams could energize even the most reluctant learners. When Belcher asked her how she did it, Adams said she had a different strategy for each child, built on whatever it took to entice them to love school. She arrived early or stayed late to tutor or just to talk, she rewarded milestones with treats tailored to particular students, and most important, she had a talent for persuading the adults in children's lives—if not a parent or grandparent, then a family friend—to get involved in helping them learn. At the end of that year, Belcher pulled Adams out of the classroom and asked her to develop individualized help for all struggling students, in the name of removing barriers to learning. Adams worked with teachers, parents, the school's social workers, outside service providers

—serving as a designer, coordinator, and dispatcher of student support, drafting detailed assignments for everyone involved. "The systems queen," Belcher called her.

Some cases took a team, if not a village. Belcher herself provided dedicated assistance. One morning late in 2011, a mother of three SPARK students was badly beaten by her boyfriend while her children were in school. The mother appeared in the school office, her face bruised and swollen, clutching her newborn baby and desperate for help. Belcher accompanied her and the baby to the hospital, persuaded her to file a police report, and went with her to the courthouse, where they sat together for hours waiting for a lawyer to be assigned. "I'd never seen that in all my career—a principal coming to court with a victim," said attorney Suzanne Groisser, a specialist in domestic abuse who handled the case.

Even more unusual was what happened back at SPARK, where the systems queen took up the case. Diane Adams created a carpooling schedule involving seven different staff members, who would pick up the three children each morning at a neutral location—the family had moved to a shelter whose address was secret—and return them each day after school. The lead social worker, Sarah Dewey, formerly a teacher in the Bronx, held counseling sessions with the children and also guided teachers on how to speak with them about the traumatic experience, to help them feel safe and able to learn. Within two weeks, the mother called with a special request: she wanted a set of SPARK banners to hang in their room at the shelter so the children would feel at home. Each letter stood for a school value: Seek knowledge, Pursue justice, Act as a team, Reach for excellence, Keep going. Not one of her children missed a day of school throughout their months in the shelter, and all finished the year above grade level.

More often, Adams worked with students who had severe behavior problems. In the case of one boy, whose home life was chaotic, she and Dewey found a willing partner in a stepfather, who recently had been released from prison and wanted to play a role in the boy's life.

Another boy experienced such volcanic anger that he slugged teachers without warning. Dewey created an "office" for him—with his own child-sized desk and chair—in a corner of her work space, and she and Adams supervised his work while his mother went through the long process of having him classified for psychiatric treatment. Princess Williams had a student at Avon with similarly violent tendencies (in his fiercest rages, he threw chairs, terrifying classmates), but it took the district bureaucracy almost eight months to deliver the support she requested.

A brother and sister at SPARK who had been model students suddenly began throwing daily tantrums, disrupting classes. Realizing that they consistently lost control at particular times, Adams assigned a teacher on break shortly before their meltdown times to pull each of them out of class for ten minutes of one-on-one attention. That got them through the rest of the day. It also protected the learning atmosphere for their classmates.

Although many district teachers voluntarily gave long hours to help struggling students, this kind of administrative flexibility would not have been possible in district schools, where the union contract barred the assignment of teachers to nonteaching tasks, such as carpooling or spending break time with children who needed to calm down. At SPARK, being available and responsible for all students was part of every job description. Rather than cite the student-teacher ratio as a defining statistic, Belcher referred to the ratio of adult staff to students, 61:520. "EVERY ADULT IN THE BUILDING (from lunch aides to custodians to teachers) is 100% responsible for every single child," she wrote in an email to the staff.

For its 520 students, SPARK had two full-time social workers and a third who worked half-time—a stark contrast to larger district schools that had only one or sometimes two. Together, they conducted group therapy sessions with a total of seventy children a week and individual therapy with fifteen. Dewey started a grief group one year for five children who had lost a parent or close family member to murder. At the same time, she provided play therapy daily for one child and three days a week for another. District social workers typically were too busy to do therapy.

The KIPP schools in Newark adopted a deliberately forgiving policy toward parents who missed enrollment deadlines after winning a lottery. If parents failed to contact most charters by the deadline, they lost their child's slot to the next student on the waiting list. But Joanna Belcher was convinced that parents who needed the most support were also likely to miss deadlines. She deployed her staff to track them down, holding their places until the opening day of school, despite the uncertainty this created for teachers. Belcher's hunch was squarely on target in the case of a kindergartner named Da'Veer Snell.

Her staff located Da'Veer's mother, Dyneeka McPherson, less than a month before kindergarten was to start, and Belcher scheduled a home visit, a standard SPARK practice to get to know families and children's needs before school began. McPherson arranged to meet Belcher at her grandmother's apartment. She was then twenty-two, and Da'Veer, age five, was her oldest of four children. The young, slender mother in cutoffs and a white top explained that she had applied to both SPARK and North Star, and that Da'Veer had been picked in both lotteries, but she had missed both deadlines. She said she recently had called North Star and learned that Da'Veer had lost his spot. When Belcher told McPherson that he was still on the SPARK roster, McPherson closed her eyes as if a prayer had been answered and said, her voice catching, "I want him to be better than me."

Beside her sat Da'Veer, lean and quiet with large, dark eyes that made him appear unusually serious as he colored a picture with concentration. He had attended preschool tuition-free for two years, thanks to a program ordered as part of the *Abbott* rulings to prepare New Jersey's poorest children to learn. But school quality varied widely, and when Belcher showed Da'Veer the letters of the alphabet in random order, he correctly identified only five. Like Williams's students at BRICK Avon, he was far behind STEP's national benchmark for literacy in kindergarten-age children.

"We're going to promise to do everything we can to help you go to college," Belcher told him, as McPherson watched with a look of wonder.

McPherson and Da'Veer's father, Kevin Snell, had faced long odds almost since birth. Both children of drug addicts and raised by their grandmothers, McPherson said they fell in love at age twelve and pledged to each other to do better than their parents. "We decided we can't raise our children the way we was raised," she said. She worked hard in school and believed she would have been successful in life with more support. But she and Snell had two children by the time she graduated from Central High School in 2007, and two more soon after. Snell had worked since age fifteen on a farm in northwestern New Jersey; he lived there four days a week.

McPherson said Da'Veer never could have attended SPARK without busing, but she had trouble getting him to the stop on time, often because of family crises. The family was forced out of its high-rise apartment building when the federal government canceled its contract with the landlord because of the property's severe health and safety hazards. Later, McPherson developed a seizure disorder and was homebound on heavy medication, unable to walk Da'Veer to the bus stop. Adams arranged a car pool, drafting the SPARK office manager, Belcher, and the school's operations director. But at one point Da'Veer was absent for a week, and calls and texts to his mother went unanswered. McPherson later explained that she had canceled her cell phone service to save money, because the family had to move yet again—this time, they would share an apartment in a high-crime corridor of the South Ward with McPherson's sister and a lifelong friend, who had two children.

Chronic absenteeism tends to be a leading indicator of a family that doesn't value education. But teachers at SPARK were struck that when Da'Veer came to school, he consistently had done his homework.

"Despite everything on her plate, his mother made sure Da'Veer's education was never going to get lost in the shuffle," said one of his teachers, Garrett Raczek.

But because of his absences, Da'Veer was not on track to be promoted to first grade. SPARK stepped up the support—daily, small-group instruction with one of his two kindergarten teachers, and daily tutoring and extra homework from learning interventionist Karen Chen. Because of continuing absences, though, he fell behind even in the intervention class.

Belcher and his teachers summoned McPherson to warn that Da'Veer could be retained. The year was almost half over, and he knew only seven letters. "He could be one of the top kids in kindergarten," Belcher said. "He's not behind because he can't, but because he's missing instructional time. What can we do to support you?"

The conference produced an action plan: McPherson or her sister would text Belcher every morning just after 6:30 to report whether Da'Veer caught or missed the bus; if he missed it, Belcher would pick him up on her way to school. Far from turning defensive, McPherson was effusive about the school and its effect on Da'Veer.

"My sister says, 'Whoever heard of a teacher who texts you? A principal who texts you?'" she said. "Da'Veer did something that amazed me the other day," she went on. "He got on the floor and started doing pushups and counting." She told them he often played school with his younger siblings, instructing them to count their toys, identify colors, or draw an animal. With the right answer came SPARK-style praise. "Thumbs-up, Daquan. Thumbs-up, Kaya," he would say.

The action plan succeeded, and Da'Veer's attendance improved. For much of the spring, he worked daily with Chen and in small groups with his teachers, reaching STEP's end-of-kindergarten literacy benchmark and being promoted to first grade. The next year his brother, Daquan, would come to SPARK, and the year after that, his sister, Kayasia.

• • •

Back at BRICK Avon, even without the resources at SPARK, about half of Princess Williams's students thrived in spite of starting out behind the national curve. These were invariably the students whose parents took an active role in their schooling and helped them with homework. In preparation for parent conferences, Williams wrote letters to every family, emphasizing the importance of a partnership with the school. So did principal Charity Haygood. The teachers prepared what they called a "BRICK plan," documenting each student's level of achievement versus where he or she needed to be to reach grade level, detailing how both the school and the family would help. The plan was simple—no more than three tasks for families to perform with the child every night, and three interventions the teacher would carry out.

Turnout for conferences was better in BRICK Avon's second year than in recent memory. Avon's longtime crossing guard, her bright yellow jacket glowing against the dusk, watched in wonder as scores of parents converged on the big, red brick schoolhouse. "Look at 'em! Look at 'em!" she exclaimed, with a smile almost as bright as her jacket. "They're coming out. This is the first time I've ever seen them support their children like they're doing today. I'm proud of them."

Parents or grandparents of sixteen of Williams's twenty-three students attended, a flood by Avon's old standards, but the young teacher was disappointed. As she feared, the children who needed the most support were the ones for whom no one showed up. And Avon had no systems queen whose job it was to recruit adults to guide them.

Williams's dedication combined with support at home made a critical difference for some children. Tariq Anderson was a slight and wiry boy with a head full of braids and boundless energy. In the early weeks, when Williams asked the class to walk quietly and sit on the learning rug, Tariq would get a running start and slide into the rug as if stealing home. "Tariq is making a bad choice," Williams would say, without a hint of impatience. Each time, she took his hand and escorted him to a red, tomato-shaped table where he was to work alone and reflect on how "scholars" carry themselves. This consumed considerable lesson time, but Williams said she had no choice, lest others follow his lead. At SPARK, the kindergarten class arrived two weeks before the older grades, and extra teachers were on hand in the early weeks to intercept and correct misbehavior, avoiding any break in instruction.

Williams noticed that Tariq knew much more than he let on. He'd ask for help spelling an easy word, then she'd hear him tell friends how to spell much harder ones. She took every opportunity to bolster his confidence, and by the end of the first month, he seemed to want nothing more than to cooperate with her. His mother and father took an interest in his education. "He's always been a smart boy," said his mother, a home health aide. At his report card conference, she told Williams that Tariq talked constantly about her at home. "I think he's got a crush on her for real!" said Keisha Robinson, the classroom aide. As time went on, Williams became more and more aware of Tariq's potential—the depth of his questions, his curiosity about how everything worked. He often asked her for help writing a sentence, but she pressed him to try it on his own. Once she returned to discover he had written a whole story, with a beginning, middle, and end. "You are brilliant," she whispered.

But when it came to children who needed intensive, specialized intervention, Williams had none of the extra resources that would have been available at SPARK. In the case of a boy who was struggling to learn letter sounds, while most students were writing elementary sentences, Williams made time to tutor him twice a week with other students at his level. At SPARK he would have had daily small-group instruction with a teacher, plus classes with an academic interventionist. In a conference with the boy's mother, Williams explained that he was in danger of failing kindergarten. In order to be promoted, she said, children had to write a story of four to five sentences with a beginning, middle, and end, although "creative" spelling was fine. "For kindergarten, don't you think it's a little bit much?" the boy's mother asked.

Williams responded that that was the national benchmark, and Newark children must reach it. The mother did not protest. Rather, she turned to her son and said, "I want you to grow up and be the scholar Miss Williams and I want you to be." Williams asked the mother to help her complement his learning by having him write two complete sentences every night and practice addition and subtraction with flash cards. She also asked her to come to class periodically to check on him, as encouragement. But the support at home was spotty, and there was no Diane Adams at Avon to shore it up. The boy did not pass and had to repeat kindergarten.

The children in Da'Veer Snell's kindergarten class at SPARK started out with literacy assessment scores comparable to those of Williams's class; of twenty-five who took the test, only four met the readiness standard for kindergarten. (In Williams's class, one of twenty-three passed.) But by year's end, twenty-four out of twenty-five at SPARK reached the national benchmark for first grade; sixteen of those surpassed it. Only eleven of Williams's students cleared the bar, with another seven missing it by one question. There were as many factors at play in the different results as there were children in each class, but given the excellence of the teaching in both, the resources available to support children and families appeared to play a large role.

Still, the teachers and leaders at Avon were bringing new hope and purpose to the school, and parents as well as children seemed well aware of that at the kindergarten graduation ceremony on June 22, 2012. Nineteen of Williams's twenty-three students were marching; four were being held back. The graduates arrived early in their Sunday best. Girls wore flower-print dresses, white dress socks with ribbons threaded through them, and braids adorned with multicolored barrettes and beads that matched their dresses. Boys wore dress pants and dress shirts. Williams wore a tailored black and white dress and heels.

The students were eager to share what they would remember about their teacher. Jonathan: "I'll remember how nice she is to us and how she always wears a nice dress." Faith: "Miss Williams is special to us

because she's a great teacher and she always has a smile on her face."
Larry: "She taught things we didn't know. She taught us to read a
book and to write." Jonathan asked to add one more thought: "My
favorite memory is I learned how to read."

The temperature outside was in the nineties, and Room 112 was
so hot that Williams turned off the lights. Wiping moisture from her
forehead and cheeks, she walked among her excited students, urging
everyone to be still. "When it's hot," she said, "friends get aggravated
faster. Please, please, please be nice to friends." Soon it was time for
her scholars to line up and walk out for the last time. "We're going to
walk like first graders!" she said with pride and a smile. As if on cue,
everyone stood up a bit taller.

BRICK Avon's three kindergarten classes entered the cafeteria to a
recording of "Pomp and Circumstance," passing a banner that pro-
claimed, "Your Choices. Your Actions. Your Life." More than a hundred family members awaited, holding bouquets of Mylar balloons.
Many raised smartphones, tablets, and camcorders to capture the moment. The children saluted the flag and sang "America" and "Lift Every Voice and Sing," also known as the black national anthem, a favorite at BRICK Avon. Swaying from side to side, the graduates belted
out the chorus, which seemed to speak directly to the mission of their
teachers and leaders: "Sing a song full of the faith that the dark past
has taught us, / Sing a song full of the hope that the present has
brought us."

Teachers called their students' names one by one, and the small
graduates walked across the stage to receive scrolls as each of their pictures appeared on a projection screen. Williams's students got something extra. For weeks, she had thought about the message she wanted
to leave with them, one that would endure long past kindergarten.
One night it came to her. She would tell them, in public, what she envisioned them becoming in the future. She hoped to plant an aspira-
tion, so that perhaps one day, as adults, they would say to themselves,
"I remember Miss Williams saying I'm going to be this, and I desired
this, and now I am this."

First she called Jessica, "our future politician, because she's always questioning and speaking up on behalf of friends." Then Zyashah, "our future meteorologist, because she loves to be our weather girl and give us the weather report." Zahmya, "our future author—this girl is into books." Keona, "our future secretary of state. She loves keeping the peace." Jonathan, "our future mathematician. He does miracles with numbers." Tavon, "our future lawyer. He loves to challenge me."

Last in line was Tariq, the gifted boy who always underestimated himself. She had thought hard about what to say to Tariq to bolster his confidence for the long haul. "This scholar says he wants to be a policeman, but the truth is that Tariq is a future genius. He's so brilliant and he tries to hide it," Williams said as the small boy crossed the stage, eyes fixed on his teacher. Extending his diploma with a flourish, she said with all her heart: "Show your brilliance, Tariq Anderson!"

9

Transformational Change Meets the Political Sausage Factory

December 2011–November 2012

N EWARK HAD THE attention of the national reform move- ment. Cami Anderson and Chris Cerf were featured panel- ists at its conferences. Anderson was named one of *Time*'s one hundred most influential people in the world, with her entry written by Booker, who made the previous year's list. In late 2011, Wendy Kopp, the founder of Teach for America, and her husband, Richard Barth, president of the KIPP Foundation, came to Newark to speak at a dinner for donors about the promise they saw in the rare alignment of a governor, a mayor, a superintendent, and bounteous philanthropy.

"Just to be real," Barth warned, "it's going to be a tragedy for the city and the country if you don't succeed. If you can't do it here, with all those things in place, we do not have a shot *anywhere* in the coun- try."

"Doing it" in education reform inevitably involved a prizefight be- tween two powerful forces in America politics: muscular and mon- ied teachers' unions with old-guard political patrons on one side and, on the other, an ascendant alliance of recently elected officials backed by education reform financiers. This conflict had fueled all the public skirmishes in Newark so far—over the leaked consultants' report, the school closings that would lead to layoffs, the expansion of charter schools into district buildings.

But nothing revealed the dimensions of the power struggle as vividly as Booker, Christie, and Zuckerberg's quest for what they called a "transformational" teachers' contract, one they hoped would become a model for attracting the nation's most talented college graduates to teach in distressed cities. The goal was to apply business-style accountability to teacher pay—abolishing the long-standing system of basing salaries on years of service, instead making student performance the measure of a teacher's worth. They wanted the contract to ease the removal of teachers with the worst evaluations and to reward the best ones with pay raises, handsome bonuses, and more remunerative career opportunities. Unlike the other battles, this one played out almost exclusively behind the scenes—in elected officials' private offices, union halls, tony corporate meeting spaces, windowless warrens in the district headquarters, and phone calls between politicians and billionaires.

In early 2012, Cerf made a trip to Washington to meet privately with Randi Weingarten, president of the American Federation of Teachers, the parent of the Newark Teachers Union. For more than two years, Newark teachers had worked without a contract and without raises. Negotiations with the previous superintendent had gone nowhere. Cerf and Weingarten had developed a cordial relationship when he was Klein's deputy in New York and she was president of the city's AFT local. Despite philosophical differences, she viewed him as an honest broker who respected the work of teachers; he viewed her as a leader who wanted to challenge the public's notion that unions served adults at the expense of children.

In Washington, Cerf was blunt. He made clear that he and Christie could use Zuckerberg's money in one of two ways: to underwrite a teachers' contract that imposed consequences on the worst and rewarded the best, or to "charterize" the city, ultimately leading to the collapse of the district.

"My view had been that the trajectory was for Newark to become a charter district like New Orleans," Weingarten said. New Orleans, which was transformed into an almost all-charter system after Hurricane Katrina destroyed the vast majority of its schools in 2005, was the ultimate threat to teachers' unions. Teachers in the school district were unionized; those in charters were not. After talking with Cerf, she saw the contract—despite the compromises involved—as a path to save the district, and with it, union jobs.

Weingarten had been national president of AFT since 2008, but having worked in New York for decades, she was painfully aware of the failure rate in Newark schools and was convinced that the district's teachers had to unite behind an improvement strategy. "One of the first things I did when I became national president, I went to Newark and met with Joe, and I said we have to help. We need to do something to help you."

"Joe" was Joseph Del Grosso, president of the Newark local for almost twenty years. A relic of Italian American hegemony in a now black and brown city, he had helped create the system the reformers wanted to dismantle, having won his members handsome raises, sizable pay "bumps" for longevity, and enough paid sick and personal time to cover almost one in ten school days. A onetime firebrand who in 1970, as a second-grade teacher, went to jail for three months for participating in a strike, Del Grosso was now sixty-five, with a white hatband of hair. He still delivered blistering speeches against state control and the charter school "conspiracy," but he was visibly tired, struggling against Crohn's disease. "Joe and I thought this was an important step," Weingarten said of Cerf's proposal, "to get the principals who controlled the district to be willing to invest and support as opposed to destabilizing a public system."

Weingarten was wary of Christie, who had rocketed to national fame as basher in chief of the state teachers' union. But she and the governor had a chance encounter at a New York ceremony on the tenth anniversary of the 9/11 attacks that made her think perhaps they could do business. She recalled that Christie took her aside, told her of living in Newark as a young child, and said with seriousness, "I really want to do something" in Newark. "I was incredulous," Weingarten said, "and I looked at him and asked, 'Are you telling me you don't want to do something ideological? You really want to do something about the Newark *district* schools?' And he said yes." They saw each other again the following February in Washington, at the White House Correspondents' Dinner, when negotiations were flagging, and Christie said they resolved to push their two sides harder. "What a story that would be," the governor recalled saying, "if Chris Christie and Randi Weingarten stand next to each other at a press conference in Newark, New Jersey, and announce a new teachers' contract."

In a document given to Booker on the day of the *Oprah* announcement, Zuckerberg had made clear that he wanted to use half of his gift — $50 million — to win a game-changing teachers' contract. He was influenced by a labor agreement Michelle Rhee had reached with teachers in Washington, D.C., in 2010, which electrified the reform movement. It allowed her to lay off teachers based on merit, without regard to seniority. And with $64.5 million from four venture philanthropists — Eli and Edythe Broad, Laura and John Arnold, the Walton family, and Julian Robertson — the Washington contract provided hefty bonuses for the highest-rated teachers, who could earn up to $100,000 by their fourth year if they agreed to forfeit tenure protections.

Zuckerberg's document laid out similar goals: "Restructure pay scale to increase base salaries for new hires . . . Abolish seniority as a factor in all personnel decisions and incentivize the removal of poor performers." He also wrote that he wanted the best teachers to receive bonuses of up to fifty percent of their salary, the kind of incentives paid to top workers in Silicon Valley.

The young philanthropist was unaware, however, of a key difference between Newark and Washington: tenure and seniority protections were enshrined in New Jersey state law, and contracts alone couldn't eliminate them. Cerf and Christie were working to change that statewide, but this required them to win over a legislature in which horse-trading Democratic political bosses called the shots and the New Jersey Education Association, the biggest teachers' union — a subsidiary of the National Education Association — was by far the largest contributor to political campaigns. The NJEA and Christie were already at war. The union had spent millions of dollars trying to defeat him in 2009 and recently had lost a bruising battle against his fiscal austerity package, which required public employees to contribute more to their health care coverage. Buoyed by his victories, Christie ramped up the attacks, casting the NJEA as New Jersey's version of the evil empire, a selfish, greedy "playground bully." Polls showed state residents were increasingly siding with Christie, and Democratic lawmakers were caught between restive voters and their richest patron.

After arduous negotiations, in the summer of 2012 the legislature did pass a measure that made tenure harder to achieve and much easier to lose — an example of laws then being passed in many states to qualify for the Obama administration's Race to the Top education grants. Modeled in part on a recent Colorado reform measure, the New Jersey law empowered districts to strip tenure from teachers with two consecutive years of poor performance ratings and made student growth on standardized tests a factor in their evaluations. In return for union support, however, New Jersey lawmakers kept seniority protections intact. Union leaders had argued that in a time of tightening school budgets, many districts otherwise would lay off their most expensive (read: senior) teachers, without regard to merit. "It would've put this union and all unions out of existence," said Del Grosso. The measure passed both houses unanimously, with strong support from the NJEA and Weingarten's AFT, which included few New Jersey locals other than Newark's.

At the time, there was growing skepticism nationally on the validity of grading teachers based on the annual growth in their students' test scores. In fact, one of the leading skeptics of this brand of high-stakes accountability was Dr. Damian Betebenner, a statistical analyst who developed the system used in New Jersey and about thirty other states to measure that growth. Reached in his office at the National Center for the Improvement of Educational Assessment in Dover, New Hampshire, Betebenner said the system, known as Student Growth Percentile, was designed to measure student gains or losses, not to assign blame or credit for them. "Simply focusing on teachers as being the only potential cause of growth of students is pretty obviously myopic," said Betebenner. The data would be more useful, he said, as a starting point for discussions with teachers on the reasons individual students are improving or losing ground, which could include many factors in and out of school. "A lot of high-stakes accountability has become self-defeating—focusing solely on the identification of bad schools, the bad teachers, as opposed to creating a signal and involving teachers in processes that lead to investigations and changes," he said.

Nonetheless, test-based teacher accountability for student performance remained a primary goal of the reform movement, and Christie touted the law nationally as yet another bipartisan victory in a blue state. But the law's preservation of seniority rights dealt a blow to Zuckerberg's vision for the Newark contract. Negotiations were under way at the time among Cerf, Anderson, and Del Grosso, and seniority protections for teachers were suddenly off the table. "If this is our one shot at reform, this is a terrible disappointment," Cerf told lawmakers. With charters expanding, district enrollment shrinking, and the pool of excess teachers swelling, Anderson would have no way to downsize except to lay off the most junior teachers and keep all senior ones in place, regardless of who was better at reaching kids.

"There is no way we can have a transformational contract without eliminating LIFO," Anderson said at the time, referring to the seniority system known as Last In, First Out.

With a crucial goal now out of reach, Cerf and Anderson nonetheless won significant teacher accountability measures in the contract, again thanks to the power of Zuckerberg's purse. As long as anyone could remember, Newark teachers—like most teachers nationally—had received virtually automatic pay hikes regardless of performance. "Keep breathing another year and you get your raise" was the way Cerf and many other reformers derided the status quo. Del Grosso, with Weingarten's blessing, agreed to Cerf and Anderson's demand that his members no longer would get pay raises unless they were rated effective or better under a new and much more rigorous evaluation system. All others would have their pay frozen. In addition, teachers rated at the top of the scale would receive merit bonuses ranging from $5,000 to $12,500—the first use of merit pay in New Jersey. But as his price for all this, Del Grosso demanded $31 million in back pay for the two years that his 3,600 members had worked without raises. In fact, he made it a condition of even staying at the table, on a bet that the reformers wanted a contract at least as much as he did. He turned out to be right. After conferring with Zuckerberg's representatives, Cerf and Anderson added $31 million to the philanthropists' tab.

The cost of labor reforms was growing increasingly extravagant. Anderson put the price of the teachers' contract at about $50 million —with back pay by far the biggest component and the rest going to merit bonuses and one-time stipends to encourage teachers to switch to a universal pay scale. The existing system had three scales, with higher pay for teachers with master's degrees, and still more for those with PhDs. Under the universal scale, teachers would no longer receive higher pay for earning degrees. Instead, they would get tuition support, but only for graduate programs Anderson deemed relevant to their effectiveness—adding another $8.5 million to the bill. Anderson also asked for a $20 million buyout fund to encourage weak teachers to leave, and another $15 million for an anticipated new principals' contract modeled on the teachers' agreement.

Anderson estimated the total cost of the labor agreements at $100 million, far more than Booker and Zuckerberg had expected. This came to half the anticipated philanthropic bounty of $100 million from Zuckerberg and $100 million in matching gifts. The FNF staff's strategic plan had called for investing heavily in ongoing community organizing around reform efforts and also in early-childhood programs. But these plans were canceled to make way for the labor costs as Anderson had calculated them.

Also gone was a plan to spend $50 million on programs for an estimated four thousand teenagers and young adults who had dropped out of school, with few skills and less hope, becoming a recruiting pool for Newark's proliferating gangs. Booker had made "disaffected and at-risk youth" his personal project—Zuckerberg hadn't committed to it—and he spoke eloquently of the urgency of connecting young dropouts with learning and economic opportunities, lest they swell the school-to-prison pipeline. But he ended up not raising the money to pay for the initiative, which was quietly shelved, even as intensifying gang violence seemed to validate the mayor's concern.

This meant the contract would be the signature play to transform the Newark district. But as the deal came together in the summer of 2012, Booker hadn't raised enough money to match the young billionaire's gift—the condition for unlocking his dollars.

At the time of the announcement on *Oprah* in September 2010, Bari Mattes, Booker's chief fundraiser, had predicted Booker would raise the full $100 million by Thanksgiving or Christmas. He didn't. "We're almost there," he said in early 2011. The following summer, Booker said he believed the Texas-based John and Laura Arnold Foundation, major donors to charter schools and to the Washington, D.C., contract, was on the verge of donating $25 million. But the Arnolds didn't give. "The truth of the matter is I'm not that concerned about that now," Booker said in an interview as the one-year anniversary of the announcement approached. "When Facebook goes public, Mark is going to create about ten billionaires, and there's a lot of interest among them in helping out." Facebook went public in May 2012, but the new billionaires didn't donate to Newark.

One challenge was that many reform-oriented philanthropists

viewed school districts as unfixable and, unlike Ackman and Zuckerberg, were willing to donate only to charter schools. John Doerr, the Silicon Valley venture capitalist, gave $10 million to Newark charters through his NewSchools Venture Fund. The Walton, Fisher, and Robertson foundations gave $14.25 million through the Newark Charter School Fund. Both conditioned their gifts on a commitment that Zuckerberg match them. He did, and combined with other donors' gifts to individual schools, about $60 million of the $200 million in philanthropy went toward the expansion and support of charter schools. Indeed, Zuckerberg and matching donors helped put the sector on track to enroll a projected sixteen thousand students by 2016, an increase of more than eleven thousand since 2009. The city's two top-performing charter networks, TEAM and North Star, now had enough money to double in size, ultimately adding ten thousand students. Many reformers saw charter growth as the fastest way to raise the quality of education citywide and considered this the crowning achievement of the Zuckerberg gift, but there was no public announcement of the total contribution to charters. At the time, public resistance to school closings was mounting, and Cami Anderson was wrestling with a $57 million budget gap—largely a result of the exodus of students to charters and the related, swelling cost of her excess teacher pool. In private sessions, the FNF board concluded that it would be the epitome of bad "optics" to announce a $60 million gift to charters as the district struggled to plug a budget hole of almost precisely the same size.

In late July, Booker, Cerf, and Anderson gathered representatives of some of the nation's wealthiest education philanthropists to ask for $27 million to complete the $100 million match, unlock Zuckerberg's full gift, and finance the teachers' contract. To make the sale, they had to argue that Newark's contract would be "transformational" for the country, but as Anderson had acknowledged privately, it wasn't particularly transformational, even for Newark, because of its seniority protections. For the presentation, William Ackman made available the conference room of his hedge fund, Pershing Square Capital Management, on the forty-second floor of a Manhattan office tower, with windows overlooking Central Park.

"I want to welcome everyone to an extraordinary moment," Booker said, kicking off the presentation. "We can really seize a victory, not just for the children of Newark, but for the country. This is the one moment in time, the one place in America we can win this opportunity or lose it." At times, Booker sounded like an auctioneer: "It's a game-changing contract that raises the bar for the nation. We're twenty-seven million dollars away."

"Winning will set the contract standard and grease the wheels for the rest of the country," Cerf said.

Representatives of the Walton, Robertson, and Fisher foundations and other leading philanthropists sat around the conference table watching PowerPoint slides on two television screens. Their questions revealed considerable skepticism. Where was the data to show the district could afford to sustain the bonuses when Zuckerberg's money ran out? How could there be transformational change if Anderson couldn't fire the worst teachers unless they were also the most junior ones? What is transformational about paying $31 million—the bulk of the $50 million for the teachers' contract—just to get a union to come to the table? An executive of one of the philanthropies asked this: "I've heard the fear that philanthropy in Newark is creating something that's not replicable because it costs so much. How many cities can raise a hundred million dollars?"

"They could just hire Cory," Anderson cracked.

No one laughed. Nor did they volunteer to write checks—yet.

"A lot of time was spent telling us this would be transformational versus concretely showing where the funding gap exists that demands this level of investment," said one of the foundation executives at the table.

• • •

In the end, it was Christie who came up with pledges of about $25 million, in the fall of 2012, to finish matching Zuckerberg's gift, tapping some of his political donors, including Home Depot founder Kenneth Langone and hedge fund titans Stanley Druckenmiller and Julian Robertson, who were prominent supporters of education reform causes. Christie's national star was rising rapidly at the time. The previous year, key Republican fundraisers, including Langone, billionaire conservative industrialist David Koch, former Morgan Stanley chairman John Mack, and dozens of other business executives, had privately urged him to run against Barack Obama in 2012, vowing to raise whatever money the plain-talking governor needed, as recounted in the book *Collision 2012* by Dan Balz. Christie demurred, instead becoming a surrogate for Mitt Romney's presidential campaign and delivering the keynote address at the Republican National Convention.

When Christie called to ask for help matching Zuckerberg's gift, Langone said he was eager to pitch in. "It was important for Newark to pull this off. I went to others and got commitments," he said. Langone said he was particularly impressed by the plan to use philanthropy to buy out the weakest teachers. Julian Robertson mistakenly deemed the plan a *fait accompli* in a Bloomberg TV interview: "We actually bought out the bad teachers and kept the good teachers."

Booker was enjoying a boom of his own in national attention, touring the country as a prominent Obama surrogate. He cochaired the platform committee for the Democratic National Convention in Charlotte, North Carolina, where he dropped well-publicized hints that he might challenge Christie in the governor's race the following year. The idea won enthusiastic encouragement from party activists.

Christie met with Cerf, Del Grosso, and Anderson in his Trenton office on October 12 and laid plans for a triumphal contract announcement. Booker was noticeably absent. "Cory Booker will not be anywhere near this press conference," Christie announced icily, according to two people at the meeting. The governor made clear that he was furious that Booker was talking of a possible gubernatorial run. Christie was counting on Democrats to put up only token opposition, resulting in a landslide reelection, to position him as a strong presidential contender in blue as well as red states in 2016.

Meanwhile, as Joe Del Grosso campaigned among union members for the contract, the influence of the national school reform movement—and in particular Zuckerberg's money—was palpable. Touting the contract to his members, the aging union president said repeatedly that he had made the best deal he could under tough circumstances. He said he was proud of the contract because it treated educators as professionals. He emphasized that it won teachers the right of peer review, to weigh in on colleagues' evaluations—a critical protection, as he saw it, in an age of tightening accountability. But his strongest argument, to which he returned again and again, was that teachers would collect $31 million in back pay, courtesy of Zuckerberg. With New Jersey stuck in economic doldrums, Del Grosso said, more than one hundred other locals had been forced to settle for no back pay at all.

"We had an opportunity to get Zuckerberg's money," he said, in summing up the tradeoff. "Otherwise it would go to the charter schools. I decided I shouldn't feed and clothe the enemy."

The union was scheduled to vote on October 29, but nature intervened as Hurricane Sandy devastated the New Jersey shore and large swaths of the state. The rescheduled vote came on November 14. By then, the back pay provision loomed even larger for teachers and other union members because, as a telephone survey found, one in three of them had suffered storm-related losses or helped relatives who did. "People lost cars, have to get a new roof, have taken in relatives who lost their homes," a union official explained. "It made people think, 'Holy shit, this contract will put thousands of dollars in my pocket.'" The contract passed with sixty-two percent of the vote.

From Facebook headquarters, Zuckerberg issued a statement: "Our hope was always to support and reward effective teachers in all they do to give kids the great education they need and deserve, and this is the most important step yet."

The contract indeed increased accountability for Newark teachers, and Cami Anderson aggressively used the new tools to mete out consequences to those with the lowest ratings and reward those with the best. Throughout the district, there was new, if uneven, focus on teaching quality, with the strongest principals following the new evaluation system as a guide to coach teachers on lesson design, strategies to engage all learners, the use of data to guide instruction, and the creation of "cultures of achievement" in classrooms.

But the fine print in the contract revealed that many costly union perks remained securely in place, such as fifteen paid sick days and three paid personal days—putting the district on the hook to hire substitutes one of every ten days for every teacher. Also intact were long-standing annual pay bumps for veteran teachers—from $2,025 at fifteen years to $8,950 at thirty—skewing the pay scale dramatically in favor of more senior members, of whom 560 earned more than $92,000 a year. Zuckerberg had wanted a contract that quickly raised the salaries of promising young teachers as an incentive for them to remain in Newark. But the district couldn't afford pay bumps at both ends of the scale. A new teacher consistently rated effective would have to work nine years before making $60,000 in base pay—hardly a magnet for the star-quality graduates Zuckerberg had hoped to attract. Even with bonuses, fourth-year teachers wouldn't come close to making the $100,000 available to top performers in Washington. Nor did Zuckerberg realize his goal of paying merit bonuses of up to fifty percent of a teacher's salary. The cash-strapped district couldn't have afforded them after his money ran out.

Moreover, in the wake of the fundraising scramble to finance labor reforms, millions of dollars ended up not being spent. The proposed buyouts for weak teachers—touted by both Langone and Robertson as the key reason for their contributions—never materialized. Neither did the new contract for principals, whose union refused to negotiate. Anderson used more than $300,000 of that money to pay retention bonuses to principals and assistant principals in schools with the greatest academic need. But more than half of those who received the bonuses left their positions within a year.

The official announcement of the new contract, on November 16, 2012, resembled a Christie coronation. He and the AFT's Randi Weingarten appeared on MSNBC's *Morning Joe,* accepting plaudits from host Joe Scarborough for putting children's interests above politics. Invoking Christie's fortitude during Hurricane Sandy, Weingarten said, "This is the way government should work, whether at the collective bargaining table or in face of natural disaster."

Christie's political capital was soaring in Sandy's wake. National television broadcasts showed him trudging the shattered shoreline day after day, comforting victims and, in a tableau that irked many Republicans, advocating for federal help as he and Obama surveyed the wreckage on the weekend before the presidential election. His approval rating would soon pass seventy percent, with almost half of New Jersey Democrats saying he deserved reelection. Booker later announced that he would pass up the governor's race to run for the U.S. Senate in November 2014, to succeed the eighty-nine-year-old incumbent, Frank Lautenberg.

Even Christie's vision of standing side by side with Weingarten at a news conference came to pass. It took place in the gymnasium of Newark's Speedway Elementary School with hundreds of children sitting behind him in uniforms and dozens of television cameras recording his every word. Christie, Weingarten, Cerf, Anderson, Del Grosso, and the CEO of the Foundation for Newark's Future, Greg Taylor, all had turns at the microphone, declaring victory for the children of Newark. Booker, on Christie's orders, sat in the audience.

An effusive Del Grosso, in a charcoal-gray suit with a white silk handkerchief in the chest pocket, spoke as if peace was at hand in the long war between unions and education reformers. "For my city to become better, education has to be better," he said. "It's time for all of us to say where did we fail, what did we do wrong, and how do we fix it?"

Anderson followed Del Grosso at the podium, hugging her once and future nemesis as they passed. Christie kissed Anderson on the cheek as he followed her. "This is by far the most gratifying day of my governorship—by far," Christie said with obvious emotion. "The kids of this city deserve better, and teachers, by voting for this contract, said they want to give it to them." It was a remarkable peace offering from a governor who rose to national prominence three years earlier decrying the greed of teachers' unions.

"Hell," Christie said, trying out what sounded like a presidential campaign theme in the aftermath of Obama's reelection, "if Randi Weingarten and I can come together, for God's sake, President Obama and John Boehner and the rest of them can come together, too . . . Someone asked me this morning what's the future of government in the aftermath of this election. And this is what it is right here."

Asked afterward if his union was likely to vote to continue the accountability reforms when the contract expired in three years, Joe Del Grosso responded, "Let's pray there's another Zuckerberg."

10

Alif Rising

September 2012–June 2013

E VEN AS MONEY and power poured into the battle for a transformative teachers' contract, equally high-stakes battles were being waged in schools across Newark to improve education student by student. One such effort, at BRICK Avon, aimed to rescue a single child, Alif Beyah.

Bernadette Scott had immediately noticed Alif's profound weakness in reading when he showed up in her sixth-grade literacy class in 2010. Conditioned to failure, he had built a popular persona to camouflage it: the lovable goof-off. Scott recognized immediately that Alif loved football and made a deal with him: when she assigned the class a writing prompt, he was to write about the game he loved, and she would work with him to develop an expository essay that earned a passing grade. "I remember the day he looked at me and said, 'I got it, Miss Scott,'" she said. She taught him to follow the same format to complete other writing assignments. In Scott's view, "he was crying out, 'I want to learn, but I need you to see me for me and not another black male sitting in your classroom.'"

Still, in most classes he continued to disrupt and often got kicked out. The BRICK leadership team vowed not to promote students who couldn't perform at their grade level, and Alif was held back a second time. When he arrived in seventh grade in the fall of 2012, he was old enough to be a high school freshman but far behind most of his classmates. However, his mother, Lakiesha Mills, noticed changes in his attitude. He told her how much he liked the new principal, Charity Haygood, even on days when she disciplined him for disrupting class. During recess, which Haygood supervised daily, she insisted that students line up on time, quietly, in a straight line to reenter the building after playing. "I expect you to line up *well*," she would say. "I'm asking you to make a decision to be disciplined, to be mature. If you're not in place by the end of the countdown, you stand with me." Alif did a lot of standing with her. "My boys learn that I do that out of love and concern," she said. "I want them to do better. I want them to *be* better. The purpose is to make sure they can learn, they understand their value, they know they *are* somebody." Even after Haygood flunked him, Mills said Alif was eager to go to school the next fall instead of having to be dragged there. He'd tell his mother, "Mrs. Haygood needs to *see* me. She said she *wants* to see me."

In the fall of 2012, Kathleen Carlson, a special-education teacher who normally taught students with cognitive impairments, was completing her training in a reading program for students who had failed to learn to read in conventional classrooms. Her final requirement for certification was to teach the program, the Wilson Reading System, one on one, to a student who had a considerable reading deficit but no diagnosed disability. Assistant Principal Melinda Weidman paired Carlson with Alif. After teaching special education in Newark for almost twenty years, Carlson was accustomed to encountering students with terrible behavior histories who changed dramatically as their learning problems were addressed. She told Alif she wasn't judging him, but she wanted to hear, in his own words, why he got in trouble so often.

His answer burned itself into her memory. "I get frustrated when

I don't understand what's going on," he said. "If I get thrown out of class, nobody finds out I can't read."

"I was blown away that he could verbalize that," Carlson said. As with many of her students, the learning issue was tangled up with disruptive behavior, but in her experience, few kids were able to recognize that connection, much less articulate it. To Carlson, Alif seemed like a fugitive, tired of running, who finally had found a safe place to turn himself in—a teacher with real, nonjudgmental interest in what he was feeling.

Carlson tested Alif on the Woodcock Reading Mastery index to gauge his baseline skills. At fourteen, he was reading at a second-grade level. In a test of word attack—or sounding-out—skills, he was able to read only four percent of words expected for his grade level. He stumbled on words as simple as "duck" and "quack." He knew only eighteen of twenty-four consonant sounds, seven of fifty-six vowel sounds. Of 120 sounds in the English language, he knew only forty, or thirty-three percent. "He was missing all the basic skills for kindergarten to third grade. Why?" Carlson asked. His math scores on standardized tests, by contrast, had been on grade level every year, and in some years above.

Weidman rearranged Alif's schedule so that he met daily with Carlson at 2 p.m. in her special-education resource room. For the first week or so, Alif was persistently late or absent, but Carlson tracked him down and coaxed him to try. Working one on one in the privacy of the resource room, he no longer ran from what he was: a second-grade reader. Like Princess Williams's kindergartners—who used another Wilson program for pre-readers—he tapped a finger to his thumb as he verbalized each letter sound, creating a sensory connection. Starting over as a reader, he learned how letters combined to make sounds, and sounds to make words. For Carlson, short-circuiting Alif's frustration and hopelessness was at least half the battle. She fought daily to turn his attention away from how far he had to go and toward however far he had come. The Wilson program came with bar graphs that Alif filled in every week to illustrate the ground he was gaining. Carlson used the weekly ritual as an occasion to celebrate his success, something he'd never known as a reader. It didn't hurt that she also brought snacks, which her lean and growing student eagerly devoured. Soon he was arriving on time, even early. One afternoon, Carlson was absent to attend a workshop and sent word they would not meet. The following day, Alif was waiting at her door, demanding to know where she had been. He began to talk of her not just as a teacher but as someone "who came into my life." He encouraged friends to go to a remedial class Carlson taught, telling them about his experience. "She'll help you — really," he said.

In January, on a follow-up Woodcock test, after one semester working with Carlson, he registered a fivefold increase in the number of words he could sound out. He was still years behind, but he finally believed Carlson's assurance that he was on his way to becoming a proficient reader. Weidman and Haygood noticed a marked improvement in Alif's behavior in general. This was in part because it was basketball season, his favorite time of year. Alif had loved the game since age six, showing up on courts around the public-housing complex where he lived with his two brothers and his mother, playing anyone who was there. His mother had been Newark's most valuable player among middle school girls back in the day, and his father had played varsity basketball in neighboring East Orange. Besides that apparent genetic advantage, what distinguished Alif as a player, said Shawn McCray, who had coached him since first grade in a local league known as the Zoo Crew, was his furious determination to get to the basket, no matter who stood in his way. By middle school, he was a standout on Newark's neighborhood courts, where grown men spoke of him as a kid with a future.

Seventh-grade science teacher Marc Harris, who coached the Avon Rams basketball team, noticed a change in Alif as the 2012 school year got under way. "Last year, he was just as athletic, but it was like he disappeared in some games. He wasn't consistent. This year, he is like my quarterback every game. He gets everywhere he needs to be — defense, rebounding, slashing, driving to the basket," Harris said. His teammates voted him captain, and Harris noticed that he led with humility, never showboating. Under Harris's direction, the boys gelled into a squad of team players, passing rather than hogging the ball, producing unusually balanced scoring game after game. It was a winning combination, and Avon went into the citywide playoffs undefeated, marching straight to the championship game on June 6, 2013, in the Weequahic High gymnasium, Newark's newest and showiest basketball venue. Alif made a point of dropping by the Avon school office after dismissal on the day of the big game to make a promise to his principal: "Don't worry, Mrs. Haygood, I'm going to bring this home for you tonight."

By game time, the Weequahic bleachers were packed from floor to ceiling with family, friends, and alums of the competing schools, Avon from the South Ward and Dr. E. Alma Flagg from the Central Ward. Shawn McCray, the Zoo Crew youth coach who now was head coach at Central High, announced the game, keeping up a patter about how hard this player had worked since age six, what speed and grace that one had developed. The mood was celebratory, but Newark was experiencing a spasm of street violence, and unease was palpable. Wearing the Newark chip heavily on his shoulder, McCray said during one time-out, "Let's see if they put this game on the front page of the *Star-Ledger* tomorrow. They put our faces there when someone gets arrested, but never for something positive." He also issued a warning about outsiders peddling big promises—a familiar Newark theme. "Those private schools tell parents negative things about our district schools to lure your sons away. They want to take all the talented kids out. Stay home! Newark needs you!"

The Flagg squad was taller and more muscular, but Avon opened a double-digit lead in the first half. Then Flagg roared back to within three points with less than two minutes left in the game. Alif later recalled being seized at that moment by a single thought: "Every time they inbound, I have to steal or score. Don't let the game slip away."

In the next thirty seconds, the skinny shooting guard wearing number 2 stole the ball three times and scored eight points, streaking like a guided missile past everyone between him and the basket. He made one steal as he staggered to his feet after being knocked to the floor, one basket by lofting the ball into the net underhanded while he was trapped under the goal. Coach Harris called a time-out, and as Alif ambled into the huddle, everyone shoved his shoulder, slapped his back, rubbed his head. "Alif is whilin'!" his mother yelled from the stands.

When the clock ran out and the game ended, Avon was the champion, and McCray was announcing that Alif was the tournament's most valuable player. Looking stunned and ecstatic, he was ushered to center court along with Coach Harris, and each was handed a towering trophy—Alif for MVP, Harris for the championship. Asked by the emcee what basketball means to young men in Newark, Harris responded: "A lot of my players, if they don't have this, I don't know what they'd be doing right now. It's better to be here than to be out in the streets." Harris was on the mark. Alif, his mother, and his younger brother would arrive home that night to learn someone had been shot and killed behind their apartment building.

The emcee asked Alif what he told his teammates in the final huddle with the game on the line. "I just put in their head we didn't come this far to lose," he said. "We never gave up and we fought to the end."

Alif fantasized about playing college basketball, but he had known for years that he likely wouldn't make the grades required by the NCAA because of his reading. "No coach wants a dumb player. They'll take a smart, okay player over a dumb player any day," he said. For years now, he had seen himself as dumb, unfit for the life he longed for. But that was changing. One afternoon, sitting in Kathleen Carlson's classroom, he said, "I don't want to go on with my life and not read. They say you need to read to do everything. I want to play basketball and I got to be able to read my contract so my lawyer won't be able to take money from me."

Hope was taking root in Alif, and Weidman, Haygood, and Carlson were determined not to let it die this time. They felt that the Newark Public Schools had allowed that to happen once—or certainly hadn't tried to stop it—and it was their obligation to combat this horrible legacy of illiteracy in Alif. Their two-pronged strategy was to work with his mother to get him on track academically, and to keep him playing basketball, which was his life. But now those two goals were in conflict. With Alif in seventh grade, two years behind his class, he would be too old to play high school sports as a senior, the year college scouts came prospecting. Somehow, they had to get him to high school the following fall. "This is about Alif's life as well as his academics," Weidman said. "He has a chance to get a college basketball scholarship, and we can't let him miss that opportunity." Weidman had attended graduate school at the University of Connecticut, where she knew of basketball stars who got hours of tutoring a day. She envisioned that kind of support for Alif in college. But how could they send a boy who read at perhaps a third-grade level to high school in the fall?

A few days after the championship game, Alif went to Kathleen Carlson's special-education classroom for an end-of-year Woodcock Reading Mastery test. In his BRICK uniform—yellow polo shirt and navy khakis—he sat down in a plastic chair at a wooden table, his long legs extended so that he was slightly slouched. Opposite him sat Carlson, outfitted in a black polo shirt with BRICK printed in small, pastel-colored letters above a pocket. Between them was a spiral-bound book of words, poised atop a stand. Alif trained his dark eyes, edged with thick lashes, on the book. He sat perfectly still except for his trademark fidget—twirling a couple of fingers in his thick black hair. As Carlson turned the pages, Alif read the words appearing before him.

He flew through "black," "house," "away," "wonderful," "without," and "question," but stumbled on "piece" (he pronounced it "picey"), "brought," and "cattle." As the words became more challenging, he used the Wilson technique of tapping out each letter sound on his fingers as if playing an instrument. He accurately sounded out "dangerous," "garage," "entrance," and "extinguish," but missed "cruel," "budget," and "ache." Because he had only an elementary vocabulary, relatively simple words were unfamiliar. Sounding out "pioneer" and "circumstance" proved as laborious as decoding the jumble of letters in a nonsense word. As the words got harder to read, his mood sank visibly. "I can see you're getting frustrated," Carlson said. "Yeah, you don't know all these words, but that's why we're going to continue next year. You're going to get there." He pressed on, barely missing "baroness" (he used a long "o") and struggling through "lethargic."

"Do you know what that means?" Carlson asked.

Alif shook his head.

"That's you right now," she said. "It means tired." He smiled weakly.

Alif kept going, stumbling with more frequency, and then came a stretch when he was zero for six—"transient," "edifice," "verbatim," "ptomaine," "itinerary," and "jujitsu." On that section of the exam, when a student misses six words in a row, the testing ends. He stared flatly at Carlson and sank into his chair, looking completely deflated.

"Look how much *better* you did," she said, pulling out his results from January. Then he had stalled after sixty-four words; today he got to ninety-two. "Now do you believe me?" she asked. Alif looked at her gratefully. He had to admit that he was making progress. That was Carlson's mission as much as teaching him to decode and encode vowel sounds, consonants, welded sounds, and more. She had to keep him from giving up—the way he never gave up in basketball. *We didn't come this far to lose.*

Alif took a range of other assessments, and Carlson sent all of them to the district office to be analyzed and scored. When the results arrived a week later, she had to catch her breath. His reading level had risen from second to fifth grade. In one category, word attack skills, he had moved from the equivalent of a midyear second grader to a beginning eighth grader. Rather than tell Alif immediately, she asked him to come the next morning at 7:50 with his mother to see the results. She also invited Charity Haygood and Melinda Weidman. Everyone was there on time except Alif and his mother, who apologized, saying that her son made them both late by insisting on taking a shower, even though he'd taken one the night before. Alif just stood there, rubbing his eyes as if someone had yanked him from a deep sleep. Carlson had prepared a PowerPoint slide show that she projected onto the Smart Board, showing Alif's scores in six skill clusters as well as his overall reading level. "Alif's Woodcock Reading Mastery Test Scores," the top line read. "Alif, you see your name up there in lights, right?" Carlson asked. He nodded, his eyes almost closed, fingers twirling his hair. In the left column was his initial score from September, and in the right, the latest one. She went line by line, reading the scores aloud, before and after. His jaw dropped open when she read that he was sounding out words like an eighth grader. When she reached his overall skill level of fifth grade, a jump of almost three grades, Alif covered his mouth with his hand and looked wide-eyed at the Smart Board. All evidence of sleepiness vanished, and now he was alert, a smile exploding across his face. Haygood threw out her arms like a proud mother and walked toward him, her eyes tearing. He stood to meet her, and they wrapped their arms around each other. More hugs followed: Weidman, then Carlson, and then his mother. "I worked hard and I feel proud of myself," he said, addressing himself as much as everyone else. He stood in silence for a while, savoring this wondrous experience of success in school. "Reading is going to come easier to me. Now I *have* to come back next year and make more progress."

The school district agreed to promote Alif to high school if he passed eighth-grade math in summer school. He did, with a grade of A-minus, third in the class. He also had to sign a contract with Avon, promising to read independently and do online remediation exercises for at least forty minutes a night. His mother monitored his independent reading, and Carlson checked his online work, reporting regularly to his mother, who refused to let him go out unless he kept to the schedule. The contract required him to attend high school faithfully unless he had a doctor's excuse and to return to Avon every day for tutoring with Carlson at 3:15. In addition, he had to behave himself; lapses would lead to detention or suspension—from basketball as well as school.

A few days after celebrating Alif's test results, Carlson found out that she had been rated "highly effective" under the district's new evaluation system, which entitled her to a merit bonus of $10,000—$5,000 for receiving the highest possible grade, and an extra $5,000 because Avon students ranked among the neediest in Newark, academically and economically. This was the fruit of the new teachers' contract, with merit pay that Zuckerberg and other philanthropists considered essential to attracting and retaining the best teachers. Asked if the incentive of extra money had influenced the way she worked with Alif or other students, Carlson answered, "Not at all. Don't get me wrong—the money is nice. But just the progress my students have made, and the progress Alif has made, and how it's changed his life—that's the bonus for me."

Carlson had been thinking seriously of transferring to another school because of Avon's extended day, which then ended at 4:15 p.m. She and her husband had two children, whom they had adopted and who were now ages seven and eight, and she wanted to be home when they got out of school. "I adopted these children to give them a better life," she said. "I know I'm giving them a better life than they would've had, but I could do better for them, and that's hard." In the end, she decided to return to Avon, in part because she had promised Alif she would work with him another year. "If I stayed home, I would do better for my kids, but what's happening with Alif is why I teach," she said.

As the school year ended, Haygood announced over the loudspeaker that her daughter, having just graduated from Spelman College, was going to become a teacher in Newark. She asked all students to stop by the office and compose a sentence or two in a book of advice for her. Alif was one of the first to show up. "Don't ever give up on a student," he wrote.

II

The Leading Men Move On

February 2012–June 2013

T HE TEACHERS' CONTRACT was a trophy for Zuckerberg,
Booker, Christie, and Anderson, but at the same time, Anderson had a school district to run. On a Friday evening early
in 2012, after eighteen months on the job, she unveiled her most dramatic proposal to turn around the Newark public schools. Like superintendents in many other struggling urban districts, she would
close schools to shore up finances as enrollment shrank. But unlike in
some other cities — or in Newark the previous year, when Cerf and
the consultants were calling the shots — she promised there would
be gains in return for the pain. She would consolidate the district's
twelve lowest-performing kindergarten-through-eighth-grade schools
into eight "Renew schools," each with a top principal who would be
given latitude to handpick the best teachers and preside over a longer
school day, new curriculum, more computers, enhanced training time
for teachers, and extensive engagement of parents. Anderson hoped
these eight schools would become "proof points," evidence that her
strategies could turn around all Newark schools. She and her leader-

ship team rehearsed how to answer angry parents: "Your child's school didn't have the ingredients for success. We're providing those ingredients so that children can soar."

She chose for her presentation a lecture hall at the Paul Robeson Center at Rutgers University's downtown Newark campus, anticipating an audience of about two hundred mostly invited civic and education leaders. Instead, roughly a thousand people turned out, a mix of parents whose children's schools were closing, teachers, union activists, politicians, and a cadre of hecklers who came to almost every public forum to inveigh against Christie, Booker, and purported conspiracies.

Nothing else went as Anderson had planned either. A respected Rutgers administrator who was supposed to introduce her called a day earlier to say she couldn't make it because of a sick parent. A prominent minister, who had agreed to share the stage and close the presentation, phoned in sick with laryngitis. Another influential pastor who was supposed to be there called to say he was stuck in traffic in New York City. Anderson stood alone on the podium.

The heckling began almost as soon as she started to speak. "It's great to have an opportunity to talk," Anderson said. *"We don't want you to talk!"* several voices yelled from the crowd. *"Sit down!"* others called from around the room. Anderson spoke from PowerPoint slides that appeared on a projection screen beside her, as if addressing a business conference. One slide, a quote from Martin Luther King Jr., said, "This is no time to engage in the luxury of cooling off or to take the tranquilizing drug of gradualism."

Anderson did manage to get through some of her talk, including a recitation of dismal student test scores at the twelve schools she had targeted. Most had shrinking enrollments, she said, leaving buildings one-third to one-half empty, too expensive to maintain. In some of them, only twenty percent of students were reading at their grade level. "We have to have a frank conversation about what it's going to take to put our kids on a path to success so they can access the twenty-first century," she said. This seemed to earn her a few moments of attention.

But the heckling resumed when she proposed to close schools. She bowed her head for a moment, then looked up with lips tightened, holding the microphone in both hands, fixing her gaze on the angry crowd. "We're proposing . . ." Anderson said loudly, as dozens of people in the crowd shouted her down. "WE'RE PROPOSING . . ."

"*Cami must go!*" a woman shrieked above the din. "*Send the devil back to New York!*" yelled a union activist.

No one came to her aid, not even to ask everyone to be civil, to hear her out—much less to state the obvious: Newark was failing its children on a massive scale and something had to change. In all the years the crisis had been building, there had been no comparable public outcry. In 2005, a lone school board member, Richard Cammarieri, had demanded urgent action, citing high schools where fewer than twenty students passed the state proficiency test, and elementary schools—particularly in the South Ward—that had become dumping grounds for the weakest teachers, rendering them "voids of academic exercise." He had called for an "urgent, systemic response." The district had ordered up studies, but nothing had changed. "It was just utter passivity. It was hard to explain," Cammarieri recalled. "We literally manufactured the bullets the charters are now firing at us."

As the noise level rose in the Robeson Center, the school board members sat in silence. Police officers stood in place. Anderson's executive team, almost all white, from New York City, and unknown to the crowd, sat motionless in the front row. Cerf, knowing he would have fueled the furor had he intervened, remained seated and silent too. Booker was not there. Anderson, in fact, had asked him not to come, assuming that his presence would have provoked even more opposition.

Anderson hurried through the rest of her presentation, proposing to lease the closed schools to charters—providing they eliminated practices that had the effect of screening out the neediest students.

"Charters are *not* equity!" screamed a teacher from a school targeted for closure.

By then it was impossible to hear anything but angry voices yelling all at once. Amid the cacophony, Anderson said something about wanting this to be the beginning, not the end, of a community discussion. "I look forward to coming together on behalf of our kids," she added, barely audibly. "So I thank you and I look forward to additional conversation." With that, she left the podium and the room, exiting by a side door. Her final PowerPoint slide remained on the screen: "Our kids can't wait. We must act now. Get involved."

The scene oddly recalled her showstopping theater performance at age eleven, when she stood alone and triumphant onstage, having bested the bad guys. But this time, the opposition was still standing, and she was gone.

The Robeson Center audience was an especially stark example of the growing opposition to top-down reform in Newark. Anderson was certain that the teachers' and principals' unions had packed the house, since school closings and expansion of charters threatened hundreds of jobs. Indeed, unions were there in force, including teachers and principals but also cafeteria workers, clerks, security guards, janitors —workers who had few options for secure employment outside the school district. So were parents, fearful that children whose schools were closing would have to walk through gang-ruled territory or cross highly trafficked thoroughfares to reach their reassigned schools. Affected principals had learned of the plan only that morning, alerting staffs, who alerted parents, who came to protest what they saw as a violation of their right to a voice in the fate of their children's schools. There it was again: disrespect. The word rose from conversations all over the auditorium.

It didn't take unions to stir up fears that school closings and charter schools were part of a conspiracy by wealthy profiteers. "Some people believe that sincerely, and some people use that belief," Richard Cammarieri said. As Councilman Ron Rice Jr. had said in 2010, soon after the Zuckerberg gift was announced, Newark suffered from "extreme xenophobia," particularly toward white outsiders who sought to change the city's direction. The victimization narrative stretched back to urban renewal and white flight. "We drink it with our mother's milk," as a prominent civic leader had told Booker and Cerf during the uproar over reform a year earlier.

Despite the obvious barriers, many leaders in the city saw the potential to change the conversation about education. "I've not met one person who does not believe we should improve our schools—grassroots activists, single mothers, agitators, quiet school retirees, librarians," said Reverend William Howard, a respected Baptist pastor who had come to Newark after having played a prominent role in the anti-apartheid movement. At first he was supportive of Cami Anderson, counseling her to work patiently and humbly to nurture change from within. "I'm judging from the revolution in South Africa and Zimbabwe," he said. "I know that no abiding change in human communities is imposed."

Two days after the public battering, Anderson was undeterred, certain that parents would embrace her vision once they understood it. At home in Newark, preparing for a Super Bowl party and sporting a well-worn Giants football jersey, she said of the presentation at the Robeson Center, "I'd give it a B-minus. If I could change three or four things, it would've been an A." Sitting at her dining room table beside a stack of district documents, she said she had no intention of turning back, and in fact was already laying plans with her leadership team to hold information sessions with parents from each affected school. Just as Cerf had said of her, Anderson had the capacity to "get the shit absolutely kicked out" of her and keep going. She said she had learned her lesson from Friday night: when she met with parents, she would have district security guards block access to others. She wanted to talk with the real community.

Anderson's first opportunity came at Thirteenth Avenue School. It was to be consolidated with nearby Martin Luther King Jr. Elementary, which the superintendent was closing. At both schools, barely twenty percent of children were reading at grade level. Thirteenth Avenue had about six hundred students, from kindergarten through eighth grade, but only twenty-five parents showed up to learn about the big changes afoot. If this was the real community, it appeared to align with neither Anderson nor the angry protesters. Rather, parents seemed constitutionally incapable of trusting anyone who promised to fix public education. "I went to school here myself. So did my nieces, my brothers, my sisters, and now my daughter. I don't see why it has to change," Seleta Carter, mother of a seventh grader, said afterward. Asked about the dismal proficiency scores, Carter said they were indeed a concern, but she pointed out that her own daughter was proficient in both reading and math. How did she account for that? "I choose her teachers," Carter said. "If I don't like the teacher, I move her." Carter estimated that forty percent of the school's teachers were below par, and she considered it her responsibility as a parent to steer her daughter clear of them. If other parents were equally engaged, she said, their children would perform better.

In other words, Carter viewed dysfunction as a given in the Newark schools, and she spent her social capital shielding her daughter from it. The same was true for most of the two dozen other parents at the meeting. Among hundreds of Thirteenth Avenue School parents, they were the small core investing time and energy in classrooms. When they had concerns, administrators tended to listen. This was their definition of school choice: the ability to maneuver a child out of the path of inevitable disaster. Anderson's and the reformers' vision of choice—replacing the dysfunctional system with a "portfolio" of excellent schools from which parents could choose the best "fit" for their children—sounded like yet another promise that never would materialize. Anderson's mantra, "All means all," rang noble, but in Carter's life, her daughter was her all, and she couldn't imagine a system that would do right by her, much less kids who ran with gangs, were years behind grade level, or cut class. If Anderson scrambled the staff, sending away some teachers and recruiting others purported to be more effective, how would Carter know where to move her daughter in the likely event that the upheaval changed nothing?

Soon after the Thirteenth Avenue meeting, Anderson also made a presentation to the Newark Trust for Education, an umbrella organization of local foundations and nonprofits that had been working in the schools for decades. Several of Newark's more esteemed leaders warned Anderson against moving full speed ahead without the community behind her. Robert Curvin spoke with the authority of a lifelong Newark resident with a Princeton PhD in political science who had been a civil rights leader in the 1960s, an editorial writer for the *New York Times,* a vice president of the Ford Foundation, and a dean at the New School. "I urge you to back up and think about implanting a deeper understanding," he admonished. "This is Newark. There's a lot of history, particularly the episode last year with the leaked report. There's deep anger about what school closings mean."

"I use the word 'trauma,'" said Clement Price, the Rutgers professor of Newark history. "This is a city that perceives itself as always losing things."

"I get it," Anderson responded. "But there's real tension between talking about it and doing it. This requires a leap of faith and moving faster than is comfortable."

"Leaps of faith are not possible under these conditions," Curvin said. "You have to be very concrete."

"I hear you," the superintendent said, "but I lose sleep over kids stuck in a school when they're losing ground."

A month later, Anderson held a redo of her Renew schools announcement, a press conference with invited guests only and several speakers with Newark credentials: a prominent minister, a respected district principal, Booker, the district's Newark-born preschool director, school board president Jeffries. It was held at Quitman Street Community School in the Central Ward, one of those targeted for renewal.

In her turn at the microphone, Anderson made an astonishing prediction for the Renew schools: "We are striving for fifty percent proficiency within two years, seventy-five percent within four . . . If we pick the right principals, my hope is that we're actually going to do better than that." At none of the schools were more than thirty percent of students then performing at grade level in reading or math. And Anderson would not name the new principals until May or June, leaving them at most three months to recruit teachers, engage parents, and reimagine their schools in time for the fall.

The following Monday, Alison Avera, Anderson's interim chief of staff, strode into the leadership team meeting with arms raised Rocky-style, declaring that the media event had "really kicked ass." Everyone around the table agreed it was infinitely better than round one, but some team members were troubled that parents were not invited. One senior deputy had stayed outside talking to Quitman's PTA president and local activists, who were not on Anderson's guest list and were barred by security guards from attending. "It fed into the old Newark story: big things are happening and we're the last to know," he remarked.

Despite the rushed time frame, principals selected by Anderson to lead Renew schools viewed them as the opportunity of a lifetime. In the past, none had been allowed to select their own teachers or to build a staff around a shared vision of transforming a school. Chaleeta Barnes, at thirty-two, was the principal of Dayton Street School, which was closing and merging into Peshine Avenue School, a mile away in the South Ward. Simultaneously plucky and business-like, Barnes kept school interesting, even down to her hairstyle, which changed every few weeks, from bouffant to doobie to ponytail. Barnes was tapped to lead the consolidated school, and she chose as her vice principals Tameshone Lewis, a Newark-born teacher and administrator, and Sabrina Meah, a former district teacher who had helped lead a Newark charter school for a decade.

It was striking to witness a conversation about school closings led by trusted local educators rather than by Anderson. At first Dayton parents were enraged by the announcement that their neighborhood school was closing. "My baby is *not* going to ride a bus," one mother after the next declared to Barnes, upon learning their children would be bused to Peshine. Dozens of parents converged for a meeting at Peshine's library, where the petite principal greeted them with a dazzling smile, wearing her Dayton uniform of light blue polo shirt and navy slacks. She radiated excitement, but also firm insistence.

"I know with all the changes we feel unsure, fearful. I get it. I hear you: 'They're pushing us around — *again!*'" she said, airing the issue of disrespect before anyone had a chance to raise it. "But trust me, this is our time. This is where you want to be. This is where you want your *children* to be." She told them about the advantages of a longer school day, a team of dedicated teachers, more computers in every classroom, field trips to reinforce classroom learning.

"It's very evident we are low-performing schools. But we are going to change that together," Barnes went on, with conviction. "Nobody wants to drop a child off at a failing school. Nobody wants to work at a failing school. No longer will anyone in this school accept failure and think it's okay. It is so *not* okay." She answered all of the parents' questions with candor. Several, including early opponents, rose to say they were now on board.

"It is going to be a lot of work, but are we ready for it?" Barnes asked. "*Yes!*" the parents chorused, and several applauded. The district had ordered a dinner for the parents, and as they filed out of the library, heading for the cafeteria, the caterer waited to have a private moment with Barnes. Patting the young principal's arm, she flashed a smile of admiration and declared, "Honey, I love your attitude. You're like Joe Clark without the bat!"

Chaleeta Barnes had a level of influence with parents that Anderson couldn't muster, even with Christie's state powers at her back. She was a true daughter of Newark. Her mother had taught at Dayton for more than thirty-five years, and both of her parents were products of the city's public schools. Barnes herself had taught for five years at Peshine and five at Dayton before becoming its principal. Peshine parents remembered her organizing a cheerleading squad, then sewing all the uniforms when the district couldn't afford to pay for them. Dayton parents recounted how she had overseen movie nights and after-school dance classes in a community where children had nowhere safe to go after school. And she had a reputation as a hawk on excellence for all students, including those with serious learning disabilities.

Tameshone Lewis, the vice principal, was known for persuading even the most rebellious children to try their best. She had survived a harrowing Newark childhood — daughter of a crack addict, the only one of five children to graduate from high school and college. She told students that if she could make it academically, they could make it too. Their survival depended on it, she said.

"Kids tell me they can't succeed because they've been abused, and I say, I understand that. They say they've been rejected by their parents, and I say, I understand that. They say they don't know their father, and I say, I understand that. They say, 'Come on, Ms. Lewis, no way you grew up in a dirty, filthy house,' and I say, I understand that. Then they'll say, 'Ms. Lewis, can you bring me a toothbrush? Can I get a water from your fridge? Can I call you when I need to talk?'"

Barnes and both vice principals, Lewis and Meah, knocked on every door on all four blocks surrounding Peshine, inviting neighbors to attend a summer barbecue with parents and kids. Lewis seemed to know someone in every building. A woman in a nightgown called down from atop a flight of stairs to say that she couldn't come because she was sleeping in. "Fran, get your behind in a dress and come out here!" Lewis yelled, prompting screams of laughter. The two had worked together at the Department of Motor Vehicles when Lewis was in high school.

Barnes formed a partnership with BRICK, the teachers leading the turnaround effort at Avon Avenue, and they offered lessons from the front lines, particularly on selecting teachers. Dominique Lee, the BRICK founder, told Peshine's leaders to look primarily for ability and mindset—teachers deeply concerned about the injustices of poverty and also eager to improve their instruction. "If the mindset and the intelligence are there, we can coach them into being good and then great teachers," he said. "Don't expect ready-made greatness. Most teachers in NPS haven't been coached. How many principals are instructional leaders?"

All summer, Barnes, Lewis, and Meah held weekly parent meetings at the hulking, hundred-year-old Peshine building, soliciting input as they designed the new school program. How many nights a week should students have homework? Every night, came the answer. How can we ensure parents check it? Tell the kids we have to sign it, the parents said. Fewer than thirty parents came to the first meeting, but more than fifty came to the second, and by the last meeting, in late August, the auditorium was packed with more than two hundred parents, who cheered loudly as Barnes introduced the leadership team and teachers. Crystal Williams, the mother of a fifth grader, asked to address the crowd. "My husband and I came here not too happy with our experience with the last principal," she said. "At that first meeting, we came at Ms. Barnes growling, and she said, 'Calm down and give me a chance.' We kept coming and we saw changes, we saw excitement. We saw people who were happy. I said maybe there's going to be a change here. And look at us tonight, Ms. Barnes! Look at all these people! What happened before is before. Now, we can really do this. Yes we can!"

Having won the battle for hearts and minds that had bested Anderson, Lewis, Barnes, and Meah turned to the challenges of education in the city's lowest-income ward. They coordinated efforts to support struggling students, address discipline, and increase the rigor of instruction. They won the parents' endorsement for raising expectations, for both achievement and behavior. They cultivated esprit de corps among teachers, who said they had rarely felt so much support from supervisors.

But as at BRICK Avon, teachers did daily battle with the legacy of poor schooling, poverty, and Newark's permeating violence. Shakel

Nelson, a fifth-grade math teacher who graduated from Newark schools and had taught for fourteen years, brought notable skills and determination to the challenge. She persuaded struggling learners to articulate what confused them, then drew classmates into helping them over the hump, with a result that students of all skill levels were engaged. When she realized that few students knew their multiplication tables, which typically were taught by third grade, Nelson turned them into rhyming chants—". . . sixteen, twenty, twenty-four, that is how we roll our fours"—to make them easier and more fun to learn. Her devotion to her students was evident in how hard she worked, and they rewarded her with consistent attention and excellent behavior. When results of state tests arrived in 2014, fifth-grade math students, of whom Nelson taught all but a handful, had by far the highest proficiency rate at Peshine—fifty-seven percent. Based on their scores from the previous year, the fifth graders' growth outpaced that of sixty percent of the state. This was a tremendous achievement. But it also meant that, even with the benefit of an extraordinary teacher, more than forty percent of the fifth grade still came up short.

Nelson's students' difficulties went well beyond academics. One boy's father had been murdered early in the school year. When Nelson stood beside his desk and encouraged him, the boy tried hard and sometimes solved problems. When she moved on to help another student, he put his head on his desk, dropping his pencil on the floor. A girl from a particularly troubled family who was acing tests stopped trying when her estranged, emotionally disturbed parents resumed contact and began fighting.

As a Renew school, Peshine had been given the added resource of a math coach, who met regularly with Nelson and her fellow math teachers to go over student assessment data and pinpoint skills they needed to reteach. The bulk of the test questions on one assessment were word problems, and most of Nelson's students had missed more than half of them. Out of curiosity, Nelson had converted the word problems to number problems, then tested students again. Scores went up at least thirty points. "They do much better when there's no reading," she told the coach. As it turned out, Nelson's students had a reading problem as well as a math problem. Only one in five fifth graders were reading at grade level, according to their state tests, but under the new Common Core State Standards, reading was increasingly important to math mastery, with new emphasis on logical reasoning, demonstrating "why" as well as "what."

One math teacher shook her head, looking over the failing grades of a boy named Emanuel, who had a more urgent problem than reading or math. "His sister was shot at Essex County College," she said. "It's always on his mind."

In a school of 612 students, Peshine's lone social worker couldn't begin to support all the teachers who tended daily to troubled children. Barnes and her teachers created a special class for children who had suffered trauma, incorporating relaxation, tai chi, yoga, dance, stretching, deep breathing, and movement with gentle musical accompaniment. All teachers were to seek out children in their classes who were especially sad or angry, and urge them to attend. There was no shortage of candidates. Students loved the classes, visibly relaxing to the music and movement, opening up about their feelings in conversations with each other and teachers. All but two children in one class on one day were motherless. One boy's brother had been murdered. A girl had become homeless when she and her drug-addicted mother and twin infant siblings were evicted from their apartment.

There was no question that Anderson had equipped the Renew schools to serve children better. She had given them stronger principals and teachers, assessments to measure what students were and weren't learning, curriculum aligned to the Common Core standards, online learning programs that individualized instruction. Principals were evaluating teachers with a new and demanding rubric—paid for with millions of dollars in philanthropy—identifying specific steps that each should take to better reach students, then following up with coaching. There was a new team of assistant superintendents observing all of the district's principals to ensure that evaluations, curriculum, and the exacting Common Core standards were being implemented consistently from school to school. But as experiences at Peshine and other Renew schools made clear, students who were years behind in reading skills or struggling with emotional problems— legacies of poor schooling, poverty, and pervasive violence—needed more than new and improved systems, no matter how well implemented.

One problem was that the quality of the teachers at Renew schools was mixed. Charter schools searched nationally as well as locally for the best talent, with generous support from Zuckerberg and the matching donors. They got up to $17,500 to spend recruiting and training each new teacher and more than $200,000 for each new principal. But district schools had to choose mostly from Newark's existing supply, since leftover teachers in the excess pool already were bursting the budget.

Also, while Anderson recognized that students needed more social and emotional support, she told Renew principals that the district couldn't afford it. She asked principals to shift funds within their budgets—for example, by consolidating small classes to eliminate a teaching position, then using the savings to pay for a counselor or tutors. But that fell far short of the resources that reached KIPP's SPARK Academy in the form of extra teachers, tutors, social workers, and a dean dedicated exclusively to family support.

On their own time, Peshine teachers and staff found ways to brighten the children's outlook. Salimah Gordon, the school's liaison to parents, came up with the idea of a "Daddy-Daughter Dance" —not father-daughter, which she feared would leave girls with absent biological fathers feeling excluded. "A daddy can be any male figure in your life—your father, grandfather, uncle, older brother," she explained to girls in every class. Gordon had been planning the April 2013 event since Peshine opened the previous fall as a Renew school. She wanted to create "a moment the children will never forget—something they'll always have as a happy memory from child-hood."

The response exceeded her wildest hopes: girls signed up by the score, listing uncles, cousins, neighbors, family friends—and of course fathers—as their escorts. Some girls told her with excitement of usually uninvolved fathers who had said yes.

Finally the night arrived, and sixty-three daddy-daughter pairs passed under an archway of pink, white, and black helium balloons into the Peshine cafeteria, which was transformed for the evening into a ballroom. Huge sashes billowed from the ceiling, creating a pink, white, and black canopy—the work of a parent volunteer who had spent all day creating it, balanced on a stepladder. Peshine music teacher Steve Pittman, the deejay for the night, spun slow and fast love songs of every pop genre and decade. Barnes led a procession of girls—dressed in a rainbow of satiny and silky gowns—as Pittman played Stevie Wonder crooning "Isn't She Lovely." Daddy-daughter pairs lined up for hours to pose for photographs, taken by Joanne Rutherford-Pastras, a first-grade Peshine teacher by day.

One dad after the next expressed amazement to see so many Newark men in one room, honoring daughters. Muraad Abdus Salaam, a city firefighter escorting his stepdaughter, looked around at one point and said, "In fifty-three years in Newark, I've never seen a school do anything like this. They're showing the men it's time to step it up."

Gordon, the parent liaison, another daughter of Newark, pur-chased thin silver bracelets with her own money for each man to give each daughter, and Barnes instructed the men to face the girls and re-peat a pledge to love, lead, and encourage them as they snapped the bracelets—featuring two hearts coming together in a clasp—onto their wrists. She asked them to declare their love publicly, and many did.

One man stepped forward in a white dress shirt and pink satin tie, matching his daughter's pink and white party dress. "I'm here to sup-port you in whatever you do," he said into the microphone, holding her hand. "I've got your back. Daddy loves you and I'll always be here for you. You understand that?"

In a burst of emotion, the girl buried her head in her father's chest as he wrapped her in his arms.

The budget crisis Cami Anderson foresaw upon her arrival in Newark hit with full force in 2013. Announcing a $57 million revenue gap in March, she cut over $18 million from school budgets and laid off more than two hundred attendance counselors, clerical workers, janitors, parent liaisons, and security guards, most of them Newark residents with few comparable job prospects. "We're raising the poverty level in Newark in the name of school reform," she told a group of funders, unhappily. "It's a hard thing to wrestle with." At the same time, she was awarding significant raises to her own leadership team, which she did not make public.

The painful budget cuts were met with an increasingly frequent chorus from critics of the reform effort: "What happened to the Zuckerberg money?" Wilhelmina Holder, the grandmother and ubiquitous reform critic, tartly observed, "The sweet potato pie is looking more like a sliver."

The layoffs fueled rising resistance to Anderson's plans for the district, but she further riled opponents by arriving at the annual budget hearing in March 2013 with a spending plan that was noticeably short on information. School board members pressed for specifics on which positions and services would be eliminated by her cuts. Would schools lose art or music teachers? Would they have even fewer social workers? But Anderson's staff said the information wasn't available, and the board—with mere advisory status—had no authority to demand it. In addition, the budget understated by more than half the cost of the excess teacher pool, which was a major cause of the funding gap. The board proceeded to vote down Anderson's budget for the coming year, and also voted no confidence in her—in both cases unanimously, but without effect because of the state's control.

Anderson overrode the budget vote, moving ahead with her spending plan. She said she saw the votes as a backlash against layoffs, not a rebuke for delivering a less-than-transparent budget. She later referred to board member Shavar Jeffries, a supporter of charter schools, as a "hypocrite." She accused him of voting against the budget because he intended to run for mayor and couldn't defend a vote for layoffs, even though the layoffs were necessitated by the district's loss of revenue to charter expansion, which he supported. Jeffries sternly defended his vote, saying he couldn't support a budget without knowing its impact on schools. "She was asking for a billion dollars without telling us how she was going to spend it," he said. Increasingly, Anderson characterized opposition to her as opposition to reform, asserting that even allies who questioned her approach weren't sufficiently committed to doing what was best for kids.

In the spring of 2013, Ras Baraka declared his candidacy for mayor, with a fiery address vowing to "take back Newark" from the control of outsiders. He made clear that Anderson would be a prime target. "We are witnessing a school-reform process that is not about reforming schools," he told a packed auditorium in his South Ward district. He gave no hint that although he detested the reformers' tactics, he shared a number of their goals. "We have to reform our own schools and find good-willed and fair-minded people to help us, not hedge fund groups and special interests," he said. As the city council's education committee chairman, Baraka introduced a resolution calling for a moratorium on all of Anderson's initiatives until she produced data showing that they were improving student achievement, taking a page from the reform movement's insistence on accountability. The resolution passed unanimously, without effect because the council had no power over schools. Within days, Anderson sent an aide to suggest to Baraka that he take a leave of absence, arguing that he had a conflict of interest because he was opposing initiatives as a mayoral candidate that he was supposed to carry out as a principal.

He refused, and the following day a video of his defiant account of the incident was emailed to supporters with this question: "Are we going to stand by like chumps, and allow this 'Interloping Outsider' to harass one of our own?"

The staff at Peshine, proud of their hard work and commitment, soon had cause to feel that they were being seriously undervalued. In June 2013, when Anderson sent something called an "Election to Work Agreement" to the turnaround and Renew schools, they learned that an appendix to the new teachers' contract required them to work longer days and years for a flat $3,000 stipend. The previous year, teachers at Peshine, Avon, and several other schools with extended schedules had been paid $12,000 to $15,000, or about $50 an hour, for the extra time, under a federal school improvement grant—a sweet deal the teachers' union had struck with the previous superintendent. The teachers said they knew the bonanza wouldn't last. But they calculated that the new stipend amounted to less than $10.50 an hour for working two weeks in the summer, an extra hour every day, and three weekend days annually. Joe Del Grosso, the union president, had not mentioned the flat-fee stipend in campaigning for the contract, and many teachers acknowledged they had overlooked it. The contract required teachers at turnaround schools to sign the agreement and accept its terms or leave for the excess teacher pool. Teachers called their union in alarm, only to discover that the union was party to the deal.

Longer school days were becoming more common across the country as one of many approaches to boosting student achievement, and Anderson wanted to extend the hours of many Newark schools. Paying hourly wages for the extra time would be prohibitive, she said— particularly at the $50 rate agreed to by her predecessor. "That created the problem by setting totally absurd expectations. In what universe are you going to be able to pay up to fifteen grand forever?" she asked. "I was not going to do hourly pay. It sends the message of clock-punching. It doesn't treat teachers like professionals." The contrast with her defense of $1,000-a-day pay for long-term consultants was not lost on teachers.

"They should have the same deal we have," Davis Hannah, Peshine's visual arts teacher and union rep, said of Anderson and her executive team at a meeting of union members. "If we have to get slave wages, they should, too." Zuckerberg had wanted the contract to raise the status of teachers in society, certainly not to make them feel exploited.

After venting anger toward Anderson and their union for more than an hour at a meeting in the Peshine auditorium, teachers, one by one, rose to say they didn't want to leave Peshine even if they had to accept what they considered degrading pay. What emerged was a devastating picture of working conditions in much of the district. They said they felt unspeakably lucky to have leaders who supported them, who wanted to help them become better teachers. They had worked for too many principals who were ineffective at best, bullies at worst. "This is the best year I've had in almost thirty years in the district," said the school's music teacher. Another teacher said her stomach used to tighten when her classroom doorknob turned, a signal that a previous principal was arriving to conduct an observation that invariably would be harsh and provide no useful feedback. With Barnes, Lewis, or Meah, she said, observations were constructive, not punitive.

It was a window onto why teachers consistently tell researchers that, given the choice, they would opt for a good principal and supportive working conditions over merit pay. Indeed, research had found no correlation between merit pay and student achievement, although reformers and venture philanthropists were fighting hard to make it a staple of new teacher contracts.

Shakel Nelson, the gifted fifth-grade math teacher, came close to leaving Peshine because she and her husband needed more family income. She calculated that she would be financially better off moving to a school with a shorter day and finding a part-time job in the evening. With fourteen years in the district, she fell into a cohort of teachers whose salary on the new pay scale — $66,000 — would be $20,000 less than if the old one had continued. Even if she won every merit bonus, she'd still be behind.

"It makes me feel afraid," Nelson said. "You kind of look down the road and you plan your life, and you think, 'I'll be okay.' And then you're not where you thought you'd be. But I've had horrendous administrators in the past who were more into putting teachers down than supporting us. Life can be hell in those situations. I have to have my sanity to make it through the day, and being here is better for my sanity. So as much as the money pains me, I'm going to stay."

The teachers' union held elections several weeks later, and Del Grosso came within nine votes of being ousted, largely because of a backlash over the contract. A caucus seeking to remake the union along the lines of a left-wing social movement won control of the executive board. The brief moment of comity between labor and reformers on the teachers' contract was over. Del Grosso and his union became hardened opponents of Anderson and every aspect of her agenda.

Despite the strife in Newark, Anderson was ebullient when she appeared before the board members of William Ackman's Pershing Square Foundation in Manhattan in June 2013. The board was eager to hear how the foundation's $25 million gift to Newark—the biggest donation other than Zuckerberg's—was spurring reform of the district.

"As someone who's anal retentive about setting levers and milestones, I'm feeling pretty awesome about milestones reached versus goals set," Anderson began.

She rattled off accomplishments. The new contract, made possible by philanthropy, was a signal achievement for teacher accountability. She had made concrete changes in the workings of the district—recruiting five new assistant superintendents who now supervised and coached all principals. There were new evaluation systems for teachers and principals and eight Renew schools—"my most proud accomplishment." Asked about results in the classroom, she said a number of schools had improved from the lowest performance ranking to the middle, and some in the middle were now at the top. Emphasizing strong principals as the heart of her improvement strategy, she reported that she had replaced almost fifty of the district's seventy-five school leaders, calling her last round of hires "so phenomenal I'm pinching myself."

The real story was more mixed, as would be expected in a district with such profound challenges. But that wasn't the way Anderson—or many reformers in pursuit of transformational change—tended to tell their stories. The school improvements she reported were based on her own school-rating rubric. But based on state standardized test scores, Newark children had declined in proficiency since her arrival, in math in all tested grades, and in language arts in all but two. And Anderson neglected to report that students in all eight Renew schools were "falling behind" the rest of the district, according to her own rubric. By the end of the next year, she would lose confidence in five of her "phenomenal" new principals and remove them.

Although Anderson focused almost exclusively on the positive, the board was well aware of virulent resistance to her reforms, which had made news in New York City. "So, everything's going great except you need bodyguards," summed up Pershing board member Whitney Tilson, a prominent advocate of education reform nationally.

At that very moment, a large, athletic figure could be seen moving down the corridor toward the conference room. Heads turned as everyone realized it was Cory Booker. "There he is—my bodyguard!" Anderson declared with a laugh. "What timing!" Tilson exclaimed.

It was a remarkable entrance, but in fact it marked the beginning of Booker's official exit from Newark. Senator Frank Lautenberg had died two days earlier, and Booker was arriving from his funeral at a nearby synagogue. Within days, Booker would be running for Lautenberg's open Senate seat, traveling the country to amass what would become an $11 million campaign war chest for a special election in October.

He assured the Pershing Foundation's board that his departure would not hinder the reform effort, regardless of who succeeded him, because the governor still would hold the reins and no Newark mayor had the power to interfere. With Anderson able to count on at least two more years of Christie at her back, he said, "we can get two school years from now where every school is a school of hope, promise, and performance." Once again, Booker was shifting into his high rhetorical gear, soaring far above facts on the ground.

Booker wasn't alone in turning his attention from Newark. Christie was laying the groundwork for a presidential campaign. And Zuckerberg, with almost all of his $100 million now spent or committed—half of it on the hard-fought contract and a quarter of it on charter schools—was beginning to look for his next big philanthropic move. Anderson was about to be left largely on her own, carrying on the mission they had started three years earlier.

12

One Newark, Whose Newark?

June 2013–May 2014

T HE TIME HAD come, Chris Cerf told Cami Anderson, to
"rip off the Band-Aid." That meant putting in place the radical reorganization of the school district that had been looming since Christie and Booker's late-night conversation in 2009 in the
back of the mayoral SUV. In a sweeping use of gubernatorial power,
Anderson, as Christie's agent, would significantly downsize the school
district to adjust for years of falling enrollment and make way for the
expansion of charter schools. With parents demanding them, Christie
authorizing their expansion, and Zuckerberg and other donors funding their start-up costs, charters were now on a path to enroll forty
percent of Newark students within the next three years.

Newark was on its way to becoming a "hybrid" district, like Washington, D.C., with forty-four percent of children in charters, Detroit
with fifty-five percent, and Philadelphia with twenty-eight percent.
This was the emerging shape of public education in more and more
urban districts. While charter schools nationally had produced mixed
results, there was little question that children in Newark charters were

performing better than those in district schools, in some cases far better, although the lower concentration of needy students remained a factor. But the increasingly pressing question, in Newark and in cities around the country, was, What would become of the children left behind in district schools? School systems in Philadelphia and Detroit were struggling to avert fiscal collapse. Now Newark was at a tipping point, with more and more children and state dollars exiting for charters.

Booker, Christie, and Zuckerberg hadn't planned for this impasse. The biggest challenge, Booker had said at the outset, "is breaking this iceberg of immovable, decades-long failing schools. They'll melt into many different school models. They're going to flower, just like the cherry blossoms in Branch Brook Park." Clearly no one had a road map for the treacherous path from failure to utopia. That, in a sense, was the assignment Anderson had taken on. On the horizon were huge disruptions in children's lives, adults' jobs, and long-standing community relationships with neighborhood schools. Nonetheless, she gave her plan a name that conveyed harmony and optimism: One Newark.

Anderson announced her vision at an invitation-only cocktail party in June 2013 in the spacious lobby of the New Jersey Performing Arts Center. Remembering the drubbing she took the previous year, when hundreds of uninvited residents heckled her speech at Rutgers about Renew schools, she hired private security guards to bar gate-crashers.

The audience was stocked with leaders of Newark's charter schools, education reformers from New York, and consultants whose firms were collecting millions of dollars in philanthropic funds by working for Anderson. While numerous Newark clergy and civic leaders were present, missing from the invitation list were the parents and parent leaders whose children would be most affected by the reorganization. The omission was the subject of whispered disbelief among the locals in attendance.

After admiring testimonials to her from a charter leader, a district principal, and Cerf, Anderson delivered a twenty-minute speech, promising to create an online, unified enrollment system for all district and charter schools. Similar systems had been adopted in charter-heavy New Orleans, Washington, and Denver. By replacing charter lotteries, she said, the new system would make it as easy to apply to charters as to district schools, greatly reducing the selection bias toward the most motivated families. Dousing the caution light she had held up to charters for the past two years, she said in the strongest terms that parents deserved the right to choose charter schools for their children. "Who can blame them?" she asked, adding, "How dare we . . . say they should be trapped in failed schools while we get our act together?" Acknowledging that the district would shrink, she called on the reform movement's leaders and funders to lobby alongside her for laws giving the district the flexibility charters had to hire and fire teachers based on merit. Only then, she said, would district schools be able to compete and survive, albeit on a smaller scale. She received a sustained standing ovation.

Anderson had only the outline of a plan, with details yet to be developed, but the logo, "One Newark," was everywhere, on folders and materials handed out to guests, on wall posters, and beaming from flat-screen televisions around the room. Having handpicked her audience, Anderson used her speech as an opportunity to reframe her raucous two years in office as a major success that had been obscured by unfair, politically motivated attacks. Along the walls were large posters that she called her "accomplishment storyboards," each with a large, red ink stamp declaring, "DONE." Raising student achievement — "DONE." Turning around failing schools — "DONE." Engaging the community — "DONE." In fact, the initiatives were seriously un-done.

A few days after her speech, Anderson sent an email to all who attended with a link to a questionnaire seeking feedback on her vision and the event. Like the evening itself, it seemed designed to come out positively. Each question offered six possible answers, five of them laudatory. For example, "What did you think of the 'accomplishments' storyboards (check all that apply)?" was followed by these choices:

- They were awesome!
- It's amazing how much has been accomplished.
- They were informative.
- They were a nice addition to the room.
- I wish you had covered more accomplishments.
- I thought they just took up space.

Anderson spent much of the fall working in her tenth-floor office on a master plan for the district's survival. To guide the analysis, she turned to the Parthenon Group, which had advised other school systems experiencing aggressive charter growth. "Districts across the United States are passing the buck till they end up like GM," with dwindling revenue and crushing costs, one of the consultants said. "The goal is to adapt over three years to changes you can foresee."

Anderson wanted the plan to address the many overlapping complexities of urban education—considerations her superiors had neglected to consider. How to ensure that charters, as they expanded, enrolled a representative share of Newark's neediest children. How to improve district schools fast enough to persuade families to stick with them. How to close underpopulated schools without adding to neighborhood blight. How to retain the best teachers, given that she estimated she would have to lay off a thousand of them in the next three years. How to find money to modernize schools that on average were eighty years old. How to stabilize the district's finances for long-term survival. "This is sixteen-dimensional chess!" she said often.

Demographic data essentially pointed a dagger at the district. In the next three years, its schools would lose 5,600 students and $249 million in state funds to charters, requiring the closure of up to twelve district schools. Half would be in the South and West wards, home to the highest concentration of African American families, most of the lowest-performing schools, and, not coincidentally, the largest exodus to charter schools. The district, still responsible for educating a majority of Newark children, would face a structural deficit of $100 million, requiring extensive layoffs. "You look at the data, and all you see is a train wreck," Anderson said.

Surrounded by artifacts of superintendents past on the walls of her conference room, Anderson and her staff scripted the most sweeping rearrangement of education in Newark history. In a matter of months, more than a third of district schools would be closed, renewed, relocated, phased out, repurposed, redesigned, or taken over by charters. Rather than sending children automatically to a neighborhood school, as they had for a century, families would select from fifty-five remaining district schools and sixteen charter schools that had agreed to forgo lottery admissions. Parents were to enter up to eight top choices online, and an algorithm would make school assignments. Preferences would be given to children whose schools were closing and those with the lowest family incomes or learning disabilities—giving the highest-need students a better shot at their top choices. As part of her plan to broaden access to charters, she asked them to take over district schools in some of the city's poorest neighborhoods.

Anderson and her team held more than a dozen meetings with charter school leaders to vet the plan. But there were no comparable meetings with parents of schoolchildren to preview the tumultuous changes. Anderson said she feared that any public hearings, like school board meetings, would have been co-opted by "political forces whose objective is to create disruption." And she said it would have been impossible to address individual concerns without unwinding the whole design. "That is the nature of sixteen-dimensional chess," she said. "You can't create concessions in one place that then create problems in another."

Convulsive change was inevitable in a district facing fiscal ruin, massive overcapacity, and an urgent need for improvement. And some version of Anderson's ideas—particularly her emphasis on requiring charters to enroll more of the neediest children—might have won public support if residents had been given a voice in the process. But effectively imposing a dramatically rearranged school system on families and communities, after a number of unfulfilled promises of "bottom-up reform," triggered a predictable uprising.

District parents were cryptically alerted to the radical reconfiguration on December 16, 2013, one day before Anderson announced it publicly. A letter went home in students' backpacks inviting parents to school-by-school meetings the following night to learn of "bold and urgent actions." With only one day's notice, the meetings were poorly attended, although word of the changes spread swiftly. Anderson was braced for an uproar—"December-palooza," she called it to her staff—and she got one. Parents immediately began picketing schools that were designated to close. Many said they feared for the safety of their children, who would be forced to attend schools in unfamiliar neighborhoods. Fears were rampant in the South Ward, where murders had increased seventy percent in four years. Jacqueline Edward, a mother of two children in district schools, blurted out one afternoon, as if addressing Anderson in absentia, "Can you guarantee me my daughter's safety?" She described gang activity and drug dealing near the school where her daughter would be reassigned. "My twenty-eight-year-old started off in a gang, and we fought to get him out," she said. "My twenty-two-year-old has a lot of anger issues because Daddy wasn't there. I just refuse to see another generation go that way."

Although One Newark offered parents for the first time the chance to opt out of any failing neighborhood school, the overall shape of the plan left many Newark families convinced that their children were not being handled with care. Neighborhood schools were part of a delicately balanced ecosystem that served many needs for families. Anderson persuaded charter schools to take over three neighborhood K–8 schools, portraying the move as an opportunity for some of the lowest-income children to attend the most sought-after programs. But the charters agreed to serve children only in kindergarten through fourth grade. Children in the upper grades had to go elsewhere. That removed a trusted source of child care for parents who relied on older siblings to accompany younger ones to and from school. In a focus group arranged by the district, parents from both district and charter schools complained that they felt poorly informed, inconvenienced, and dissatisfied with the new enrollment system. Two representative comments from the focus group summary: "The community would've received the changes better if it was not shoved down their throats" and "It felt like one big experiment." Anderson's staff distributed performance ratings for each charter and district school to help parents make their selections. But as one parent said in the focus group, "The ratings for most schools were failing." Anderson had delivered on the reformers' goal of increasing parental choice and expanding high-performing charters, but as before, good choices remained in short supply.

One reason for this was the disappointing results at Anderson's first round of eight Renew schools. She had hoped they would flourish and attract parents who otherwise would enroll children in charters. Indeed, almost every aspect of the schools had improved: stronger teachers and principals, more rigorous curriculum, longer school days, and noticeably better learning environments. When test scores arrived in 2014, Anderson called a press conference to announce "incredible gains" over the previous year. She neglected to report that, when viewed across the two years since she had designated them in urgent need of renewal, scores at all but one of the schools had fallen, in some cases by double digits, in either literacy or math or both. Nonetheless, Anderson insisted that the strategy eventually would bear fruit and designated eight more schools for renewal as part of One Newark.

In effect, Anderson was asking parents and the community to trust that her strategies, in time, would deliver results for their children. Indeed, it was reasonable to assume that progress would come slowly, as teachers and students adjusted to multiple changes at the school and classroom levels. But trust was an early casualty of the top-down approach that Booker and Christie embraced even before Anderson's arrival. And Anderson's declarations of victory, based on less than complete presentations of data on student performance, only exacerbated unease. She announced a ten percent increase in the graduation rate —an accomplishment Christie touted in his State of the State address —but results from the ACT college admission test, taken by all juniors, showed that only two to five percent of students in nonmagnet high schools were prepared for college. Meanwhile, throughout the district, proficiency had declined in both literacy and math in every tested grade on the state standardized test since 2011, the year before Anderson arrived. The state had made the tests more difficult over those years, but students' results statewide hadn't suffered.

Although she had vowed to bring accountability to a district that long resisted it, Anderson said she should not have to answer for the declining test scores. She called the state test "fatally flawed," adding, "If we had a better test, we'd have better gains." Her defense spoke volumes about the muddle that reform had become at the ground level. Anderson had relied on state test scores to decide which schools to close for poor performance, but now—echoing many union leaders and opponents of test-based accountability—she was saying that those tests didn't accurately measure whether children were learning.

Anderson also argued that by using new powers in the teachers' contract to weed out weak teachers and reward the best ones, she was raising the quality of the teaching corps across the district, which would eventually translate into higher student achievement. There again, progress was slower than advertised. Anderson bullishly announced that only five percent of teachers rated effective or better had left the district in the past year, compared to almost forty percent of those rated ineffective. But the actual numbers, which she did not announce, painted a different picture. So many teachers had gotten effective ratings that the departures included more of them than those at the bottom. Nonetheless, Anderson hailed the overall trend as an important shift. In the coming year, using the new state law to bring tenure charges against the lowest-rated teachers, she and her staff would move to shift the balance further.

With no data yet showing that the district's students were improving under Anderson, it was perhaps not surprising that almost half of the applicants to kindergarten listed charter schools as their first choice in the One Newark enrollment process. But the popularity of charters didn't translate into support for One Newark. Many charter parents had relatives who worked for district schools or other children who attended them, and they too were adamantly against closing schools and eliminating jobs—even though both were inevitable consequences of the growth of charters. "You see parents dropping their children off at charter schools and then joining a picket at Two Cedar Street [the district headquarters] because I laid off their cousin," Anderson said.

Christie remained steadfastly committed in public to Anderson and her agenda, though not in a way that helped her in Newark. Asked during his 2013 reelection campaign about local resistance to Anderson, he responded, "I don't care about the community criticism. We run the school district in Newark, not them." The governor cruised to a twenty-two-point victory, solidifying his status as a GOP presidential contender. On the day after Christmas, he and Anderson met privately in his Trenton office, and he promised his support, no matter how intense the opposition. "I left thinking, 'He's totally engaged,'" Anderson recalled.

Two weeks later, the scandal known as Bridgegate broke, with revelations that senior Christie appointees caused a massive traffic jam at the George Washington Bridge in September 2013—an apparent payback to the Democratic mayor of Fort Lee, whose town was snarled with cars for days, for refusing to support Christie's reelection. The governor said he knew nothing of the plot. As the United States attorney investigated, Christie had his own career to worry about.

With Christie weakened, and opponents emboldened, resistance to

Anderson's plan grew so fierce that a prominent pastor told the governor he feared civil unrest. Anderson moved out of Newark, telling friends that she was concerned for her family's safety. In late January 2014, she stopped attending public school-board meetings, saying the vitriol directed at her had made them counterproductive.

That March, Anderson lost her most ardent defender when Chris Cerf left his job as state education commissioner to join Joel Klein at Amplify, the education technology business within Rupert Murdoch's News Corp. The next month, seventy-seven pastors signed an open letter to Christie calling for a moratorium on One Newark, citing "venomous" public anger and "an overwhelming sense of frustration, community disenfranchisement and alienation."

The rage engulfed the mayor's race, which was by now in full swing, and it fueled Ras Baraka's rallying cry against outside control. "When I become mayor, *we* become mayor" was his slogan, repeated in every speech and emblazoned on a campaign bus in which he traveled the city. Baraka fashioned Anderson into a stand-in for all outsiders—a universal "they." Attendance at his Saturday breakfast rallies doubled immediately after the announcement of One Newark. "They want to close our schools. Their idea of fixing Newark is getting rid of you!" he declared to loud cheers at a packed rally in the North Ward, where previously he had had little support. "We have to look the devil in his face and say, 'Not only are you wrong. We don't want you here.'" The festering resistance to Anderson, the backlash against One Newark, and the first mayoral campaign of the post-Booker era became one and the same. "Cami Anderson has handed Ras Baraka the most powerful weapon in his arsenal," said a city councilman running on a slate opposed to Baraka's.

The election became a proxy for the national battle between reformers and unions for control of public education. Baraka had the solid support of every union representing Newark school employees —teachers, principals, custodians, clerks, security guards, cafeteria workers. They and national unions raised just over $600,000 for his race. The national education reform movement raised almost $5 million for Baraka's opponent, Shavar Jeffries, the former school board president who advocated closing the worst district schools and leasing them to the best charter schools. New Jersey's most powerful Democratic political bosses also rallied behind Jeffries, viewing Baraka as a threat to their own power.

While Jeffries had publicly supported the reformers' agenda throughout his years on the school board, he was harshly critical of their approach. Since the announcement of the Zuckerberg gift, he had spoken out repeatedly against the top-down strategy for spending it. He too was a Newark native, with an inspiring life story—an orphan at age ten when his mother was murdered, he went on to be a top student at Duke University and Columbia Law School—and he insisted that reform could succeed only if the community embraced it. "Education reform comes across as colonial to people who've been here for decades," he said. "It's very missionary, imposed, done *to* people rather than in cooperation with people." He called Anderson a detriment to her own cause—and his. "She behaved like an enemy out of central casting, the disrespectful way she treated our community," he said.

Although Jeffries won the fundraising battle by miles, Baraka won the war, foiling both the billionaires and the party bosses with a decisive victory in May 2014. At his filled-to-capacity victory party, the candidate and his supporters spoke as if they were waging a liberation movement as much as a political campaign.

"Today we told them that the people of Newark are not for sale!" Baraka declared as the final tally was announced. "That people outweigh money in a democracy! That Broad Street should be more important than Wall Street!" Surrounding him on the stage were leaders of every education workers' union, dozens of his former students at Central High School, and a phalanx of campaign workers.

"*We* are the mayor," Baraka rasped above the cheers. The crowd echoed the slogan, the words resounding through the ballroom of the historic Robert Treat Hotel, named for Newark's colonial-era founder.

And yet when Baraka, in one of his first acts as mayor, met with Christie and asked him to return control of the schools to Newark, the governor responded with an emphatic no. "We are the deciders on what happens in the school system," Christie said. It was an assertion of authority in the face of a rising tide of resistance that seemed destined eventually to have its day. But not now, and not—as long as Christie held the cards—in the person of a mayor backed by every union in the school district. Newark's tattered prize—its district schools and all that they represented to so many, from the youngest kindergartner in Princess Williams's class to the leading politicians, from the dwindling ranks of public workers to the most ambitious philanthropists in the land—was in fact still in play.

Conclusion: No Excuses

O N NOVEMBER 5, 2014, all of Newark seemed to stand still and stricken as word spread of the untimely death of its civic steward, Professor Clement Price, at age sixty-nine from a massive stroke. In a stirring eulogy at Price's funeral, Mayor Ras Baraka said the city already missed the sound of his "distinct, calming voice . . . forcing all of us to deal with each other, to see each other in one collective narrative—our story—our Newark."

Newark needed that voice more than ever amid the polarizing rancor over education. In an interview shortly before he died, the usually optimistic Price had delivered a grim summation of the reform effort. "At the outset," he said, "this was an opportunity, I thought, to put public education at long last at the center of Newark's civic agenda. I think that opportunity was lost. There was a huge consensus here that schools needed dramatic reform. Now the space for that conversation has almost disappeared."

For four years, the reformers never really tried to have a conversation with the people of Newark. Their target audience was always somewhere else, beyond the people whose children and grandchildren desperately needed to learn and compete for a future. Booker, Christie, and Zuckerberg set out to create a national "proof point" in Newark. There was less focus on Newark as its own complex ecosystem that reformers needed to understand before trying to save it. Two hundred million dollars and almost five years later, there was at least as much rancor as reform.

Newark illustrated that improving education for the nation's poorest children is as much a political as a pedagogical challenge. Redirecting large district bureaucracies—for decades, the employers of last resort in distressed cities—in the service of children in classrooms is a treacherous process, activating well-organized public workers, political organizations, and unions invested in the status quo. Voter backlashes against education reformers in mayoral elections in New York City in 2013, in Newark in 2014, and in Chicago in 2015 revealed the tenuous nature of disruptive changes made without buy-in from those who have to live them.

Howard Fuller, the former Milwaukee superintendent and the first African American to become prominent in the education reform movement, happened to pass through the city in the fall of 2014 on a promotional tour for his memoir, *No Struggle, No Progress.* He literally cringed at the political spectacle that reform had fostered. "I think a lot of us education reformers—and I include myself—have been too arrogant," he said. "It's not even what you do sometimes, it's the way you treat people in the process of doing it. If your approach is to get a lot of smart people in the room and figure out what 'these people' need and then we implement it, the first issue is who decided that you were smart? And why do you think you can just get in a room and make decisions for a community of people? You don't think they'll respond the way they responded? I'm not saying you can ever create this level of change without resistance, but I don't see how this is politically sustainable over time."

Even in the aftermath of the uprising against One Newark, Chris Cerf, the state's chief architect of the Newark effort, said he had no regrets about imposing changes unilaterally. A more inclusive process, he said, would not have yielded as much progress—in particular, more schools run by high-achieving charter networks. "You have no chance of giving these kids the lives they deserve if you don't essentially override the local political infrastructure—no chance at all," he said. "I honestly don't think there's a logic-based counterargument to that . . . There's no chance this political culture would have been able to rise above the question of who gets what. They had their chance."

But a year later, in the summer of 2015, the state announced a sudden and stunning change of strategy. Despite his plummeting popularity, Christie was making a run for the White House. Opposition to Anderson and her agenda was drawing national attention—with more than one thousand students marching out of class and into downtown traffic, teachers refusing to carry out her latest reforms, and Baraka taking his fight for local control to the *New York Times* op-ed page. In early June, Christie covertly invited Baraka to Trenton to discuss education. Days before his formal campaign launch, the Republican governor and the Democratic mayor issued a joint announcement that they had reached an agreement to begin the process of returning to Newark long-lost control over its public school district. Anderson was not the person to lead in this new era, the governor said. She was given three hours to decide whether to resign or be fired. She resigned. "I don't blame Cami at all for coming to the decision that we did that it was time for her to move on," Christie told reporters. Anderson's former patrons moved quickly to write her out of the narrative of school reform in Newark. "She came here, she gave service, and she's now moved on," Booker said.

There was a sense of déjà vu all over again—the white Republican governor and Newark's black Democratic mayor coming together to fix the public schools, declaring in a joint statement, "The future of our children deserves no less." And to complete the tableau, Christie announced the new superintendent would be the founding leader of the reform effort—Chris Cerf, who just had left his job at the education technology firm headed by Joel Klein.

But this Newark mayor was certain to be a very different partner for the state than Booker. And now Baraka was tantalizingly close to reclaiming Newark's prize. Still, there were legislative and regulatory hurdles to be cleared, which meant Cerf would remain in charge for at least a year, probably longer. A committee with five members appointed by Christie and four by Baraka would oversee the process. Cerf sent signals immediately that he was committed in the interim to pushing ahead with the agenda of charter school expansion, citywide school choice, and increased teacher responsibility, but he also made clear he was ready to compromise on at least some grassroots concerns about One Newark. There were suggestions that Baraka would get some of his own brand of reforms—like community schools, with social services for families and neighborhoods as well as students—financed with some of the Zuckerberg bounty that Anderson hadn't spent. Indeed, since Baraka's election, some of Zuckerberg's remaining dollars had begun flowing to community-based initiatives—the mayor's summer youth-employment program, a citywide campaign to increase the college graduation rate—instead of systems reforms, a shift long sought by the staff of the Foundation for Newark's Future but only recently embraced by its board. The voices of Newark, it appeared, were beginning to be heard.

While praising the new direction of FNF, Baraka declared himself unmoved by Cerf's newly conciliatory demeanor, calling his appointment "a clear indicator that Governor Christie is still Governor Christie, and we should not expect anything to the contrary of him." He added, "We are in this fight to govern and be in charge of our lives. The Governor should expect nothing less from Newark."

Cerf appeared to be following the lessons of Washington, D.C., where Michelle Rhee's autocratic leadership gave way in 2010 to a far more collaborative chancellor in Kaya Henderson. She pursued an agenda similar to Rhee's and closed fifteen schools in 2013, but only after a yearlong vetting process with affected families, making multiple changes in response to their input. She also presided over slow, but steady, achievement gains. While the backlash against Rhee fueled the ouster of Washington's mayor in 2010, the city elected a new mayor in 2014 who promised to keep Henderson in office. "Movements that don't include beneficiaries are doomed to fail," Henderson said.

Put another way, education reform is too important to be left to reformers alone. One person who drew this lesson from Newark was Mark Zuckerberg. He had vowed at the outset to learn from his experience and to use it to become a better philanthropist. Based on his subsequent initiatives, he appears to have learned a lot. He and Priscilla Chan have said publicly that they intend to spend the rest of their lives as philanthropists working on the challenge of improving education for the nation's most underserved children. With their Newark commitment due to expire at the end of 2015, they have refocused their Startup: Education foundation on low-income communities close to home, in the Bay Area. A priority of the foundation from now on, according to Jen Holleran, is understanding the desires of the communities where they make grants. There are likely to be a lot of them. With a contribution of almost $1 billion in stock to the Silicon Valley Community Foundation for unspecified future gifts, Zuckerberg and Chan became the nation's most generous philanthropists in 2013. They announced plans in May 2014 for $120 million in grants to schools in a series of high-poverty communities in the Bay Area. The amount was similar in size to their gift to Newark, but the method was not. The couple wrote in an op-ed in the *San Jose Mercury News* that they were working through parents, teachers, school leaders, and officials of both charter organizations and school districts "so that we understand the needs of students that others miss." By contrast, in Newark they worked through politicians and arrived with little knowledge of the community, the schools, or the impediments to reform.

Well before the gift to Newark, Priscilla Chan had made a personal cause of working with children like those who struggled the most in Newark. As a pediatrician caring for underserved children, she became convinced that schools, on their own, were unlikely to meet the needs of students raised amid extreme poverty and violence. Working with educators and researchers, she is developing a school that would operate alongside a community health center, providing medical and mental health care in tandem with education and community-based services, creating a web of support for students with the greatest needs, beginning in early childhood. The school and health center would draw on neuroscience research to jointly address adverse childhood experiences—such as poverty, trauma, and neglect—that can interfere with a student's ability to learn, even before kindergarten. In contrast with the approach in Newark, Chan's starting point was children, their needs, and a school equipped to address them.

It was tempting to imagine how this kind of support system might have affected Alif Beyah. He was in free fall at BRICK Avon when a principal, assistant principal, special education teacher, and basketball coach wove themselves into a safety net in partnership with his mother and caught him. Flush with hope from his remarkable progress, Alif went to Newark Vocational High School in the fall of 2013. But his support system didn't go with him. He made the varsity basketball team as a freshman but struggled academically and quickly lost hope, despite heavy encouragement from his coach and his mother. "I'm just not on their level," he kept saying of his teachers.

The second semester was immeasurably worse. In March, a lifelong friend of Alif's was stabbed and killed at age fourteen while the two of them walked home from a pickup basketball game. It was a calamity that could have derailed any child. For one already at risk, it was all the more devastating. For weeks, his mother said, Alif cried himself to sleep and lost all motivation. He ended the year with F's in English, math, and history, and was sent to summer school.

Anderson had vowed in her first weeks on the job to fix the district's broken summer school system, but the improvements didn't make their way to Alif. He retook freshman English and math, but his English teacher quit, and he was taught by rotating substitutes who he said simply distributed work packets. He passed math but flunked English.

In the fall of 2014, Newark Vocational was relocated to unused space in West Side High School as part of Anderson's One Newark reorganization. Alif arrived for his sophomore year two credits behind, which disqualified him from playing on the basketball team, which had been his strongest anchor. Meanwhile, with the district's attention focused on implementing sweeping change, some of the most basic functions—such as student scheduling at certain high schools—had broken down. Throughout the fall semester, Alif had no English or math classes. Although Anderson's Grad Tracker program was supposed to ensure that students who failed classes regained the credits, there was no arrangement for Alif to make up freshman English and history.

Meanwhile, he was frequently late for school or absent, occasionally posting videos of himself and friends on Facebook in a haze of marijuana smoke. Melinda Weidman, the BRICK Avon vice principal, found the videos one day on Facebook. Taken aback, she contacted Alif and his mother and began visiting him at West Side, introducing herself to guidance counselors, social workers, after-school coordinators, and assistant principals, hoping to weave him another safety net. "The whole endeavor," Weidman said, "is just trying again, again, again."

Breakdowns like these led Princess Williams, the gifted kindergarten teacher at BRICK Avon, to take a dramatic and unexpected step in her path as an educator. From the time she entered teaching, she had vowed never to work in a charter school, convinced that charters didn't serve children with the greatest needs—those with troubled histories like her own, rooted in the city's pathologies. But for most of the 2013–14 school year at BRICK Avon, Williams tried without result to persuade the district to provide an aide for severely disturbed children in her kindergarten class, including two who threw furniture at her and their classmates. Other students didn't feel safe, she said, affecting their ability to concentrate and learn. In the fall of 2014, she made an emotional decision to leave the district for SPARK Academy, the KIPP charter elementary school. Williams said she wanted to become an education leader in Newark and perhaps beyond. With charters now a major presence in public education, she felt compelled to learn from the inside what the best of them could offer students like hers.

Williams had changed in other ways. She was now Princess Fils Aime (pronounced Feece Ah-*mee*), having married Ronald Fils Aime, her boyfriend of several years whom she had met at her church. And in the summer of 2014, she earned a master's degree in education leadership from Columbia University, an experience that caused her to reexamine all her premises about teaching and learning. "We talked in my master's program about ethics and the ethic of critique, and how our first priority is the child's well-being," she said. "A school district, a principal, and a teacher may all have different ideas of what is required for well-being, but as a teacher, at some point you have to stop accepting no. You have to say no, I'm going to critique the system." At the heart of her critique, she said, was the district's failure to get more of its money to classrooms and children who need it.

So instead of Room 112, Fils Aime is now in Room 202 at SPARK. Echo the owl has come too, helping her as always to teach letters and sounds to five-year-olds. Her new classroom is known as Lincoln University, for the nation's first degree-granting historically black college. As at BRICK Avon, if her students allow their attention to wander, they hear a calm voice say, "Ms. Fils Aime is feeling sad inside because the scholars in Lincoln are not trying their best right now." And as at BRICK Avon, they snap back to work as if by magic. Her students at SPARK are as needy as those at Avon, she said, in part because she is teaching an inclusion class for children with cognitive and emotional disabilities, including some with symptoms of trauma. But here, in a class of twenty-six children, Fils Aime has considerable support. She is one of two full-time teachers and a learning specialist who instruct children in small groups of eight or nine. Fils Aime said there is less conflict than in her class at Avon because students with emotional problems get more attention. As at BRICK Avon, some of her angriest students have tried to hit classmates. But instead of having to wait months for support from district administrators, she said, a school social worker arrived almost immediately to observe the child and suggest adjustments. In some cases, the social worker conducted multiple observations, identified idiosyncratic circumstances in the classroom that triggered a child's anger, and worked with Fils Aime to alter them. Her conclusion was not that charters were inherently better, but rather that they were structured to more easily deliver money to classrooms than was the district.

"Budgets tell you a lot about values," she said. "We need to change the values of our district." She said she wants to return one day to the district to be part of that change.

It is significant that Fils Aime, now thirty, aspires to have the power to reshape Newark's public schools. She was a product of those schools, and unlike many of her classmates, she recognized their inadequacy as a grave injustice. She is part of a historic shift in the makeup of Newark in which a generation raised in the wake of riots, white flight, and the near collapse of the public schools is coming into its own. Ras Baraka is the first mayor to have been born in Newark since Hugh Addonizio—the Italian American former congressman who presided over the riots. Kenneth Gibson and Sharpe James, the first two African American mayors, were born in the Deep South and came north in the Great Migration. Booker was a child of the suburbs. But now comes a generation that inherited the tragedies of Newark and lived to tell the story, and perhaps to change it. There are teachers and principals throughout the city's schools, both district and charter, with the same convictions as Fils Aime, potential leaders who could speak both for Newark and to Newark about the difficult ways in which public education needs to change. To those engaged in the struggle, the stakes are embodied in a message Fils Aime posted on her Facebook page in January 2015: "Sometimes we lack the conviction that our success is needed, when in fact our families and communities need us to be uncommonly successful."

With her unrelenting spirit, Princess Fils Aime will be working to improve the Newark schools long after the current wave of reformers is gone. For her, the work begins with finding a path beyond the polarizing debate over charters and districts to conceive of all schools as institutions designed to meet the complex needs of children and communities.

"Finding a way to connect these worlds is my focus now," she said, "so that we can ask of every school: What does this particular school need in order to meet the challenges of the neighborhood it's situated in? And then we simply have to provide it. We have to be able to show children: Why is this education meaningful? How can you possibly do that if so many other things are not working?"

To those like Fils Aime who see education through the lens of students and classrooms, it is obvious that urban public schools are being asked to overcome nothing less that the effects of poverty. Reformers are right, she said, to insist on consistently excellent teaching and leadership, but the results in Newark and in distressed cities across the country make clear that much more support is needed. Coming from her, and from Priscilla Chan, this is not an excuse. It is a simple but urgent plea to put the real needs of children at the center of the national conversation about education reform, which in its ideological devisiveness is in danger of leaving them behind.

Author's Note

I came to know Newark as a reporter in the New York bureau of the *Washington Post* from the mid-1990s through 2008, during the mayoralties of Sharpe James and Cory Booker. I met Professor Clement Price the first time I reported a story in the city, and he became a friend whose deep knowledge and feeling for Newark kept me on the lookout for more opportunities to explore its riches and its glaring challenges. He and Robert Curvin—author of *Inside Newark,* who also became a friend—taught me to look at Newark as a metaphor for much of urban America, saddled with the long-term consequences of racism and inequality, made worse by ill-advised government policies and economic change. More and more, I saw Newark in terms of this line from James Baldwin's preface to his *Notes of a Native Son:* "I am what time, circumstance, history have made of me, certainly, but I am also much more than that. So are we all."

Mark Zuckerberg's $100 million gift to the Newark schools in September 2010 struck me as an enormously lucky stroke for the city. Like many others, I viewed education reform from a distance but as a movement full of promise, and the Newark schools as desperately in need of change and support. I was eager to follow what would come of this generous gift and to explore how it would interact with and perhaps mitigate some of the forces that had dragged the city down for so long. The story that emerged was less promising than I expected. The reasons, as I discovered, could fill a book. That almost everyone on all sides was well intentioned made the failures as well as the successes of the enterprise that much more important to wrestle with. I have worked to portray all of this with fidelity to events, context, and the many people who entrusted me with their experiences and perspectives. Over four and a half years, I chronicled the unfolding story from the back seat of Cory Booker's mayoral SUV, dozens of classrooms, homes, and neighborhoods of Newark students, windowless rooms where policymakers labored in the school district headquarters, opulent offices of wealthy philanthropists, gatherings of education reformers around the country, Chris Christie's gubernatorial office, Mark Zuckerberg's Facebook conference room, and scores of public meetings, rallies, and coffee klatches in Newark. All characters are identified by their real names except Tariq Anderson, which is a pseudonym.

In the spirit of full disclosure, I want to reveal that one of my sons, Sam Purdy, is in ways a participant in the school reform movement. He is a middle school teacher who began his career through Teach for America in a public school district in the Rio Grande Valley of Texas. He also taught for two years at a KIPP charter school in New York City. However, at the time that I reported and wrote about SPARK Academy, the KIPP elementary school featured in this book, he was not employed by KIPP.

A disclosure of another sort is that I embarked on this book out of a lifelong interest in race and inequality, having come of age in Birmingham, Alabama, as a white child during the final years of legal segregation. I attended all-white suburban schools and have vivid memories of drinking from "white" water fountains, riding in whites-only elevators, and attending the state fair on nights reserved for white residents. I had parents who—unusual in white Birmingham then — regarded all of this as profoundly wrong and encouraged me from a young age to question it. For this reason, I dedicated this book to their memory.

I am indebted to many people who believed in this book and in my ability to write it. Deanne Urmy, my editor at Houghton Mifflin Harcourt, emailed on a Saturday night in 2011 to convey her excitement after reading my book proposal. Her commitment never wavered, nor did her exceptional skills, both professional and personal. I am grateful also to Joëlle Delbourgo, my agent and friend, for guidance, insights, and encouragement. Dorothy Wickenden patiently and brilliantly helped me elevate the narrative as editor of the first serial in *The New Yorker.* I benefited tremendously from the wisdom and time of David Barstow and Sara Mosle in conceptualizing the book.

Cory Booker, Mark Zuckerberg, Chris Christie, Chris Cerf, and Cami Anderson gave me rare opportunities to witness the unfolding story of education reform in Newark. I'm grateful to them for seeing the value in patient, in-depth journalism and for tolerating my lurking presence and ceaseless questions for four and one half years.

I am lucky to have many gifted writers as friends, and several of them generously read and commented on the manuscript. Major thanks to Michael Sokolove, Natalie Wexler, Carol Rodgers, and Emma Sokoloff-Rubin. Thanks also to Nicholas Lemann for sharing his wealth of knowledge about education in multiple conversations. I deeply appreciate the help of Don Graham and Bill Bradley in vouching for me to key people in the Newark effort.

It would be impossible to name everyone who helped shape my understanding of Newark and the events in this book. Many of them are quoted in the narrative, but there are scores of others, some of whom chose to remain anonymous. Thanks to Princess Fils Aime, Joanna Belcher, Charity Haygood, Dominique Lee, Chris Perpich, Milagros Harris, Ras Baraka, Shavar Jeffries, Chaleeta Barnes, Tameshone Lewis, Shakel Nelson, Winston Jackson, Alif Beyah, Lakiesha Mills, Dyneeka McPherson, Junius Williams, Richard Cammarieri, Kathleen Nugent, Jen Holleran, Paul Bernstein, Kimberly McLain,

Kevin Callaghan, Renee Harper, Matthew Frankel, Dan Gohl, Chuck Crafts, Gordon MacInnes, Ryan Hill, Steve Small, Ben Cope, Norman Atkins, Khaatim Sherrer-El, Bashir Akinyele, Jamani Montague, Irene Cooper-Basch, Barbara Reisman, Mashea Ashton, Tynesha McHarris, Mike Maillaro, Bruno Tedeschi, Cynthia King Vance, David Sciarra, Rob Reich, Lizabeth Cohen, Jelani Cobb, Rick Hess, and Robin Lake. I benefited from the work of fellow journalists David Giambusso, Jessica Calefati, John Mooney, Tom Moran, Paul Tough, Sara Neufeld, Kate Zernike, Lyndsey Layton, Jonathan Alter, Elizabeth Green, Dana Goldstein, Bob Braun, Nicolas Stavros Niarcos, and Aaron Miguel Cantú. And I am grateful to good friends who were exceptionally thoughtful listeners at key points along the way — Joanmarie Kalter, Donna Rifkind, Felicity Barringer, Michael Taubman, Trish Perlmutter, Gabrielle Glaser, Meg Campbell, Sara Rimer, Steve Luxenberg, Carolyn Acker, and David Greenstein. This is especially true of my parents-in-law, Arthur and Thelma Purdy. On a personal note, I owe immeasurable thanks to Drs. Manjit Bains, David Ilson, and Karyn Goodman of Memorial Sloan Kettering Cancer Center for their medical genius and humanity.

I have saved the biggest debts for last. My husband, Matt Purdy, a bottomless source of faith and love — in sickness and in health — played every imaginable role along this journey. It was his idea that I write this book and, despite having a fairly demanding day job, he was always by my side as unofficial editor, thought partner, cheerleader, in-house humorist, and just-in-time supplier of the bon mot. I am thankful every day for the gift of our sons, Sam and Adam, whose love and confidence lifted me over every hurdle.

Appendix I

Where the $200 Million Went

LABOR AND CONTRACT COSTS: $89.2 million committed
- Teachers' contract: $48.3 million, including $31 million in back pay for teachers and $18 million in other incentives, including less than $6 million for merit pay; $4 million for teachers' graduate school tuition support

- Principals' contract: $13.7 million committed but not yet spent;* about $1 million awarded to selected principals

- Buyouts for unwanted teachers, principals, and support staff: $21 million committed†

- Administrative fees: $1.7 million

---

* The principals' union had refused, through January 2015, to negotiate with Superintendent Cami Anderson, so the Foundation for Newark's Future allowed Anderson to spend some of the $13.7 million committed to the teacher contract on rewards to individual principals.

† Anderson wasn't able to buy out only unwanted teachers because of restrictions in federal benefits legislation. This money will probably be redirected.

CHARTER SCHOOLS: $57.6 million to expand and support Newark charters, including $14.25 million raised by the Newark Charter School Fund, $10 million from the NewSchools Venture Fund, and smaller donations by individual funders

CONSULTANTS (MOSTLY TO THE SCHOOL DISTRICT): $21 million for communications, data systems, strategic planning, financial analysis, human resources management, reorganization of district offices, teacher and principal evaluation frameworks, advice on teachers' contract negotiations, design of universal enrollment system, analysis of student performance data

PROJECTS OF LOCAL PHILANTHROPIES: $12 million

TEACH FOR AMERICA: $1 million to train teachers for positions in Newark district and charter schools

COMMUNITY GRANTS FROM THE FOUNDATION FOR NEWARK'S FUTURE:

- Start-up costs for four new district high schools: $2.1 million
- My Very Own Library: $3 million literacy initiative, giving books to 12,000 elementary school students to start home libraries and engaging parents to read with them
- Newark City of Learning Collaborative: $1.5 million to community initiative to double the number of Newark residents with college degrees in ten years
- After-school and extended-day programming: $1.2 million
- Early-childhood grants: $1 million
- Teacher Innovation Fund: $600,000 in grants of up to $10,000 each to classroom teachers for innovative projects with potential to be replicated
- BRICK and South Ward Children's Alliance: almost $500,000

for home-grown school improvement effort linked with wrap-around services for families

- Youth Leadership and Development: almost $1 million on three programs: College Summit, the Future Project, and the Center for Supportive Schools

- Support for local education foundations: $650,000 donated to a fund created by local philanthropies to pool and coordinate local support for education

Note: The total of the philanthropic funds spent or committed as of January 2015 comes to less than $200 million because some funding decisions were still pending and smaller grants are not listed.

Source: IRS Forms 990 filed by Foundation for Newark's Future (2011, 2012, 2013), FNF website, documents supplied by staff of Newark Public Schools

Appendix II

Newark Schools by the Numbers

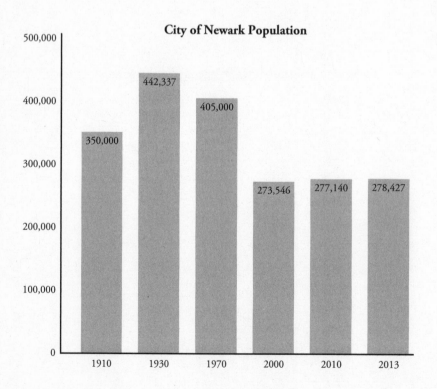

City of Newark Population

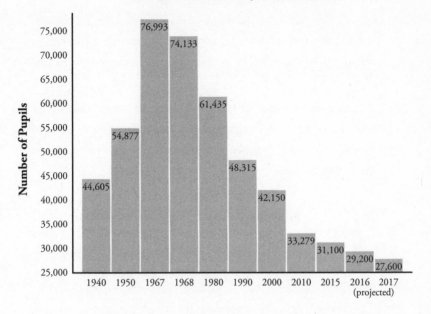

Newark Public Schools, Total Enrollment

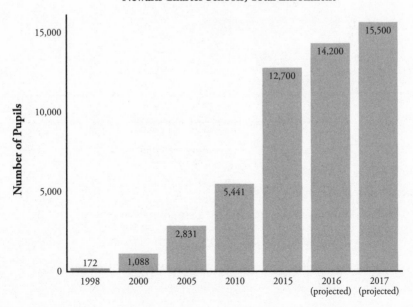

Newark Charter Schools, Total Enrollment

SPENDING PER PUPIL, 2014–2015

- Newark district schools: $19,650 (This amount represents remaining per-pupil sum after payments to charters and pre-K are subtracted; of the $19,650, an average of $9,604 per pupil reaches schools.)

- Newark charter schools: $16,400 (There is no available data on average amount reaching charter school classrooms. According to Newark's KIPP schools, $12,664 reaches its SPARK Academy elementary school.)

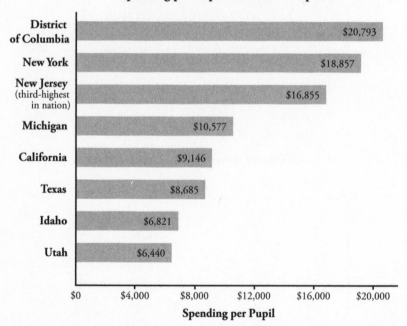

Spending per Pupil, National Comparison

	Spending per Pupil
District of Columbia	$20,793
New York	$18,857
New Jersey (third-highest in nation)	$16,855
Michigan	$10,577
California	$9,146
Texas	$8,685
Idaho	$6,821
Utah	$6,440

NEWARK POVERTY STATISTICS

- 71% of households headed by a single parent
- 42% of children live below poverty level (2010)
- $27,038 median income for families with children (2010)

NEW JERSEY POVERTY STATISTICS

- 30% of households headed by a single parent

- 14% of children live below poverty level (2010)

- $83,208 median income for families with children (2010)

Sources: Newark Public Schools, Newark Board of Education, New Jersey Charter Schools Association, Parthenon Group, KIPP schools, http://nces.ed.gov/pubsearch/pubsinfo.asp?pubid=2014301.

Notes

I researched this book primarily through interviews and firsthand observations. The notes below refer only to information on Newark and education that I researched in books, journals, newspapers, state and school district records, and online.

1. The Pact

page

4 *Christie had made urban schools:* David Halbfinger, "Christie Aims at Democrats Unhappy with Poor Schools," June 18, 2009. http://www.nytimes.com/2009/06/19/nyregion/19choice.html.

"We're paying caviar prices": John Mooney, "Spotlight Video: Isaac," February 11, 2011, town hall meeting in Union City, New Jersey. Christie was responding to a mother named Yvonne Moore, who said her son couldn't get services for his disability in Newark schools. http://www.njspotlight.com/stories/11/0210/2248.

Only 12.5 percent: United States Census Bureau, "State and County Quick Facts" for Newark, New Jersey. http://quickfacts.census.gov/qfd/states/34/3451000.html.

Newark was an extreme example: Newark Public Schools, "School Snapshot

for Families." See, for example, http://www.nps.k12.nj.us/wp-content/up
loads/mdocs/FamilySnapshot_K8_ThirteenthAvenue.pdf.

5 *Forty-four percent of city children:* Advocates for Children of New Jersey,
"2012–2013 Newark Kids Count: A City Profile of Child Well-Being," pp.
26, 29, 40. http://acnj.org/downloads/2013_02_01_NewarkReport.pdf.

7 *Henry Ford created the Ford English School:* "Ford Motor Company Socio-
logical Department and English School." www.thehenryford.org/research/
englishSchool.aspx.

*"If an unfriendly foreign power": A Nation at Risk: The Imperative for Educa-
tional Reform* is the full title of the 1983 report of President Ronald Reagan's
National Commission on Excellence.

8 *Beginning in 2000:* Foundation Stats: The Foundation Center's Statistical
Information Service, "Top 50 Foundation Awarding Grants for Elementary
and Secondary Education, Circa 1998, 2000, and 2006." foundationcenter
.org/findfunders/statistics.

15 *the fastest and most tumultuous turnover:* Robert Curvin, "The Persistent Minority: The Black Political Experience in Newark," PhD dissertation, Princeton University, 1975, p. 13.

Newark cleared more slums: The displacement of Newark residents is dis-
cussed in *Report of the National Advisory Commission on Civil Disorders*
(Washington, D.C.: U.S. Government Printing Office, 1968), also known as
the Kerner Report, p. 142; Curvin, "The Persistent Minority"; and Mindy
Thompson Fullilove, MD, *Root Shock* (New York: Ballantine Books, 2004),
pp. 52–70.

16 *"Good houses make good citizens":* Brad R. Tuttle, *How Newark Became Newark: The Rise, Fall and Rebirth of an American City* (New Brunswick, NJ:
Rivergate Books, 2009), p. 127.

A state investigation later found: "Report for Action," Governor's Select Commission on Civil Disorders, State of New Jersey, February 1968, p. 55.

"one of the most volatile": Quoted in Curvin, "The Persistent Minority," p. 15.

17 *"In schools with high Negro enrollments":* United States Commission on Civil
Rights, Hearings Before the United States Commission on Civil Rights,
Newark, New Jersey, September 11–12, 1962 (Washington, D.C.: U.S. Government Printing Office, 1963), p. 403. http://babel.hathitrust.org/cgi/pt?id=
mdp.39015012165851;view=1up;seq=425.

18 *Former U.S. representative Hugh Addonizio:* Jean Anyon, *Ghetto Schooling: A
Political Economy of Urban Educational Reform* (New York: Teachers College
Press, 1997), p. 107.

Newark exploded in six days: Accounts of the riots were taken from "Report
for Action," pp. 30–38; and Robert Curvin, *Inside Newark* (New Brunswick,
NJ: Rutgers University Press, 2014), pp. 100–127.

Its report stated, of urban renewal: "Report for Action," p. 55, 82.

19 *"I think somewhere along the line":* Ibid., p. 75.
20 *In the early 1980s:* Curvin, *Inside Newark,* pp. 280–82.

2. Seduction in Sun Valley

33 *"Mark is following up":* The emails sent by Sheryl Sandberg and Bari Mattes were obtained in an open-records lawsuit by the ACLU of New Jersey.

3. The View from Avon Avenue

43 *Nearly half of the children:* The data is taken from Table 10 and explanatory notes on page 27 of *Barriers to Upward Mobility: A Spatial Analysis of Newark and the Challenges to Human Development,* a report by the Cornwall Center of Rutgers University. https://www.cornwall.rutgers.edu/sites/default/files/files/Assesments/barriers_to_upward_mobility.pdf.
   "A generous description": "Rescuing Avon Avenue School," http://www.thechadschoolfoundation.org/avon-report2011.pdf.
49 *"an inability to captivate student interest":* This assessment comes from Avon Avenue School's April 29, 2010, application for a federal School Improvement Grant, under a section titled "Curriculum and Quality of Instruction," pp. 8, 9.
52 *In a series of rulings:* For a history of the *Abbott v. Burke* litigation, see http://www.edlawcenter.org/cases/abbott-v-burke/abbott-history.html.
53 *Research had shown that children:* B. Hart and T. R. Risley, *Meaningful Differences in the Everyday Experiences of Young American Children.* (Baltimore, MD: Brookes Publishing, 1995), p. 132. Follow-up studies have found that these different experiences had lasting impacts on children's performance in later years.

4. Engaging the Community

57 *"Education reform is not about":* Michael Lomax, "Education Reform: What Adrian Fenty and Michelle Rhee Got Wrong," September 21, 2010. http://www.theroot.com/articles/politics/2010/09/what_dc_mayor_adrian_fenty_and_schools_chancellor_michelle_rhee_got_wrong_about_school_reform.html.
58 *a study revealed that in the 2012–13 school year:* The Southern Education Foundation found that fifty-one percent of students in pre-kindergarten through twelfth grade in the 2012–13 school year were eligible for the federal program that provides free and reduced-price lunches. http://www.southerneducation

.org/getattachment/4ac62e27-5260-47a5-9d02-14896ec3a531/A-New-Majority
-2015-Update-Low-Income-Students-Now.aspx.

60 *Akbar Pray, a notorious drug kingpin:* Examples of Pray's messages are online
at http://akbarpray.com/articles. The quoted passage was taken from a letter
he wrote to students in a social studies class at Central High School. Copy
in possession of the author.

64 *The total bill for the firm:* The amount paid to Global Education Advisers
and its individual consultants is recorded on the website of the Foundation
for Newark's Future, under "Newark Public Schools Diagnostic and Transition Phase." http://foundationfornewarksfuture.org/grants/school-options.

65 *Bari Mattes, Booker's fundraiser:* The FNF's payments to Mattes and Wright
are reported in the foundation's federal tax return, Form 990, for the years
2010 and 2011. See http://www.guidestar.org/organizations/27-3453412/
foundation-newarks-future.aspx#forms-docs. Mattes's city hall salary
for 2010 was obtained through an Open Public Records Act request, and
Wright's pay from the Newark Charter School Fund is recorded in that
organization's federal tax return for 2010. See http://www.guidestar.org/
organizations/26-2224940/newark-charter-school-fund.aspx#forms-docs.
Almost all philanthropy is by definition undemocratic: See, for example, Rob
Reich, "What Are Foundations For?" *Boston Review,* March 1, 2013. http://
bostonreview.net/forum/foundations-philanthropy-democracy.

66 *This was not what Shavar Jeffries:* The FNF board promised to appoint a
community advisory board to inform its decisions, but it took two years to
select the board, which included distinguished Newark experts on children,
education, and community development — the kind of people who might
have been expected to be involved from the beginning. At the same time, the
advisory board's chairman, Dr. Robert L. Johnson, dean of the University of
Medicine and Dentistry of New Jersey and a national authority in pediatrics
and psychiatry, was made a full voting member of the board of trustees. But
by then, most of the money had already been allocated.

5. The Rise of the Anti-Booker Candidacy

79 *Based on their eighth-grade standardized test scores:* This data comes from
Central High School's April 29, 2010, application for a federal School Improvement Grant, under "Eighth Grade Performance," p. 11.

6. Searching for Newark's Superman

97 Waiting for Superman *had its own:* http://bits.blogs.nytimes.com/2010/10/07/
mark-zuckerberg-at-the-movies/?ref=todayspaper.

101 *The* Star-Ledger *reported:* David Giambusso, "The Absentee Mayor? Cory Booker's Endless Travel Schedule Pulls Him Away from Newark," July 15, 2012. http://www.nj.com/news/index.ssf/2012/07/the_absentee_mayor_cory _booker.html.

Sandberg had taken charge: The quotation comes from a document written by Mark Zuckerberg and dated September 24, 2010, "Declaration of Intent to Grant," laying out his understanding of the goals for his $100 million gift. Document in possession of the author.

7. Hi, I'm Cami

126 *After pressing Anderson:* The grant is described on the foundation's website, http://foundationfornewarksfuture.org/grants/school-options.

127 *In less than eighteen months:* Payments to Avera and Breslin are reported in FNF's tax returns for 2011 and 2012.

8. District School, Charter School

132 *Fewer than thirty percent:* "State of New Jersey, NJ School Performance Report, Overview: George Washington Carver." http://www.state.nj.us/ education/pr/2013/13/133570435.pdf.

134 *Children with more than one:* For a discussion of the effects of adverse childhood experiences, see Paul Tough, *How Children Succeed: Grit, Curiosity, and the Hidden Power of Character* (Boston: Houghton Mifflin Harcourt, 2012), pp. 9–27.

135 *the vast amount of money:* See Mark Dixon, *Public Education Finances: 2012 Census of Governments,* Figure 4, Public Elementary-Secondary School System Per Pupil Current Spending by State (U.S. Department of Commerce, Economics and Statistics Administration, U.S. Census Bureau), May 2014, p. xiv. http://www2.census.gov/govs/school/12f33pub.pdf.

136 *When district officials tried*: Antoinette Martin, "Newark School Office Plan: From Lease to Lawsuits," *New York Times*, March 2, 2003.

137 *According to financial documents*: "NPS Budget Presentation." http://www .nps.k12.nj.us/wp-content/uploads/2014/08/BudgetHearing_FY1415.pdf . See p. 28 for Avon Avenue School budget and enrollment data for 2013–14.

138 *North Star had by far the highest:* In reporting test scores for charter school networks, the New Jersey Department of Education reports an average score for all schools in a network. As such, it aggregates the test scores of North Star schools and TEAM schools as if each network were an individual school.

138 *A Stanford University study:* Center for Research on Educational Outcomes, Stanford University, "Charter School Performance in New Jersey,"

November 1, 2012. http://credo.stanford.edu/pdfs/nj_state_report_2012_FINAL11272012_000.pdf.

Of the high-performing charter networks: Statistics on the number and percentage of students who qualify for free lunch, by district and school, are available on the website of the New Jersey Department of Education. The percentage of free-lunch recipients in charter schools is reported as an average for all schools within a charter network. http://www.state.nj.us/education/data/enr/enr14/stat_doc.htm.

9. Transformational Change Meets the Political Sausage Factory

151 *The goal was to apply:* Zuckerberg, "Declaration of Intent to Grant."

153 *In a document given to Booker:* Zuckerberg's "Declaration of Intent to Grant" stated, "Recognizing the importance of achieving contractual reforms to the NPS district-wide effort, $60M will be directly tied to (and conditioned upon) reaching new teacher and principal contract agreements." Fifty million dollars would be allocated "upon the negotiation and ratification" of a new teachers' contract, $10 million for a principals' contract. The district didn't reach an agreement with the principals' union, however.

Zuckerberg's document laid out similar goals: "Declaration of Intent to Grant."

154 *After arduous negotiations:* The New Jersey law, known as TEACHNJ, is available at http://www.njleg.state.nj.us/2012/Bills/PL12/26_.pdf.

there was growing skepticism: Two years later, the state reduced the role of standardized tests in teacher evaluations from thirty to ten percent, in recognition of the uncertainty surrounding new tests due to be given for the first time in 2015.

158 *Indeed, Zuckerberg and matching donors helped:* The charter enrollment data came from the Newark Charter School Fund and the New Jersey Charter Schools Association.

160 *Julian Robertson said the same:* Robertson was interviewed on Bloomberg TV's *This Matters Now,* July 23, 2013. A video is available at http://www.bloomberg.com/video/a-new-approach-to-investing-in-u-s-education-TDgorP76QjaPzB2BTmctWw.html.

10. Alif Rising

167 *Carlson tested Alif:* The results are taken from Carlson's records of Alif's performance on his first Woodcock Reading Mastery assessment in the fall of 2012.

11. The Leading Men Move On

177 *In 2005, a lone school board member:* Cammarieri distributed a four-page paper, "Regarding Strategic Reform for the Newark Public Schools: An Open Statement," at an education summit in Newark on June 4, 2005. He declared the system in crisis, addressing the statement to "Any and All Concerned with the State of Public Education in Newark."

183 *"You're like Joe Clark without the bat":* The reference was to the movie *Lean on Me,* about an inner-city high school whose principal, Joe Clark, carried a bat to keep order.

188 *Charter schools searched nationally:* The operations budget for the Newark Charter School Fund designated $3.5 million to place up to two hundred new teachers at an average cost of at least $17,500 each, and $3.25 million to recruit and place up to fifteen new school leaders at an average cost of at least $217,000 each.

193 *Indeed, research had found:* A 2012 study of teachers in Nashville, Tennessee, who were promised bonuses of up to $15,000 for gains in their students' scores on state standardized tests found no impact over a three-year period on the students' scores. https://my.vanderbilt.edu/performanceincentives/research/point-experiment.

12. One Newark, Whose Newark?

197 *Newark was on its way to becoming:* National Alliance for Public Charter Schools, "A Growing Movement: America's Largest Charter School Communities," December 2014, p. 3. http://www.publiccharters.org/wp-content/uploads/2014/12/2014_Enrollment_Share_FINAL.pdf.

200 *Demographic data essentially pointed a dagger:* The information in this paragraph comes from a PowerPoint presentation, "Building a System—One Newark," developed from district data by the Parthenon Group, October 2013.

203 *In a focus group arranged by the district:* The focus group of sixteen parents and guardians of children in district and charter schools was conducted on April 15, 2014, by United Way on behalf of the district's Office of Family and Community Engagement. Quotes were taken from a district document summarizing the questions and answers.

205 *With no data yet showing:* An internal NPS document summarizing the results of the 2014 One Newark enrollment process, "Data Request: Enrollment Data," reports that 48.6 percent of all applications to kindergarten—1,560 of a total of 3,211—listed charters as a first choice.

Asked during his 2013 reelection: Jeanette Rundquist, "Christie to Newark: We Run the School District," *Newark Star-Ledger,* September 5, 2013. http://

www.nj.com/news/index.ssf/2013/09/christie_to_newark_we_run_the_
school_district.html.

206 *They and national unions:* The campaign contributions to Baraka, Shavar
Jeffries, and independent expenditure campaigns waged on their behalf
are available at www.elec.state.nj.us. A list of financial-industry contributions to Jeffries and union contributions to Baraka was compiled by a blog-
ger, Darcie Cimarusti: http://mothercrusader.blogspot.com/2014/05/newark
-mayoral-race-wall-street.html.

Index